*Loving God and
Disturbing Men*

Loving God and Disturbing Men

Preaching from the Prophets

Donald A. Leggett

BAKER BOOK HOUSE
Grand Rapids, Michigan 49516

All scripture quotations in *Loving God and Disturbing Men* are taken from the New International version of The Holy Bible unless otherwise indicated.

Library of Congress Cataloging-in-Publication Data

Leggett, Donald A.
    Loving God and disturbing men : preaching from the prophets /
Donald A. Leggett.
        p. cm.
    ISBN 0-8010-5660-8
    1. Bible. O.T. Prophets—Homiletical use. 2. Bible. O.T.
Prophets — Sermons — Outlines, syllabi, etc. 3. Bible. O.T.
Habakkuk — Homiletical use. 4. Bible. O.T. Habakkuk — Sermons —
Outlines, syllabi, etc. 5. Bible. O.T. Haggai — Homiletical use.
6. Bible. O.T. Haggai — Sermons — Outlines, syllabi, etc. 7. Bible.
O.T. Malachi — Homiletical use. 8. Bible, O.T. Malachi — Sermons —
Outlines, syllabi, etc. I. Title.
    BS1505.5.L44 1990
    251—dc20   90-32753
                                                                      CIP

Printed in Canada

Contents

Preface

Preface

Some time into my teaching career I began to realize how much time and attention is often given to answering the arguments of higher criticism concerning the Old Testament and how little time is given to enabling students to preach and teach from the Old Testament. This book seeks to combine the fruits of scholarly study of the prophets with the teaching and application which would come to the flock of God Sunday by Sunday. The three chapters on the minor prophets have been preached and taught in both my seminary classes and at Village Green Baptist Church in London, Ontario, where I co-pastor.

I wish to thank Ontario Theological Seminary, Toronto, for the gracious provision of a sabbatical term in January 1987, when a good part of the writing and research was done. I am indebted to the congregation at Village Green Baptist Church for the support which also allowed me to be away for the six months in Cambridge, England. While I had the help of several libraries and staff, I am particularly indebted to the librarians and friends at Tyndale House, Cambridge, England, where much of the research and writing was done. One of the additional bonuses of being present in Cambridge was the opportunity to sit under the stimulating and challenging preaching from the Old Testament of Dr. Roy Clements. His expositions of the first twelve chapters of Isaiah in 1987 were a spiritual oasis to me and confirmed for me the indispensability of the Old Testament for the life of the church.

I owe a debt of gratitude to Linda Boswall, my secretary, for her excellent work in typing, and to Ian and Anne James, for "a second set of eyes" in reading the manuscript. My wife Linda has also put in long hours reading and discussing the manuscript and I appreciate her labor prompted by love.

My desire is that the message and example of the prophets will increasingly impact the lives of God's people.

I. Introduction

There are a good number of excellent academic commentaries available on the prophets. Recent works in the major commentary series (Anchor Bible, Old Testament Library, the Fortress Press Hermeneia Series, Word Biblical Commentary, New International Commentary) are being produced and such helps are to be welcomed. In contrast to those are the smaller volumes that treat the prophets "devotionally." In such works the author tries to get to spiritual lessons as quickly as possible in the interests of edification and spiritual growth. In the academic commentaries practical application and spiritual lessons are usually de-emphasized since the purpose of such works is primarily to educate. In the "devotional" type of commentary, application often comes prematurely and sometimes almost falsely because one can properly apply only what the text actually says, and that is just what is often missing. No great pains have been taken to arrive at the intended meaning of the text, yet somehow spiritual blessing is supposed to come.

I have come to the conclusion that there is a place (dare I say need) for something between the strictly academic and the strictly devotional. A busy pastor doesn't have time (or perhaps hasn't been trained) to read academic-type commentaries. It's something like trying to get modern pastors to read the Puritans! They are heavy and tedious and hard to follow even though worthwhile, but the kind of mental energy needed to gain from them something valuable for a sermon isn't seen to be worth the effort. Thus, often the devotionalizers win out. Being easier and viewed as being more practical and relevant, they win the day in the interests of cranking out a quicker and more relevant message. It's not easy, of course, to strike a balance between these two extremes. John Bright's wise words

about the relationship between preaching and exegesis are
surely pertinent to this issue:

> Biblical preaching, we hold, begins with exegesis. And exegesis
> may proceed only along grammatico-historical principles. This
> involves the preacher, it goes without saying (or should go without
> saying), in a minute scrutiny of the text. There is no escaping from
> this. For it is his task neither more nor less than to lay hold of, and
> so to expound, the mind of the writer with whom he is dealing . . .
> To be sure, preaching does not end in exegesis, lest preaching be
> an antique, irrelevant thing. But it must begin there, in a serious
> wrestling with the text, lest the little preacher's little words be con-
> fused with the Bible Word . . . But he who will not take pains to
> arrive at the meaning of the text, he who advertises by his careless-
> ness that he does not care what it means, cannot do biblical
> preaching, for he will not begin seriously with the Bible. Biblical
> preaching and the refusal of exegesis can no more mate than God
> and Baal! (J. Bright, "The Book of Jeremiah," in *Interpretation* 9,
> 1955, p. 260).

Bright's emphasis is much needed today. One cannot apply
to today a text that isn't understood! What is needed, therefore,
is an approach that sees both the text and its application as
important. But is it possible to go to the academic commentaries for exegesis and to the devotional ones for application? Such a practice is impractical. Wouldn't it be better to at
least attempt to give serious and sufficient attention to both
aspects of the preaching task? This combination of tasks
appears to be the goal of two new modern commentary series,
The International Theological Commentary, and *Interpretation: A
Bible Commentary for Teaching and Preaching*. The stated nature
of the latter is "a commentary which both explains and applies, an interpretation which deals with both the meaning
and the significance of biblical texts."

There are many reasons for a dearth of preaching from the
Old Testament. One might be the lack of suitable tools and
helps in the form of commentaries. That is why Walter Kaiser
calls for a "whole new genus of commentary writing," combin-
ing some technical material with legitimate application and
exposition (W. Kaiser, *Malachi: God's Unchanging Love*, 1984,
p. 9). He argues that "the selection of biblical commentaries,
which normally make up the bulk of that (minister's) library,
will be extremely critical for the spiritual life and health of the
congregation" (Kaiser, *Malachi*, p. 147).

Kaiser lists four characteristics of a good commentary. It should "exhibit the plan, design and scope of the biblical writer's thought." It will set forth a clear outline of the train of thought and "it will clearly indicate all digressions, subordinate details, along with the main train of thought that contributes to the central aim of the book." Most important it will seek to set forth the "*meaning of the words*, phrases, and idioms of the original text." It will engage in theological exegesis; i.e., the "comparison of the teachings and sentiments found in one book with (1) those that preceded it in time (the analogy of antecedent Scripture) and (2) those that followed it in the progress of revelation (the analogy of faith)" (Kaiser, *Malachi*, pp. 147–149.)

I have made a modest attempt in this book to bridge the gap between the two types of commentaries — academic and devotional — and to make the Old Testament come alive for the church and the life of faith. I have attempted to write for my fellow ministers and for "the thinking layperson," one who believes his or her mind matters and that we are to love God with our minds as well as our hearts.

The expositions on three of the minor prophets are not, technically speaking, a commentary since the intent is to include a significant amount of application. Nor are they really sermons since they are much too long and not many illustrations are included. They are sermonic in form, with a detailed outline constructed from the text itself to serve as an extensive homiletical outline.

At the end of each of the sections dealing with the prophets is a bibliography. This list is by no means exhaustive but includes commentaries that I consider most helpful for preaching. In addition, there is a bibliography of books relevant to the *themes* found within the prophetic books. Obviously the choice of the particular books in this latter bibliography reflects my own opinions and limited perspective. In my experience of preaching from the prophets I have found that commentaries serve only a limited usefulness in expanding on the meaning of a theme. For example, in Malachi 3:17–18 those who are mentioned by the Lord as his "treasured possession" (see also Ex. 19:6) are described as those who serve God. The prophet says, "You will again see the distinction between the righteous and the wicked, between those who serve God and those who do not" (Mal. 3:18).

I doubt whether any commentaries at this point will expound and expand on the Old and New Testament meanings of *service*. But if the pastor-preacher is familiar with books that examine this theme in a biblical and pastoral way, then it will be possible to expand on what it really means to serve God. Even if he or she knows only the smallest amount of Hebrew it will be clear that the term "treasured possession" in Malachi 3:17 is being used in an unusual way. Having found that it is used only eight times in the Old Testament, the reader will notice that in the final stages of Old Testament revelation Malachi uses a word that originally signified the whole of the covenant community and has now applied it to the remnant! "They will be mine in the day when I make up my treasured possession" (Mal. 3:17a). "They" are not the whole of the covenant community but only those who feared the Lord and honored his name (Mal. 3:16). But what details will a commentary give about the concept of the remnant? If the pastor-preacher knows something of Old Testament theology, this concept will ring a bell. Perhaps even G. Hasel's book, *The Remnant*, will be familiar. My point is that, besides commentary helps, what we need are intermediate level thematic studies that can serve in a general way as background for expounding the intended meaning of the text.

The chapter entitled "How to Preach from the Prophets" is not an attempt to provide a detailed approach to going from text to sermon. This has been done for the Old Testament very capably in Douglas Stuart's *Old Testament Exegesis*, Walter Kaiser's *Toward an Exegetical Theology* and more recently in the helpful works of Sidney Greidanus, *The Modern Preacher and the Ancient Text* and Elizabeth Achtemeier, *Preaching from the Old Testament*. These books will be rewarding reading if studied and can be used to great benefit in one's preaching. My purpose is much more general when it comes to the sections on exegesis and application.

The section "Why Preach From the Prophets?" is a modest attempt to provide a motivation and rationale for the importance of this part of the Word of God. We need to take more than a superficial glance at the prophets. We need to cover all of the prophets, not just the same favorite books to which our sermons are limited year after year. The prophets need to be studied in connection with the Pentateuch for they expound and expand the theology of law and the covenants found within the Pentateuch. We need to be able to relate the thematic content of their messages to the New Testament and its perfected revelation in Christ.

The questions at the end of each chapter dealing with the prophets were used in group Bible studies at Village Green Baptist Church, London, Ontario, where much of the material in these chapters was preached. They focus on some of the main ideas in these chapters plus additional biblical texts that relate to the prophetic themes.

Many fine and helpful books have been written on preaching which cover this subject generally. Of those, John Stott's *Between Two Worlds* includes a definition of preaching as building a bridge between the biblical world and the contemporary world, and is well worth considering:

> We should be praying that God will raise up a new generation of Christian communicators who are determined to bridge the chasm; who struggle to relate God's unchanging Word to our ever-changing world; who refuse to sacrifice truth to relevance or relevance to truth; but who resolve instead in equal measure to be faithful to Scripture and pertinent to today (John Stott, *Between Two Worlds*, 1982, p. 144).

This approach seems to fit well within the prophetic model which sees the prophets as being intimately involved in the present with their contemporaries, as well as announcing the biblical word for the future. If this understanding of preaching is sound it is an awesome responsibility. To become a master of the biblical word is a high and holy calling, requiring continuous study and prayer. To be a person who "understands the times" (I Chron. 12:32) is to add a dimension and a magnified challenge. As we seek to assume these awesome responsibilities, we can only ask, Who is equal to such a task? (II Cor. 2:16). Let us pray that we may be enabled to say, "Our competence comes from God. He has made us competent as ministers of a new covenant" (II Cor. 3:5b, 6a).

My hope is that this material will be helpful and stimulating to those seeking to understand and expound the message of the Old Testament prophets and that God will raise up preachers with a contemporary message from the prophets "not simply with words, but also with power, with the Holy Spirit and with deep conviction" (I Thess. 1:5).

II. Who Are the Prophets?

In order to preach and teach from the prophets we must know who the prophets are and their roles in the history of redemption.* Today many dabble in the prophets to capitalize on the current interest among churches and societies in social justice. Unfortunately, such dabblers totally divorce the prophetic emphasis on "social justice" from its basis in the covenant of grace which the prophets proclaimed, but that severs the fruit from the root. The prophets cannot be seen as mere social reformers. Social reformers *generally* have too optimistic a view of human nature and its potential for change. On the contrary, the prophets say things like, "Can the Ethiopian change his skin or the leopard its spots? Neither can you do good who are accustomed to doing evil" (Jer. 13:23).

If our interest is in obtaining the blueprint for the future, if we are immersed in eschatology, we will see the prophets largely as predictors who give us insider information on things to come! Prophecy in this context will be almost entirely equated with prediction. While there are many clear prophe-

---

* A very recent study categorizes six ways in which Old Testament prophets may be interpreted:

"The prophet is a person who has had a special sort of religious experience and/or a special sort of relationship to the deity.
The prophet is a person who speaks or writes in a distinctive way.
The prophet is a person who acts as a prophet in a particular social setting.
The prophet is a person who possesses distinctive personal qualities, namely charisma.
The prophet is an intermediary between the divine and human worlds.
The prophet is a person who has a distinctive message."
(David Peterson, editor, *Prophecy in Israel,* 1987, pp. 10-17)

7

cies of the coming of the Messiah which the prophets
announce, they should not be interpreted through this lens.
The prophets were not the forerunners of Jeanne Dixon. Only
a very small percentage of their writings concerns the future:

> The prophets spoke of the future, but the future as the arena in
> which God exercised his kingship in bringing life out of death and
> forgiveness in spite of rebellion. The Old Testament prophets were
> not soothsayers, but proclaimers of the will of God who both kills
> and brings to life (B. Childs, *Old Testament Theology in a Canonical
> Context*, 1985, p. 132).

Perhaps their uniqueness was in their genius for religion, in
their strong individuality which allowed them to stand alone
against the tide of evil within their society (cf. Jer. 15:17). This
is too narrow a confine in which to fit them. They were more
than brilliant religious individualists with a bent for mysti-
cism. One reason for the inadequacy of this perspective is that
their writings do not contain large amounts of information
about their personal lives, and so personality studies of the
prophets are difficult to reconstruct. "In the prophetical books
. . . we hear *from* God *via* the prophets and very little about the
prophets themselves" (D. Stuart and G. Fee, *How to Read the
Bible for All Its Worth*, 1982, p. 150).

Without ignoring what can be learned from the religious
experience of the prophet, it is best to see them as bearers of
the traditions of the covenant, or "covenant enforcement
mediators" (Stuart and Fee, p. 151). They interpreted the covenants made with Abraham, Moses and David, and in addition
became the recipients of the promises of the new covenant
(Jer. 31:31–34; Ez. 16:59–63). The prophets are men of the past
as well as the future. They knew and applied God's law to the
people. When Hosea brought the Lord's covenant lawsuit
against the people and tried to show them that they didn't
know God, he said: "There is no faithfulness, no love, no
knowledge of God in the land. There is only cursing, lying and
murder, stealing and adultery" (Hos. 4:2).

Hosea links knowledge of God with obedience to the Ten
Commandments. God wants mercy, not sacrifices; knowledge
of him, not burnt offerings (Hos. 6:6).

Amos applied the covenant curses of Lev. 26 and Deut. 28 in
his powerful five-fold call to repentance (Amos 4:7–11).

Jeremiah knew that people were trusting in deceptive words (Jer. 7:4) because they were thieves, murderers, adulterers and perjurers (violating the covenant stipulations) and yet were worshipping as if there was no connection between their lives and their worship. "The prophets are not inspired to make any points or announce any doctrines that are not already contained in the Pentateuchal covenant" (Stuart and Fee, p. 154).

The form and application of their messages vary but the essence of their messages is the same as revealed in the Abrahamic, Mosaic and Davidic covenants. To understand the prophets thus requires us to understand the law and the covenants, i.e., the Abrahamic, Mosaic and Davidic covenants.

Yet the prophets cannot be understood as mere preservers and conservers of earlier covenant traditions. It would be false to ignore the new thing that was revealed to them. The prophets were the messengers proclaiming the end of the old era and the beginning of the new.

> God was about to do a new thing in history, to make a radical change in his relationship to his people. It first took the form of judgment, of bringing something old to an end, and so the downfall of Israel and then of Judah was proclaimed . . . When the end did come God also sent men with the message that the new era was about to begin (D. Gowan, *Reclaiming the Old Testament for the Christian Pulpit*, 1980, p. 124).

This "new" thing that God was going to be doing is part of the decisive content revealed at the time of the prophets' call. Jeremiah saw the end of the old era coming. Thus his ministry was "to uproot and tear down, to destroy and overthrow" (Jer. 1:10a). But afterwards he would be able to build and plant (Jer. 1:10b). Amos expressed the radical idea of the dismantling of the old with his sober word, "The end has come upon my people Israel" (8:2). Yet he too was given a message of hope for the future (Amos 9:11–15). Hosea uses the very words of the covenant formula but in a devastatingly negative way: "You are not my people and I am not your God" (Hos. 1:9b). Yet he also sees a new future.

> I will betroth you to me forever;
> I will betroth you in righteousness and justice, in love and compassion.
> I will betroth you in faithfulness, and you will acknowledge the Lord. (Hos. 2:19, 20)

Jeremiah gives us the most extensive statement on the new thing God is doing. He announces the promise of the new covenant (Jer. 31:31–34). Though he employs the phrase "new covenant," there is good reason to believe that a number of other expressions contain the same meaning. The phrase "everlasting covenant" (Is. 24:5; 55:3; 61:8; Jer. 32:40; 50:5; Ez. 16:60; 37:26) also refers to the glorious new era promised by God. In connection with that era the prophets promise a "new heart and a new spirit" (Ez. 11:19; 18:31 and 36:26). Sometimes the term "covenant of peace" is used (Is. 54:10; Ez. 34:25; 37:26). Occasionally the phrase "in that day," which describes the indefinite messianic future, is employed in connection with the covenant (Is. 42:6; 49:8; 59:21; Hos. 2:18–20).

> The seventh century was the greatest moment of impending destruction for the nation; yet in the midst of the faithful warnings of God's servants came one of the most spectacular series of promises of hope (W. Kaiser, *Toward an Old Testament Theology*, 1978, p. 235).

For further development of the prophets as the announcers of God's "new thing," see III, B, 6.

It is common to hear words to the effect that the church needs to assume a prophetic posture in society today. Should we be calling for prophets in 1990? The complexity involved in the task of being an Old Testament prophet should caution against simplistic transpositions from the Old Testament to today.

> Because of the complexity of the prophetic roles in ancient Israel, attempting to identify individuals as prophets in our time — especially if this identification presumes one fundamental feature, for example, spokesperson for social justice, or messenger — is risky indeed . . . It is not appropriate to think about *being* a prophet. One should rather speak of having a prophetic perspective, or better, of having one prophetic perspective (D. Peterson, "Ways of thinking about Israel's Prophets," in *Prophecy in Israel*, D. Peterson, editor, 1987, p. 17).

Certainly there are no prophets in the sense that Paul could say that the church was "built on the foundation of the apostles and prophets, with Christ Jesus himself as the chief cornerstone" (Eph. 2:20).

Whatever is meant by a prophetic ministry, it is not the case that today's "prophets" stand in the council of the Lord to see and hear God's word in the same sense that an Old Testament prophet did (cf. Jer. 23:18, 22). They were privileged to be organs of revelation in a unique and once-and-for-all sense.

We can see some general correspondence, however, between a prophetic ministry "then" and a prophetic ministry "now." Guided by the Old Testament prophets one would look for the following elements:

A sense of vocation, of responsiveness to God and responsibility to and for the world.

A sense of the power of the Word, and even of human words, to change history.

A deep awareness of historical concreteness in religious life.

A profound sense of the social, corporate, and institutional dimensions of human life. Such an awareness is especially important in a society which tends to stress radical individualism, which likes to think of itself as a nation of self-made men.

A moral decisiveness which is both specific and courageous (G. Tucker, "The Role of the Prophets and the Role of the Church," in *Prophecy in Israel*, D. Peterson, editor, pp. 172, 173).

III.   Why Preach From the Prophets?

In any attempt to explore what is involved in "preaching from the prophets," a critical assumption must be made — that today's pastor regards preaching as something still relevant to our generation. There is a biblical case to be made for the ongoing importance of proclaiming and expounding on the Bible. The pastor-preacher will find a powerful presentation on that issue in J.I. Packer's recent article "Why Preach?" in *The Preacher & Preaching*, edited by S. Logan, 1986, pp. 1–29. There is no substitute for the motivation that comes from seeing the relevance of proclaiming the message of the prophets. The "why preach" from the Old Testament question precedes the "how preach" from the Old Testament. If the "why" is not answered satisfactorily, the "how" won't matter! Some might argue that more help in methodology would lead to more preaching from the Old Testament. We welcome all such helps, but the most critical question remains, Why preach from the Prophets?

A. Their Importance to the Christian Faith

1. *Jesus and the Old Testament*

The question "Why preach from the Old Testament?" could yield many answers. Perhaps the most fundamental reason is that it's part of the Scriptures that Jesus often used and always regarded as his Father's Word. The Old Testament testifies to Jesus Christ and he testifies to it (Luke 24:27):

> Jesus Christ is the fulfillment of God's word to Israel . . . If we would be true to the New Testament, then we must proclaim Jesus Christ as the New Testament writers proclaimed Him — in terms

13

of God's history with Israel and the fulfillment of that history
(E. Achtemeier, *The Old Testament and the Proclamation of the Gospel*, 1973, pp. 115, 116).

Jesus' view of the Old Testament has been the subject of
detailed examinations, and this is not the place to open up that
discussion. The reader may wish to consult J.I. Packer's *Fun-
damentalism and the Word of God*, 1958, pp. 54–62; John
Wenham, *Christ and the Bible*, 1972, pp. 11–39; or R.T. France,
Jesus and the Old Testament, 1971, for more thorough
discussion:

> Jesus claimed to exhibit in Himself what the Old Testament actu-
> ally meant. He appealed to it as providing the warrant for what He
> said and did, and the sphere of reference in terms of which alone
> He could be understood. He saw Himself as the key to it and it as
> the key to Himself (Packer, *Fundamentalism*, p. 60).

The Old Testament witnessed to him (Luke 24:25–27, 44) and
he witnessed to it (John 5:39). The well-known words, "The
New is in the Old concealed; The Old is in the New revealed,"
though simple, are still true.

2. *The New Testament Writers and the Old Testament Scriptures*

The New Testament itself tells us by its own practice that we
should be preaching from the Old. Paul argues that the Old
Testament "announced the gospel in advance to Abraham"
(Gal. 3:8). The words of the prophets are cited at the first ecu-
menical conference in Jerusalem to confirm the experience of
the Gentiles coming to faith in Jesus Christ. "The words of the
prophets are in agreement with this" (Acts. 15:15). "*All* the
prophets testify *about him* that everyone who believes in him
receives forgiveness of sins through his name" (Acts 10:43).
    It seems clear, in reading Acts 3:24, that the messages of the
Old Testament prophets focused on the new era that had
dawned in Jesus Christ. "Indeed *all* the prophets from Samuel
on, as many as have spoken, have *foretold these days*" (Acts
3:24; cf. Acts 3:18). While in our generation we have seen the
folly and emptiness of the "date setters" and those who see
prophecy as a blueprint for the future, we can't ignore the clear
New Testament teaching that the prophets spoke of the grace

that was to come in Jesus Christ. They searched in their own minds to understand the "time and circumstances to which the Spirit of Christ in them was pointing when he predicted the suffering of Christ and the glories that would follow" (I Peter 1:11). The church has always believed in the essential unity of the Old and New Testaments. That idea is based on the New Testament itself:

> Not simply by quoting the OT as Scripture but also by continually accepting and reasserting OT content and ideas the NT attests the unity between the testaments. To reject the OT or to deny its basic unity with the NT not merely casts doubt on the OT but also charges the NT with being deeply in error, for to the NT writers the OT is truly Scripture; to them it is an indispensable witness to God, his work, and his will for men. These NT writers think that their message is in basic accord with the OT (F. Filson, "Unity Between the Testaments," in *Interpreter's One Volume Commentary*, C.M. Layman, editor, 1971, p. 989).

A text often cited when the question of divine inspiration is discussed but seemingly overlooked in the debate over the relevance of the Old Testament for today is II Tim. 3:16-17:

> All Scripture is God-breathed and is useful for teaching, rebuking, correcting and training in righteousness, so that the man of God may be thoroughly equipped for every good work.

Paul speaks in v. 15 of the Holy Scriptures which Timothy knows from his earliest childhood and which are empowered by the Lord to bring salvation. Certainly the Holy Scriptures that he refers to are the *Old Testament* canonical writings! Paul tells us then that these Old Testament Scriptures are useful to us in four ways. The first is for teaching or doctrine. Paul uses the term "sound teaching" or doctrine (I Tim. 1:10, II Tim. 1:13; 4:3; Titus 1:9,13; 2:1, 2) to indicate the doctrine about God that produces spiritually healthy and wholesome people. Imagine saying that spiritually healthy people are the result of teaching from the Old Testament! If one wishes to teach the doctrine of Christ's substitutionary suffering, is any passage clearer than Isaiah 53? How about the doctrine of the greatness of God or his incomparability, "To Whom then, will you compare God?" Can one afford to ignore Isaiah 40? How depleted our doctrine of divine holiness is without Isaiah 6. Yet as Kaiser warns:

. . . the church spurns three-fourths of God's inscripturated revelation — a massive amount of biblical teaching — if she persists in
constructing all of her theology from the New Testament, while
shamefully neglecting the Old Testament. It is this practice that
will leave lacunae and imbalances in her teaching ministry (W.
Kaiser, *Toward Rediscovering the Old Testament*, 1987, p. 29).

Paul adds another point to his list of useful things about the
Old Testament: it is profitable for reproof or rebuke.*

Paul gives us a second "negative" use of Old Testament
Scriptures when he adds the word "correction." Hebrews 12
speaks of the disciplinary influences God brings to bear upon
us (Heb. 12:1-11). The prophets speak of the curses of the covenant (Amos 4:6-12; Lev. 26; Deut. 28) which were designed to
get people's attention and lead them to repentance. Hosea
speaks of the divine corrective of the thornbush and the wall.
When Israel hotly pursues her lover the Lord responds, "I will
block her path with thornbushes; I will wall her in so that she
cannot find her way" (Hos. 2:5, 6).

Finally, the great apostle tells us that Old Testament Scriptures are a manual for training in righteousness. The prophets
speak prolifically about this key word. Isaiah alone uses the
word "righteousness" about fifty times. What a critical source
of instruction we miss if we fail to investigate the teaching of
the Old Testament prophets on the subject of righteousness.
The literature on this concept of righteousness and justice in
the Old Testament is vast.** Part of God's manual for instruction in righteousness comes from the Old Testament and in
particular from the prophets. To fail to preach and teach adequately from the Old Testament prophets is tragic and equivalent to beginning to read the manual at the half-way point.

When the God-breathed Scriptures of the Old Testament are
examined and studied and followed, Paul promises that "the
man of God will be thoroughly equipped for every good work"
(II Tim. 3:17). These combined verses indicate that the Old
Testament Scriptures are instrumental in salvation (wise unto
salvation), sanctification (teaching, rebuking, correcting,

---

* See chapter VI Haggai and the second point of application on the reproving nature of the word of God as well as III, C, 3 on the prophetic task of
  unmasking spiritual hypocrisy.
** One work, of several that could be recommended, is N. Snaith's *The Distinctive Ideas of the Old Testament*. See also Bibliography at the end of
  Chapter III, A.

instruction in righteousness) and service (equipped for every good work). That pretty much exhausts the whole of the life of faith!

3. *The Church and Its Relation to Old Testament Israel*

⚹The issue of how one sees the new covenant people (the church) in relation to Israel (God's old covenant people) will affect the *way* in which one preaches from the Old Testament. While recognizing the difficulty and complexity of this issue, our purpose here is not to argue this question in great detail. It surfaces because it is evident that if one is operating with a theology that radically dissociates the New Testament people of God from the Old Testament people of God there will be less impetus and motivation to preach from the Old Testament part of canonical Scripture.

The New Testament writers believe that the church has become in some sense the inheritor of the promises to Israel. "If you belong to Christ, then you are Abraham's seed and heirs according to the promise" (Gal. 3:29). As Paul sees it, the church is the Israel of God (Gal. 6:16).

Paul connects the gospel with the covenantal promises made to the seed of Abraham in his remark, "The Scripture foresaw that God would justify the Gentiles by faith, and *announced the gospel* in advance to Abraham: All nations will be blessed in you" (Gal. 3:8; cf. Acts 3:24, 25).

Referring to Old Testament Israel, the writer of Hebrews says, "For we also have had the gospel preached to us, just as *they* did" (Heb. 4:2). In context, "they" refers to the Old Covenant people (cf. Heb. 3:16-18).

Followers of Christ are "the true circumcision" (Phil. 3:3). They are the new people of God spoken of by Hosea (Rom. 9:25–26; I Peter 2:10; Hos. 1:10; 2:23). God has grafted the Gentile branches into the tree and root of Israel (Rom. 11:17-20) so that they have now become part of the commonwealth of Israel (Eph. 2:12, 13). The privileges, prerogatives and promises of the Old Testament are addressed to Israel (Rom. 9:4, 5), but since all the promises of God find their " 'Yes' in Christ" (II Cor. 1:20), those promises are now seen as addressed to God's new covenant people. "For everything that was written in the past was written to teach us" (Rom. 15:4). The church inherits the Old Testament Scriptures and so the word addressed to God's ancient people becomes his word to us today.

There are also certain parallels between the *life* of the church and that of Old Testament Israel. The source of the church's life is Christ and his death, and this is seen by New Testament writers to be the counterpart of the Old Testament exodus. Christ's death is compared to the death of the Passover lamb (I Cor. 5:7) and liberates the believer from slavery to sin just as the nation of Israel was liberated from Egyptian bondage. In the old covenant there were two prominent ceremonies, circumcision and passover. The first was a onetime ceremony initiating into the covenant. The latter was repetitive and observed by those in covenant with God to celebrate the redemption from Egypt. In the new covenant there are also two prominent ceremonies, baptism and the Lord's Supper. The first is a one-time initiatory ceremony by which one symbolically enters into the relationship with God. The Lord's Supper is the repetitive ceremony to look back on the redemptive work of Christ on the cross.

Peter speaks of the new covenant people in terms taken from Exodus 19:5, 6: "But you are a chosen generation, a royal priesthood, a holy nation, a people belonging to God" (I Peter 2:9).

Because of the analogy between the church and Israel, the life experiences of ancient Israel were viewed as warnings for New Testament believers. "These things happened to them as examples and were written down as warnings for us on whom the fulfillment of the ages has come" (I Cor. 10:11).

Much more could be said to support this point, but we summarize with Elizabeth Achtemeier's remarks:

We must emphasize, however, that this correspondence, this analogy between the old Israel and the new, has as its sole basis the salvation history, in which the church is understood as the realization of that new people of God, created in Christ, which was promised in the Old Testament. There is no other real historical relation between Israel and the church. They cannot be compared on the grounds that men are the same in every age and that therefore Israel's experience is instructive for the church — historians have shown us how relative to its time is the human personality. Israel and the church cannot be related by pointing out similar situations within their respective histories . . . Rather, ancient Israel and the New Testament church — and indeed the modern Chris-

tian church — are all related by one fact, by our common participation in the people of God *(The Old Testament and the Proclamation of the Gospel,* pp. 122, 123).

The practical implications for preaching are clearly and
forcefully drawn by Achtemeier:

> It seems obvious, therefore, that if the modern preacher wants to
> instruct his people as to who they are and what their life as the
> people of God is all about and toward what goal they are heading,
> in a fashion commensurate with the New Testament proclama-
> tion, then he is going to have to proclaim the Old Testament word
> along with the New. We modern Christians have become mem-
> bers of the New Israel in Christ. We need, therefore, to know who
> Israel is. And our life in Christ is analogous in many respects to
> the life of Israel. It would be helpful therefore to know what
> Israel's pilgrimage was like as we journey onward in our own.
> Indeed, for the modern preacher to neglect such proclamation is
> to leave his people without a full understanding of their identity
> and to refuse to guide them along their way with the signposts and
> instructions that God has mercifully given us through two thou-
> sand years of relationship with our Israelite forebears (p. 123).

B. The Importance of Their Message

1. *Their Message Is God-Centered*

The prophets were God-intoxicated people. Though they
fulminated against sin, they were proclaimers and conveyors
of the promises of salvation. No matter how varied the forms
of prophetic utterance, they began and ended with God:

> Whether the form is that of woe oracle pronounced over the dead
> (Is. 5:8-10), legal procedure (Is. 41:21-24), parable (Is. 5:1-7),
> lamenting dirge (Jer. 9:17-22), prophetic torah or teaching (Is.
> 1:10-17), salvation oracle (Jer. 35:18-19), priestly oracle of salva-
> tion (Is. 41:8-13), or allegory (Ez. 17:1-21), the principal reference
> is to the activity of God among his people or among the nations as
> a whole, and no sermon from the prophetic literature truly deals
> with those oracles unless it deals with that dynamic of Yahweh's
> activity (E. Achtemeier, "Preaching from Isaiah, Jeremiah, Eze-
> kiel," in *Biblical Preaching,* J. Cox, editor, 1983, p. 120).

"Divine wrath and divine grace provided the poles between

whose tension the prophetic thought operated" (E. Rust, "Preaching from the Minor Prophets," in *Biblical Preaching*, J. Cox, editor, p. 135). This preaching of both divine wrath and divine grace means that the prophets stand and join hands with the apostle Paul who speaks of both "the kindness and sternness of God" (Rom. 11:22).

The radical theocentric focus of the prophets is exemplified in the little-known and hardly-ever-preached book of Nahum. (Any theological library will provide negative evidence of this from the scarcity of substantive commentaries on this prophet.) The book in its present canonical form functions

> as a dramatic illustration of the eschatological triumph of God — whose divine nature is celebrated in a hymn — over his adversaries. In Nahum the destruction of the enemy is explicitly derived from the nature of God — 'a jealous God,' 'avenging and wrathful' 'keeping wrath for the enemy' — who claims dominion over the entire world (B. Childs, "The Canonical Shape of the Prophetic Literature" in *Interpreting the Prophets*, J. Mays, P. Achtemeier, editors, 1987, p. 45).

The judgment against Nineveh does not stem from the nationalistic narrowness and bigotry of a prophet nor from some isolated historical incident in the 7th century. Judgment against Nineveh points to a larger and recurrent theme within Old Testament revelation; i.e., the theme of the victory of God, the divine warrior and the defeat of his enemies. Two prophetic books are devoted to the Assyrians and their capital city, Nineveh. God's mercy to Nineveh is the central theme of Jonah. God's wrath against Nineveh is the central theme of Nahum. At one point within Old Testament redemptive history the deliverance and salvation of Nineveh is exhibited and at another point the righteous judgment of God is seen in the destruction and downfall of that arrogant nation. Reading and preaching from all the prophets does not allow us to be selective regarding which of these twin themes we would like to proclaim!*

---

* Tremper Longman's article, "The Form and Message of Nahum: Preaching from a Prophet of Doom," in *Reformed Theological Journal* (Nov. 1985), contains many helpful insights on how to preach from this book. Cf. D.L. Christensen, "The Book of Nahum as a Liturgical Composition: A Prosodic Analysis," *Journal of the Evangelical Theological Society* 32 (1989), pp. 159–169.

One of the marks of genuine revival is that God's people come to know *him* in a deeper and fuller way. This is beautifully expressed by the Psalmist in his prayer, "Will you not revive us again, that your people may rejoice in you?" (Ps. 85:6). It is critically important to preach the character of God. It is foundational to knowing ourselves (Is. 6:5), to godly worship (John 4:24) and to effective service (Is. 6:8b). Spiritual health is impossible without doctrinal knowledge even though doctrinal knowledge can be pursued for the wrong reasons. In studying the character of God, as Packer remarks, we must seek "to turn each truth that we learn *about* God into matter for meditation *before* God leading to prayer and praise *to* God" (*Knowing God*, 1973, p. 20).

✻The writings of the prophets provide us with great and wonderful insights into the Divine Person. Where would we be in the church today in our knowledge of the Holy One without Isaiah 6? To understand the patience and long-suffering of God and the profound "tension" within God between his mercy and justice, what better passage can we turn to than Hosea's moving statement:

How can I give you up, Ephraim?
How can I hand you over, Israel?
How can I treat you like Admah?
How can I make you like Zeboiim? (cities next to Sodom and Gomorrah)
I will not carry out my fierce anger. (Hos. 11:8, 9)

It is too easy, in reading the historical portions of the Old Testament, to come away with the notion expressed a long time ago by a certain bishop that the God of the Old Testament is a dirty bully! Though the prophets paint a black picture of sin and judgment they also speak of a God whose open and outstretched arms are ready to receive wayward sinners. "All day long I have held out my hands to an obstinate people, who walk in ways not good . . . a people who continually provoke me to my very face" (Is. 65:2, 3). Jeremiah portrays God as a disconsolate parent (Jer. 31:20) and a wounded lover (Jer. 3: 12-14) who, despite extreme provocation, yearns for a relationship with his children and his wife.

The Old and New Testaments are one in pointing to the fact that God's love is not earned by those he loves nor drawn out by our loveableness, but it flows out of his nature and character. The New Testament tells us God *is* Love (I John 4:8, 16). The Old Testament prophets speak similarly but in less abstract terms. "I have loved you with an everlasting love, I have drawn you with loving kindness" (Jer. 31:3). "Go show your love to your wife again, though she is loved by another and is an adulteress. Love her as the Lord loves the Israelites, though they turn to other gods . . ." (Hos. 3:1). "I will heal their waywardness and love them freely" (Hos. 14:4).

Failure to preach from the Old Testament, in particular the prophets, results in the loss of the Bible's unique understanding of God and the development of what Elizabeth Achtemeier calls "Reader's Digest religion." She defines this as a belief in a

> mystical presence called God, and depending upon the disposition of the individual worshipper, the presence may be identified with Jesus, with some ideal such as 'love' or 'truth' or with a numinous quality permeating the world of nature. The identity and definition of the presence are largely left up to the individual worshiper, and each individual's definition is considered as valid as any others . . . The experience of the presence remains largely private, individual, undemanding, never clearly defined, and thus it may be isolated from every other realm of the worshiper's life *(The Old Testament and the Proclamation of the Gospel*, pp. 41, 42).

Against this false notion that has crept into the church and into society stands the prophetic notion of the personal God who enters into a living, dynamic relationship with people. This God is actively involved in history and is working toward the redemption of his people. His rule is present not only in history but in the personal lives of his people. He is their king as well as king of the nations (Jer. 10:7). He has clearly revealed his purposes and his person and there is nothing nebulous about him. "Surely the Sovereign Lord does nothing without revealing his plan to his servants the prophets" (Amos 3:8). He proclaims his name; i.e., his revealed character (Ex. 34:6, 7). He calls his people to a life of trust, obedience and worship. The contrast could hardly be more striking.

Achtemeier blames the degeneration into Reader's Digest religion on the loss of the Old Testament because "it is in the Old Testament that the foundations are laid for the Bible's whole understanding of God" (p. 42). If A. W. Tozer is correct when he writes . . .

Always the most revealing thing about the church is her idea of God, just as her most significant message is what she says about Him or leaves unsaid, for her silence is often more eloquent than her speech (*The Knowledge of the Holy*, 1961, p. 1).

then it will be very important to introduce ourselves to the prophets or seek a deeper acquaintance with them. They confront us relentlessly with the question of the nature and purposes of God.

2. *Their Message Portrays Evil Realistically*

In 1973 Karl Menninger, a secular psychiatrist, had to remind the church there was such a thing as sin! Thus, he wrote his book, *Whatever has Become of Sin?* We would be less prone to ignore that unpleasant but necessary topic if we were to listen to the prophets more and the positive thinkers less. It is often positively depressing to read the prophets because they take sin so seriously! We tend to think they're fanatical and overdoing things somewhat when they say things like:

From the sole of your foot to the top of your head there is no soundness — only wounds and welts and open sores. (Is. 1:6)

All our righteous acts are like filthy rags. (Is. 64:6b)

The heart is deceitful above all things and beyond cure. Who can understand it? (Jer. 17:9)

My people have forgotten me days without number. (Jer. 2:32)

Can the Ethiopian change his skin or the leopard its spots? Neither can you do good who are accustomed to do evil. (Jer. 13:23)

Using the metaphor of two adulterous sisters, Israel's disengagement from the Lord is graphically described by the prophet Ezekiel:

Oholah engaged in prostitution while she was still mine; and she lusted after her lovers, the Assyrians. She gave herself as a prostitute to all the elite of the Assyrians and defiled herself with all the idols of everyone she lusted after. (Ez. 23:5, 7)

The sinners in Zion are terrified; trembling grips the godless:

Who of us can dwell with the consuming fire?
Who of us can dwell with everlasting burning?"   (Is. 33:14)

A realistic view of sin is the divine prerequisite for the acceptance of grace. It promotes a clearer and more intense apprecia-
tion of divine forgiveness. Low views of God breed high views of
self. Low views of sin breed low views of grace (cf. Luke 7:47b).

O, How shall I, whose native sphere
Is dark, whose mind is dim,
Before the ineffable appear,
And on my naked spirit bear the uncreated beam?

There is a way for man to rise to that sublime abode:
An offering and a sacrifice,
A Holy Spirit's energies,
An advocate with God.

These, these prepare us for the sight of holiness above.
The sons of ignorance and night
May dwell in the eternal light,
Through the eternal love!

Thomas Binney (1798-1874)

The later prophets, Jeremiah and Ezekiel, wrestle with the
issue of anthropology. It is what von Rad calls their "hardest
problem." It is their radical view of sin and depravity (Jer.
13:23, 17:9; Ez. 2:3) that makes them wonder how Israel's
inbred disposition against God is to be overcome.

Ezekiel speaks of the incapacity of human beings to "live
with and belong to God" (G. von Rad, *Old Testament Theology*,
Vol. 2, 1962, pp. 268, 269). In this state of spiritual death (Ez.
37) "nothing remained for them but to cast their whole being
on the future saving act which was already imminent" (von
Rad, p. 272). In the new covenant the Lord would remove the
heart of stone and give a heart of flesh. He would give them his
Spirit and cause them to be careful to keep his laws (Ez.
36:26, 27).

The prophets remind us that grace is to be a deterrent to sin.
They affirm that privilege brings responsibility. "You only
have I chosen of all the families of the earth; therefore I will
punish you for all your sins" (Amos 3:2). Healthy and realistic
views of one's self and of divine grace are needed for a time in

which the church is tempted to peddle cheap grace. A proper diagnosis of our problem is the first step toward a remedy. The prophets can help to point us in that direction by showing us that there is a Holy Spirit-inspired ministry of reproof.

> Reproof, then, must be understood *as much more than a mere rebuke*, a chiding for sin, as a *quid pro quo*. It is an appeal from a holy God to sinful man . . . the special object of which is to awaken in him a sense of his sin, a hatred of it, and a departure from it. It is an act of mercy far more than of punishment. . . The object of reproof is to show man his failure, to point out his mistake, to lead him once more towards the real aim of his existence (W. A. Bartlett, *The Profitableness of the Old Testament Scriptures*, pp. 170-171 cited in W. Kaiser, *Toward Rediscovering the Old Testament*, p. 30).

3. *Their Message Calls for Change*

Because of their strong idea of sin, they preach much about repentance. They spell out in considerable detail what is involved in turning to God. The prophets are "covenant enforcement mediators" whose task is to remind the people of God of what it meant *to be* the people of God (Ex. 19:5, 6) in the light of his wonderful mercy and grace. God's word to his people comes by way of the prophets (Deut. 18:15, 18, 19). Tragically, his people turn their back to God and not their faces and forget him days without number (Jer. 2:27, 32).

> They refused to pay attention; stubbornly they turned their backs and stopped up their ears. They made their hearts as hard as flint and would not listen to the law and to the words that the Lord Almighty had sent by His Spirit through the earlier prophets (Zech. 7:11-13a; cf. II Kings 17:13-15).

Such reminders, pleadings and warnings of the danger of condemnation given by the prophets are overtures of divine grace and a vital part of the task of a prophet (II Chron. 7:14; Is. 55:1-5; Zech. 1:2-3). When the prophets announce disaster their announcements themselves are exhortations to repentance. A recent study by A. Hunter, *Seek the Lord*, 1982, analyzes an abundance of such calls to seek God. In the eighth century prophets alone one finds *repeated* pleadings for a change of heart, mind and ways (cf. Amos 4:12; 5:4-5, 6; 5:14-15, 24; Hos. 2:4-5; 4:15; 6:6; 10:12; Is. 1:16-20; 7:3-9; 28:12, 16; 30:15; Micah

6:8). The prophetic message concerning repentance is addressed first and foremost to the individual. Of course their
messages are also relevant to the corporate society of Israel.
The concept of the remnant, however, implies that though
Jewish society as a whole is headed in the wrong direction,
individuals within that society can go against the strong tide of
wickedness and unbelief. Amos laments the fall of virgin
Israel (5:1), but that does not prevent him from strongly pleading with individuals within corporate Israel to seek the Lord
(5:3, 6, 14).

✱The familiar statement that the task of the preacher is to
comfort the afflicted (Is. 40:1, 2) and to afflict the comfortable
(Amos 6:1-7) has biblical and Old Testament warrant, though
there is much to learn about *how* this can best be done.* The
prophets are disturbers of the peace, which likely accounts for
their unpopularity.** It is doubtful that Amos would have
ingratiated himself with his audiences after accusing some of
the wealthy women in Israel of oppressing the poor and referring to them as "cows of Bashan" (Amos 4:1, 2). Similarly,
when he addresses the notable men (the ruling classes) within
the nation with the words "Woe to you who are complacent in
Zion and to you who feel secure on Mount Samaria" (Amos
6:1), he is not in competition for being the most popular
preacher of the day! Amaziah probably regards him as a
"prophet for pay" whose message is dictated by the faces of the
audience (Jer. 1:8; Ez. 3:8 — in both cases the Hebrew for
"face" is used) or the amount of money offered (Micah 3:11).
"The land can't bear all his words . . . Go back to the land of
Judah. Earn your bread there and do your prophesying there"
(Amos 7:10, 12). We know that he doesn't run scared in the
presence of this threat but faces it boldly and courageously.

Even kings (whom Amaziah was representing) could not
control a prophet's message! Prophets resist the pressures of
conformity, popularity and majority opinion in order to call
the nation back to God.

---

* The prophets "proclaimed judgment and disaster when there was false
  hope, and announced salvation when there was false despair." (G. Tucker, *Prophecy in Israel*, D. Peterson, editor, 1987, p. 160). Ezekiel best
  exemplifies this practice. The first half is all judgment but chapter 33 forward to the end provides a new hope for a discouraged people.

** See Chapter III,C,3, "The Prophets and Spiritual Honesty."

Micaiah was prompted by the messenger to get in line with the unanimous messages of the 400 prophets who had assured Jehoshaphat that Ramoth-Gilead would be conquered. Truth, however, won out in the end when he said, "As surely as the Lord lives, I can tell him only what the Lord tells me" (I Kings 22:14).

4. *Their Message Gives a Hopeful Perspective on History*

One of the issues that contemporary man wrestles with is the question, Is there any meaning in life? Is history going anywhere? Who is in charge of world history? The wisdom books address this matter with a multi-faceted perspective. Proverbs affirms with unshakable confidence that there is a sovereign Lord of history who is in charge, who is governing and ruling in the affairs of people (Prov. 21:1). Koheleth looks at the world and is not as sure. He affirms that it will be impossible to perceive the plan of God with any kind of privileged or insider perspective (Eccl. 11:5). The prophets provide many "case studies" of God's involvement in history using wonderful imagery:

> In that day the Lord will whistle for flies from the distant streams of Egypt and for bees from the land of Assyria . . . In that day the Lord will use a razor hired from beyond the River — the king of Assyria — to shave your head and the hair of your legs and to take off your beards also. (Is. 7:18, 20)

> God summons world empires, as a man whistles for an animal . . . When an empire appears in our historical field of vision, it takes up all the space; all thoughts are directed toward it, and God who is at work in the background seems to us shadowy and uncertain . . . Just the opposite is true of the prophets! That empire beyond the Euphrates is nothing at all; it is a borrowed razor, nothing more. It exists as though it had no will of its own, no power of self-motivation; all activity proceeds from God. Men see an empire which they do not know to be dangerous or not; the prophet sees only God and God quite directly and immediately at work in history! (G. von Rad, *God at Work in Israel*, 1980, pp. 164, 165)

History is the field of divine action. "The element in which the prophets live is the storm of the world's history" (J. Wellhausen, *Prolegomena to the History of Israel*, 1885, p. 398).

The prophet Habakkuk is outraged at God for his non-involvement in Jewish history and then for his involvement in Gentile history using the Chaldeans as his instrument of discipline. The exposition of that important prophet provides an alternative perspective to Harold Kushner's *Why Bad Things Happen to Good People*:

> What distinguishes the prophetic view of history from that of other oriental peoples is not the thought that God works in historical events, but rather that the prophets regarded the history of Israel as a *coherent* history directed by *moral principles* and in accordance with a *fixed plan* (J. Lindblom, *Prophecy in Ancient Israel*, 1962, p. 325).

The footprints of God, however, are not always clearly visible in history. Fixed plan and settled purpose, yes, but the details of the plan are hidden. This hiddenness of God is expressed in a burst of praise from Isaiah: "Truly you are a God who hides himself, O God and Savior of Israel" (Is. 45:15a). The occasion of this prayer would seem to be God's mysterious ways in raising up Cyrus, a Persian king, to allow the exiles to return from captivity (Is. 45:1, 13).

Von Rad summarizes the witness of the prophets to God's ways in world history as follows:

1) God's power in history is complete. He is decisively at work in everything. Nations and empires that seem so totally dominating to us are nothing before him. "Behold the nations are like a drop from the bucket, and are accounted as dust on the scales" (Is. 40:15).

2) But God's sovereignty in history is hidden; it mocks the most clever and profound human criteria and confronts man with impenetrable riddles. But in that which seems senseless to man, like an agonizing round of affairs, God is mobilizing history for his great future. That was, indeed, one of the most remarkable illuminations of the prophets, that in the midst of a generation that was indifferent to and secure in this flow, this stream of history, they were given to perceive its end, the Day of the Lord. Much in history contradicts God's will, but God comes. He does not intend to liquidate his creation; he comes to establish his kingdom (*God at Work in Israel*, p. 167, 168).

Such a picture of God's involvement in history is in stark

contrast with the near Eastern, mythological, cyclical view of reality. For the prophets "History is moving toward the great manifestation of God in history" (von Rad, *God at Work in Israel*, p. 169). Of course this view is not without its difficulties, the problem of evil being the central issue. Prophets such as Jeremiah and Habakkuk wrestled with that concern in an impassioned way.

The prophetic view of history is not in the strictest sense a philosophy of history, but rather a matter of faith. As one looks at the figure of God's lowly servant portrayed in Isaiah, an amazing contrast is seen between the servant's humiliation and the servant's exaltation. Before God's weak and powerless servant is placed the entire world of nations represented by their kings who bow in reverent submission to him (Is. 52:13-15; cf. Ps. 2).

> Is it not true that to see history in this way, to see God's concealed sovereignty in it and its flow toward the great breakdown, is not a matter of a particular philosophy of history? It is not a possibility of human perspicacity or profundity; it is not a general truth that lies tangibly in history to be recognized by anyone who has the will to do so. Plainly stated, that perception can be only a gift of illumination, of a special revelation in which God grants us himself (von Rad, *God at Work in Israel*, p. 174).

5. *Their Message is Socially Relevant*

What more pressing issue faces our society today than that of social justice for the poor and underprivileged? The Law and the Prophets studied together will provide a wealth of information and perspective on God's concern for the powerless and disadvantaged within society. While the interpretation and application of this Old Testament material is difficult, it is unfortunately true that the Old Testament is largely ignored. Apart from occasional preaching from Amos, we are almost totally in the dark on its message in this area. We need the Old Testament prophetic word about justice to sensitize and inform us so that we perceive how public issues of justice may be related to the faith and life of God's people today. But we must first briefly examine social justice as seen by the prophets.

The eighth-century prophet Amos is well-known for pronouncements in the area of social justice. He fulminates against the cows of Bashan (the opulent women in Israel) who oppress the poor and crush the needy through the pressure they bring upon their husbands for more material comforts (Amos 4:1). The poor are turned aside in the gate (Amos 5:12), the place where judicial verdicts are proclaimed. Through unjust economic practices the needy are trampled and the poor of the land turned away while the rich get richer by making the bushels smaller and in the process the shekels greater (Amos 8:4-6).

Similarly, Micah warns against those whose bedtime scheming led them "to covet fields and seize them, and houses, and take them. They defraud a man of his home, a fellowman of his inheritance" (Micah 2:2). In the Old Testament land had religious significance. It came to each family as a gift from the Lord who was its real owner (Lev. 25:23). Each family's portion

was the sacrament of their place and right in the territory . . . to lose their inheritance was tantamount to losing their identity as a member of the people and the privileges that went with that identity . . . The land was not only the basic economic good in society, essential to well-being, but it also bestowed identity; it was the instrument of participation in the society as an equal, the foundation of freedom (J. Mays, "Justice: Perspectives from the Prophetic Tradition," *Interpretation* 37, 1983, p. 11).

Against the judicial leaders Micah uses phrases like, "who tear off their (the poor's) skin," "who eat the flesh of my people" (Micah 3:2, 3). Micah accuses these power brokers of being financial cannibals! The best commentary on these expressions is Proverbs 30:14: There is a kind of person "whose teeth are swords and whose jaws are set with knives to devour the poor from the earth, and the needy from among mankind."

Jeremiah says that pleading the cause of the poor and needy is what is involved in knowing God (22:16).

Isaiah speaks in numerous places of the Lord's concern for the poor. He speaks to the elders and princes of God's people:

'It is you who have ruined my vineyard;
the plunder from the poor is in your houses.
What do you mean by crushing my people
and grinding the faces of the poor?' declares the Lord . . .
(Is. 3:14, 15)

He speaks against evil legislation:

> Woe to those who make unjust laws,
> to those who issue oppressive decrees,
> to deprive the poor of their rights
> and withhold justice from the oppressed of my people
> making widows their prey and robbing the fatherless. (Is. 10:1, 2)

In language reminiscent of Matthew 25:34-40, Isaiah spoke of the fast that God chose:

> Is this not the kind of fasting I have chosen:
> to loose the chains of injustice
> and untie the cords of the yoke,
> to set the oppressed free . . .
> Is it not to share your food with the hungry
> and to provide the poor wanderer with shelter
> when you see the naked, to clothe him . . . (Is. 58:6, 7)

Ezekiel's definition of righteousness is remarkable. It includes things such as restoring to the debtor his pledge, giving bread to the hungry and covering the naked with clothing (Ez. 18:7; cf. also Ez. 18:12, 16; 22:7).

Zephaniah calls the unjust judges "evening wolves that leave nothing for the morning" (Zeph. 3:3).

The last prophet of the Old Testament, Malachi, is consistent with the uniform witness of his predecessors when he writes:

> I will draw near to you for judgment; and I will be a swift witness against the sorcerers and the adulterers and those who swear falsely, and those who oppress the wage earner in his wages, the widow and the orphan and those who turn aside the alien and do not fear me, says the Lord of Hosts. (Mal. 3:5)

It is understandable, in light of the prophetic mind on matters of social justice, that the Messiah's coming will bring relief for the poor (Is. 11:4; Ps. 72:12, 13). He cares for them.

We had earlier spoken of the prophets as preachers of repentance. It is important to see that the prophets connect *repentance* with the idea of *the doing of justice*.

> But you must *return* to your God;
> maintain love (hesed) and justice (mishpat),
> and wait for your God always. (Hos. 12:6)

Returning to God (repentance) is to be known by the presence of a faithful and enduring loyalty (hesed), the doing of
justice and an expectant trust and hope in the Lord. There is a
striking similarity in this verse to the well-known statement of
Micah:

> He has showed you, O man, what is good. And what does the Lord
> require of you? To act justly (mishpat) and to love mercy (hesed)
> and to walk humbly with your God. (Micah 6:8)

The verses immediately preceding this well-known passage
are an entrance liturgy (see Ps. 15 and 24; Is. 33:14, 15) that sets
out the requirements for entering worshipers if they are to be
admitted as genuine worshipers. Thus the prophet addresses
the issue of the response that God wants and expects from His
people. The reference in the text to *man* calls attention to the
great gulf between Yahweh and his creatures. It is a reminder
to the people of the great privilege of worshiping the Lord, a
privilege that becomes apparent when they consider both who
they are and who he is. "Good" is a term used by the prophets
to point to the covenantal standards:

> Put the Trumpet to your lips!
> An eagle is over the house of the Lord
> because the people have broken my covenant
> and rebelled against my law.
> Israel cries out to me, "O our God, we acknowledged you!"
> But Israel has rejected what is good . . . (Hos. 8:1, 2)

These standards have been announced to them. The verb to
"show" refers to the revelation of those stipulations (laws) that
are binding on the covenant community, which has been
redeemed by divine power and brought into a relationship
with the Lord (cf. Ex. 19:4: 1 . . . brought you to myself).
The first requirement, justice, focuses on the relationship of
the individual to the community:

> The Old Testament believer stood within a circle of other faithful
> men, all bound together by common membership of a covenant
> relationship with Yahweh . . . Commitment to Yahweh included
> commitment to the covenant community. Justice is the key word
> so often used by the prophets to sum up this social obligation. It
> covers and transcends a host of negative precepts, such as prohibi-

tion of oppression, perjury, and bribery. It calls for a sense of responsibility toward weaker members of society lest they go to the wall (L. Allen, *Books of Joel, Obadiah, Jonah and Micah*, 1976, p. 373).

The oracles against the nations in Amos 1:3 to 2:3 present a vivid scene in which the sovereign Lord's justice singles out various crimes committed by the surrounding nations, for which they will be punished. This section is followed by two other oracles entirely similar in structure but directed against Judah and Israel (Amos 2:4, 5; 6–16). Examination of the oracles against the foreign nations shows that the sins that Amos addresses are not directly committed against God but against humanity. Motyer summarizes by showing that

> Amos first examines violations of the general relationships of life, human being to human being, then the particular responsibilities of life, brother to brother, and finally the special claims of life, the attitude of the strong to the weak (A. Motyer, *The Message of Amos: The Day of the Lion*, 1974, p. 39).

Compared to these sins against conscience, Israel's sins were bold-faced transgressions of the clear voice of revelation. "They have rejected the law of the Lord and not kept his decrees" (Amos 2:4). When it comes to the mention of specific violations and indictments, we find sins against covenant brothers extremely prominent (Amos 2:6, 7a). The point of the comparison is this: Yahweh's justice is the plumb line that scrutinizes both the sins of the nations and those of his covenant people.

Many other verses could be cited to demonstrate that the relationships within the covenant were seen to be extremely important. In the Song of the Vineyard (Is. 5:1–7) we hear the anguished cry of a wounded lover:

> The vineyard of the Lord Almighty is the house of Israel, and the men of Judah are the garden of his delight. And he looked for justice, but saw bloodshed; for righteousness, but heard cries of distress. (Is. 5:7)

In this situation God asks the question:

> What more could have been done for my vineyard than I have done for it? (Is. 5:4a)

Commonly found together, justice and righteousness have an overlapping meaning. "Let justice roll on like a river, righteousness like a never-failing stream" (Amos 5:24; cf. Hos. 2:19; Is. 1:21; Jer. 22:15). These terms refer to

> the fulfillment of responsibilities that arise out of particular relationships within the community . . . Each relationship has its special obligation, and all relationships ultimately are bound by relationship to God (B. Anderson, *The Eighth Century Prophets: Amos, Hosea, Isaiah, Micah*, 1978, p. 43).

John Stek has given in overview form the central tenets of Israel's social order:
1. Everyone's person and property are to be secure.
2. Everyone is to receive the fruit of his labors.
3. Everyone is to be secure against slander and false accusations.
4. Everyone is to have free access to the courts and is to be afforded a fair trial.
5. Everyone is to share in the fruit of the ground.
6. Everyone, down to the humblest menial and the resident alien, is to share in the weekly rest of God's sabbath.
7. Every Israelite's dignity and right to be Yahweh's freedman and servant is to be honored and safeguarded.
8. Every Israelite's inheritance in the promised land is to be secure.
9. No woman is to be taken advantage of within her subordinate status in society.
10. No one, however disabled, impoverished or powerless, is to be oppressed or exploited.
11. No one shall be above the law, not even the King (Deut. 17:18–20).
12. Every person's God-given place in the social organism is to be honored.
13. Punishment for wrongdoing shall not be excessive with the result that the culprit is dehumanized (Deut. 25:1–3).
14. Concern for the welfare of other creatures is to be extended to the animal world.
    (J. Stek, "Salvation, Justice and Liberation in the Old Testament," *Calvin Theological Journal*, 13, 1978, pp. 150-154)

Why do the prophets so passionately press the issue of social justice? Why is there such an avalanche of material in their writings on this issue? It's because their passion is for God's people to *know* him (Is. 1:3ff, Hos. 4:1ff).

> Let him who boasts boast about this: that he understands and knows me that I am the Lord, who exercises kindness, justice and righteousness on the earth. (Jer. 9:24)

> God is the axiom and presupposition of all they say. Since God is the source of all righteousness and justice, knowledge of God is prior to the practice of justice (C. Wright, *An Eye for An Eye: The Place of Old Testament Ethics for Today,* 1983, p. 146).

Justice is an expression of what it means to be like God. God himself is compassionate and caring. Our concern for advocating and promoting social justice means that we may be like God (see Matt. 25:34–40). God's active intervention and involvement on behalf of the weak and oppressed form the pattern for us. It is not that the powerless are being viewed as sinless and innocent:

> Rather, this group in society receives God's special attention because they are on the "wronged" side of a situation of chronic injustice which God abhors and wishes to have redressed. For God's righteous will to be done requires the execution of justice on their behalf (Wright, p. 147).

In their moral behavior God's people must reflect the person and righteous actions of their covenant Lord. John Willis is surely correct when he writes:

> If God is so concerned that social justice be done, the idea that social justice is not "religious" is erroneous. It also follows that one cannot be "like God" in his attitude and action unless he advocates and promotes social justice and does all he can to stop social injustice ("Old Testament Foundations of Social Justice," in *Christian Social Ethics*, P. Cotham, editor, 1979, p. 26).

In addition, since the covenant Lord is the creator of heaven and earth, man's moral conduct is also rooted in creation:

> Every human person, therefore, by virtue of his humanity has a full claim on Adam's divinely appointed inheritance: his dignity, vocation, well-being and destiny. Every human person may claim that Genesis 1 and Psalm 8 speak of him. In this sense "all men

are created equal." All are to participate (each according to his
endowed abilities) in this dominion (Stek, p. 136).

The call to justice and righteousness is not only rooted in
God's redemptive activity but in the givens of creation and the
divine purpose for that creation.

We have been speaking of the prophetic emphasis on justice
and arguing that ignoring or undervaluing the Old Testament
prophetic message leads to an anemic approach to salvation.
The word justice is an abstract term, of course, and to look
even briefly at some of the Old Testament material helps to
sharpen one's thinking. A few concluding definitions may be
helpful. S. Rooy helps to clarify this Old Testament word:

> Justice is a sort of materialization of existence; i.e., it is the incar-
> nation in time and space of God's relation to his world; it is the
> creation-form of life in divinely-given structures for society with-
> out which man cannot even exist. (S. Rooy, "Righteousness & Jus-
> tice," *Evangelical Review of Theology,* 6, 1982, pp. 263-266).

Stek's summary is very useful and instructive:

> Everyone who has been "saved" by Yahweh's redemptive action is
> thereby called, as a member of the redeemed community, to be an
> agent of his redemptive purpose. That constitutes his vocation and
> defines his role in Yahweh's kingdom.

> As regards man's relationship to his fellowman his vocation is jus-
> tice (mishpat utsedaqah). And justice is man's right dealing with
> his neighbor — image-bearer with image-bearer, servant of God
> with servant of God, one assigned dominion with one assigned
> dominion, one having a vocation with one having a vocation, one
> given a place in the earth with one given a place in the earth, one
> appointed provisions from the earth with one appointed provi-
> sions from the earth, one created for blessing with one created for
> blessing, one whose divinely intended destiny is life with one whose
> divinely intended destiny is life. This, according to the Old Testa-
> ment, is the "justice" of the kingdom of God (Stek, pp. 164, 165).

At the beginning of this section on social justice we acknowledged a problem to which we must now return. It is the issue
of *how* the content of the Law and the Prophets is to be applied
and *to whom* it is to be applied. This difficulty is clearly preeminent in the comment of C. Ryrie:

> The Old Testament perspective on social ethics focuses on con-
> cern for the oppressed and on righteous living within the group. It
> does not command the establishment of justice in the world nor
> the care of all the oppressed in the world . . . It does show God's
> love for justice and holiness in personal living as well as in the
> community life of the theocracy ("Perspectives on Social Ethics,"
> *Bibliotheca Sacra*, 134, 1977, p. 122).

Ryrie's statement forces us to confront an issue of considerable importance and one that will have a major effect on the
church's use of the Old Testament content. This issue concerns the relationship of the Old Testament covenant people,
Israel, to the people of God today.*

Put in its starkest form the question is of what importance
are the statements in the Law and the Prophets concerning
justice to Christians who are no longer living within the theocracy? The massive amount of law in the Pentateuch that
bears on the social dimensions of life requires some response.
Some, of course, believe that Israel is Israel, the church is the
church and never the two shall meet. Others, on the opposite
extreme, wish to transpose literally the theocratic laws into our
twentieth-century setting.

At this point mention should be made of the recent work of
C. Wright, *An Eye for an Eye, The Place of Old Testament Ethics
for Today*. His basic thesis is that Israel was God's paradigm.
Just as the incarnation of Christ was for the purpose of revealing God, so "there was an 'incarnational' and revelational
aspect of God's creation of Israel":

> The social shape of Israel was not an incidental freak of ancient
> history, nor was it just a temporary, material by-product of their
> spiritual message. It was an integral part of what God had called
> them into existence for. God's message of redemption through
> Israel was not just verbal; it was visible and tangible. They, the
> medium, were themselves part of the message (Wright, p. 40).

Wright explains what it means to see Israel as God's paradigm:

---

* Cf. III, A. 3. The recent book of essays in honor of S. Lewis Johnson gives
  diverse perspectives on the relationship between the Old and New Testaments and is extremely helpful. Cf. *Continuity and Discontinuity*, John S.
  Feinberg, editor, 1988. See also "Israel and the Church (Two Views)". E.
  Clowney and P. Leonard in *Dreams, Visions, and Oracles*. C. Armerding,
  editor, 1977.

The choice of the term "paradigm" needs some explanation and justification. A paradigm is something used as a model or example for other cases where a basic principle remains unchanged, though details differ. It commonly refers, for example, to patterns in grammatical inflection — a verb, say, taken to exemplify the way endings or prefixes will go for other verbs of a similar type. A paradigm is not so much imitated as applied. It is assumed that cases will differ but, when necessary adjustments have been made, they will conform to the observable pattern of the paradigm (Wright, p. 43).

Wright's approach takes the middle ground between those who almost totally ignore the Old Testament teaching because it was for the theocracy (dispensationalists) and those who wish to (rather literally) catapult it into today's society (theonomists):

> This way of looking at the social life, institutions and laws of Israel protects us from two opposite dangers.
>
> On the one hand it means that we do not think in terms of literal imitation of Israel. We cannot simply transpose the social laws of an ancient people into the modern world and try to make them work as written. That would be tantamount to taking the paradigms of a grammar book as the only words one could use in that particular language. The paradigms are there, not to be the sum of possible communication ever after, but to be applied to the infinite complexities of the rest of the language.
>
> On the other hand, the social system of Israel cannot be dismissed as relevant only within the confines of historical Israel, and as totally inapplicable to either the Christian church or the rest of mankind. If Israel was meant to be a light to the nations (cf. Is. 49:6), then that light must be allowed to illuminate (Wright, pp. 43, 44).

Wright further explains:

> In the economic sphere, the Old Testament paradigms provide us with *objectives* without requiring a *literal* transposition of ancient Israelite practice into twentieth-century society. But at the same time the paradigmatic approach compels us to wrestle seriously with texts themselves in order fully to understand the models we are seeking to apply. It also prevents us from taking this attitude, "This was all given in the context of a redeemed community and is therefore irrelevant to secular, unregenerate society." For we have clearly seen that the very purpose of the provisions given in the

context of redemption was to restore a measure of conformity to the original economic purposes of God in creation. So if we believe that it is in the interests even of fallen human society to respect "the Maker's instructions," as is the view of those who strongly uphold a "creation ethic" approach, we shall advocate policies and values drawn from the ethics of that nation who knew God as both *Redeemer* and Maker (Wright, p. 89).

Wright's comparison with the incarnation of Christ is very helpful. We're called to follow Christ and to live our lives in such a way as to be like Christ. Yet this is not to be taken in a woodenly literalistic way (we must therefore practise Christ's trade of carpentry, wear the same kind of clothing, follow an itinerant lifestyle, etc.):

We tend, unconsciously or otherwise, to use the example of Jesus paradigmatically in our ethical decisions, seeking to move from what we know Jesus *did* do to what we might reasonably presume he *would* do in our changed situation. The overall shape and character of his life — comprising his actions, attitudes and relationships as well as his responses, parables and other teaching — becomes our pattern or paradigm, by which we test the "Christlikeness" of the same components of our own lives (Wright, p. 44).

In elevating the Old Testament writings as Wright does and arguing for a new importance to the theocracy as a paradigm, we shouldn't think that the New Testament directives for social thought will be overpowered. Wright comments:

They are not, of course, the exclusive paradigm for social ethics; the Christian brings this, as he does every other aspect of the Old Testament, into the light of the new age of fulfilment and the Kingdom of God inaugurated by Christ. He therefore sets his Old Testament social paradigm alongside the paradigm of the social life of the early church as well as the explicit social teaching of Jesus and the apostles. Only then is he beginning to formulate a wholly biblical social ethic (Wright, pp. 44, 45).

Wright's views open up an exciting new avenue for reflection and action and therefore have been quoted at length. Failure to employ the insights of the prophets and to wrestle with their application today seriously hampers the church in its mission and witness. Further study of the social aspect of the writings of the prophets will lead to much greater light on sev-

eral issues that continue to engage the church; i.e., the relationship between social justice and evangelism, and the question
of capitalistic vs. socialistic views of economics.*

6. *Their Message is Christ-Centered*

The uniform testimony of Jesus, the gospels and the New
Testament apostles is that the prophets spoke of the coming of
the Messiah. Exactly *how* they did so must be ascertained from
the Old Testament itself.

We will first survey some of the New Testament passages
that stress the place of the *prophets* in proclaiming Messianic
doctrine. Then we will briefly examine the prophetic teaching
concerning the Messiah.

In Jesus' post-resurrection appearances we find him putting
great stress on the Old Testament prophetic witness to his
ministry. This emphasis may be seen in his strong statement
calling those who ignore the witness of the prophets "fools"
and in his sovereign activity of opening the disciples' minds so
they could understand the Old Testament Scriptures (Luke
24:24, 45).

The conclusion to the story of the rich man and Lazarus
contrasts the need for a miraculous intervention from the dead
and its supposed effect on unbelievers with the scriptural revelation of the Old Testament:

> If someone from the dead goes to them, they will repent.
> He said to him, If they do not *listen* to *Moses and the prophets* they
> will not be convinced even if someone rises from the dead. (Luke
> 16:30b, 31)

Deuteronomy 18:15, 18 speaks of a special prophet raised up
by God to bring God's word to all who would *listen*. There is a
linkage between the coming of Messiah and the need to listen

---

* The interaction of J. Stott, *Christian Mission to the World*, 1975, and R.
  Sider on the relation between social action and evangelism is helpful and
  challenging. Sider remarks,

  "The prophets also disclosed how the God of justice responds to oppres-
  sive social structures. God cares so much about the poor that he will destroy social structures that tolerate and foster great poverty" (*Rich Christians in an Age of Hunger*,1977, p. 137). Cf. R. Sider, *Evangelism, Salvation
  and Social Justice*, with a response by J. Stott. Grove Booklet 16, 1977.

to him (Deut. 18:19). This same linkage was proclaimed by Peter in Acts 3:

> Now brothers, I know that you acted in ignorance, as did your leaders. But this is how God fulfilled what he had foretold through all the prophets, saying that his Christ would suffer. Repent, then, and turn to God so that your sins may be wiped out . . . Anyone who does not listen to him will be completely cut off from among his people. (Acts 3:17–19a, 23)

Peter goes on to connect the prophecy in Deut. 18:15–18 about God's unique prophet, and the need to *listen* to him, with two other Old Testament messianic portraits. By scriptural quotation he joins the promise of the suffering servants (Acts 3:18b, 26) to the "seed of Abraham" promise (Acts 3:25).

Stephen's speech in Acts 7 makes several general points concerning the Messiah. Messiah would be a prophet like Moses (Acts 7:37). The prophets, he says, "predicted the coming of the Righteous One" (Acts 7:52). The prophets were persecuted and killed for doing so, he says, just as the Righteous One was betrayed and murdered (Acts 7:52b).

The Ethiopian eunuch came to faith in Christ by reading Isaiah 53. This passage provoked the question, " 'Who is the prophet talking about, himself or someone else?' Then Philip began with that very passage of Scripture and told him the good news about Jesus" (Acts 8:34, 35).

At the critical juncture when Cornelius the Gentile centurion came to faith in Christ, Peter received the vision and the explanation, "Do not call anything impure that God has made clean" (Acts 10:15). Later at Cornelius' home he preached a message on the universal offer of mercy to Jew and Gentile alike based on Christ's redemptive accomplishments. This message ended with the words, "*All the prophets testify about him* that *everyone* who believes in him receives forgiveness of sins through his name" (Acts 10:43). In context this statement not only points to the messianic doctrine as the unifying theme of all the prophets but to the free offer of the gospel, to all (everyone who believes).

Paul testifies of his conversion to Christ and to his call to apostleship before King Agrippa in Acts 26:2–24. In the conclusion to his moving testimony he remarks:

> I am saying nothing beyond what the prophets and Moses said

would happen — that the Christ would suffer and, as the first to rise from the dead, would proclaim light to his own people and to the Gentiles. (Acts 26:22b, 23)

When Paul was taken captive to Rome he had an opportunity, even while under house guard, to preach and teach about Jesus. Three days after arriving in Rome Paul somehow managed to address the leaders of the Jews. They came in large numbers to the place where Paul was staying and "from morning to evening he explained and declared to them the kingdom of God and tried to convince them about Jesus from the Law of Moses and from the Prophets" (Acts 28:23, 24). The apostolic preaching centered on the reality of God's kingdom and rule as personified in Jesus; and they knew about the kingdom of God which had come in Jesus because of the Law of Moses and the writings of the prophets (cf. Acts 28:31).

Three passages in Romans suggest that the early church got its teaching concerning Christ from the Old Testament prophets as well as New Testament apostles. In Rom. 1:2–4 Paul says the gospel was promised by God

> *through his prophets* in the Holy Scriptures, regarding his Son, who as to his human nature was a descendant of David and who through the Spirit of holiness was declared with the power to be the Son of God by his resurrection from the dead.

The gospel that credits sinners with the righteousness of Christ through faith was made known and testified to by the Law and the Prophets. "But now a righteousness from God apart from law has been made known, to which the Law and the Prophets testify" (Rom. 3:21, 22).

Even in Paul's doxological statements he cannot refrain from connecting the gospel he preaches with the prophetic writings. The gospel that Paul preached was "now revealed and made known through the prophetic writings by the command of the eternal God, so that all nations might believe and obey him" (Rom. 16:26).

The evidence is thus quite substantial that the New Testament sees the prophets as being supremely important because they speak of Christ. No verse says this more clearly than the well-known passage of I Peter 1:10–12. On this text Kaiser helpfully comments:

There were five things the prophets were certain of when they wrote their texts. They knew they were predicting that (1) the Messiah would come; (2) the Messiah would suffer; (3) the Messiah would be glorified (in kingly splendour); (4) the order of events 2 & 3 was that the suffering came first, and then the glorious period followed; and (5) this message had been revealed to the prophets not only for their own day, but also for a future generation such as the church of Peter's audience (v. 12) (W. Kaiser, *The Uses of the Old Testament in the New*, 1985, p. 20).

Exactly *how* the Old Testament speaks of the coming Messiah must now be addressed in brief.*

The approach to messianic prophecy that divides the topic into three parts — the Messiah as Prophet, Priest and King — has much to recommend it. This three-fold approach was developed in the course of Old Testament revelation. The Messiah would be the Prophet like Moses (Deut. 18:15-18). He would be a Priest (Ps. 110:4; Zech. 6:12, 13) whose soul was made to be a trespass offering (Is. 53:10). He would be the descendant of David, a King given an eternal kingdom by decree of the Lord (II Sam. 7:12b; Ps. 2:6, 7; Zech. 9:9, 10).

The doctrine of the Messiah can also be studied in its historical progression. This approach would begin with Genesis 3:15 and move out to the study of "the seed of Abraham" doctrine in Genesis and elsewhere. What is the meaning of the covenant that God gave to Abraham, and how does it relate to Christ? Genesis 49:8-10 needs to be studied, and in particular v. 10: "to him shall be the obedience of the nations." The next critical passage in order of appearance would be the promise of a prophet like Moses to whom the Lord would give words and who would speak for him (Deut. 18:15-21).

The prophets elaborate on the covenant made with David in II Samuel 7 and in particular v. 13 and 14. To understand how they do this is a key to understanding their messages. Chapter 6 of F. F. Bruce's book, *This is That: New Testament Development of Old Testament Themes*, 1968, traces the progress of the promise to David through the prophetic writings in a very helpful way.

One of the most important figures of salvation which we

---

*Apart from the general references to books on messianic prophecy already mentioned, two smaller books on the servant should be consulted for help on preaching and teaching: H. Blocher, *The Servant Songs*, 1975, and F. Duane Lindsay, *The Songs of the Servant*, 1985.

meet in the prophets is the servant of the Lord (Is. 42:1-9; 49:1-7; 50:1-4; 52:13-53:12; 61:1-4).

One is tempted to say of this figure, as was said concerning the one whom the New Testament identifies as the servant, that the whole world wouldn't have room for all the books written about him (John 21:25).

In the period of the exile the messianic doctrine was prominent, expanding with Ezekiel's and Daniel's spectacular predictions about the universal triumph of God's kingdom. In light of the exile, with its demoralization of the people, one can see why these assurances were needed.

Ezekiel is given the promise of the revitalization of the people under their "one shepherd, my servant David" (Ez. 37:15-28; cf. Ez. 16:60-63). There are a plethora of similar assurances in Daniel centering on the triumph and final victory of God's messianic kingdom (cf. Dan. 2; 7:12,13; 9:24-27). Dan. 2:45 refers to Messiah as a stone, Dan. 7:13,14 as a Son of Man and Dan. 9:25 as Anointed One, the ruler. Being sorely pressed in exile with the temple destroyed, the Davidic dynasty deposed, and the people deported from the land, it was necessary for the promise of salvation to be reiterated forcefully to keep the flame of faith burning.

The post-exilic prophets continued to speak of Messiah and his kingdom in terms continuous with the past (Haggai 2:6-9; Zech. 3:8; 6:12,13; 9:9; Mal. 3:1-3).

It has not been our purpose to expound in detail the substance of the many promises concerning Christ and his kingdom. Rather, it is to outline briefly two possible lines of approach to handling messianic prophecy; i.e., topically, in terms of Messiah as Prophet, Priest and King, or tracing the progress of messianic revelation historically through the line of prophets who foretold the coming of the Messiah.

The point of our brief look at the several ways in which the Old Testament pointed to the Messiah is this: to preach the good news of Jesus Christ necessitates proclaiming the antecedent to that good news; i.e., the messianic promises of the Old Testament:

Jesus Christ is not some mysterious figure, suddenly appearing from the blue. He is not an ideal divorced from history, or simply a projection of theological speculation. He is not a myth or a symbol of a new self-understanding on the part of man. He is not a humanistic model of a righteous man for others. Jesus Christ is the fulfillment of God's word to Israel. He is the completion and reinterpretation of Israel's two thousand years of history with her God. He is God's act whereby he brings his salvation histories to their end and begins a new one (Achtemeier, *The Old Testament and the Proclamation of the Gospel*, pp. 115, 116).

C. The Importance of Their Example

The prophetic books contain limited material on the lives of the prophets. The central focus then is on their messages, not on their personal lives. Yet, having said this, we will miss out if we ignore the sections of the prophetic writings in which the veil is lifted and we are privileged to see something of how their messages impinged on their lives. Greidanus is correct when he notes that "the concentration on the prophet is not for his sake but for the sake of the message that is being proclaimed through his life and trials" (S. Greidanus, *The Modern Preacher and the Ancient Text*, 1988, p. 256).

But this would make it all the more important to consider specifically how the prophetic writings relate the personal experiences of the prophets to their messages. Von Rad argues that with the prophets of the Babylonian and early Persian periods one sees that the prophetic office "increasingly invaded their personal and spiritual lives"* (*Old Testament Theology*, Vol. 2, p. 274).

1. *Prophets and Prayer*

The prophets are not widely known for their prayers, but rather for their preaching. The fact is, however, that Israel's prophets were intercessors before the throne of grace as well as proclaimers of the word before men and women. They resemble their counterparts in the New Testament, the apostles, who are described as those who give "attention to prayer and the

---

* Commenting on how the biographical material in Jeremiah is best understood. T.E. Fretheim, *The Suffering of God*, 1984, p. 156, suggests, "It is likely, however, that these materials are not introduced for biographical purposes; they are intended to reflect the nature of the Word which Jeremiah brings. He not only speaks the Word of God; he embodies it. And all the twists and turns of his own humanity are intended to portray for the people not simply his own life, but his own life as an enfleshment of the life of God."

ministry of the word" (Acts 6:4b). The first mention of the word "prophet" in the Old Testament is in relation to intercessory prayer (Gen. 20:7). A prophet is one who speaks from God to people and to God concerning people. Prophetic intercessory prayer is not just praying *for* others, but identifying *with* others in prayer. Thus Jeremiah prays:

> Although our sins testify against us,
> O Lord, do something for the sake of your name . . .
> You are among us, O Lord, and we bear your name;
> Do not forsake us . . .
> Have you rejected Judah completely?
> Do you despise Zion?
> Why have you afflicted us so that we cannot be healed?
> . . . O Lord, we acknowledge our wickedness and the guilt of our fathers;
> we have indeed sinned against you.
> For the sake of your name do not despise us;
> Do not dishonor your glorious throne.
> Remember your covenant with us and do not break it. (Jer. 14:7, 9, 19-21)

The calling of a prophet is to identify both with God and God's people. This dual identification, of necessity, leads to tension within the prophet. In intercessory prayer the prophets stand where the people stand. Amos receives five visions of divine judgment (Amos 7-1:9). After the first two he pleads with God, "Sovereign Lord, forgive! How can Jacob survive? He is so small" (Amos 7:2, 4). In each case the judgment is averted and God spares his people. Calvin remarks on this dual identification:

> *We now see that God's servants had so ruled and moderated their feelings, that pity did not prevent them from being severe whenever their calling so required; and also this severity did not obliterate from their minds the feeling of compassion . . . He was therefore severe, because God so commanded him; it was what his calling required; but at the same time he pitied the people (J. Calvin, *Twelve Minor Prophets*, Vol. 2, 1950, p. 329).

The lesson for God's servants today may be pointedly drawn from the recognition of the prophets' intercessory role as concomitant with their proclamatory role in the declaration of God's justice and wrath.

Calvin comments:

⚹Let then all teachers in the Church learn to put on these two feelings — to be vehemently indignant whenever they see the worship of God profaned, to burn with zeal for God and to show that severity which appeared in all the prophets, whenever due order decays — and at the same time to sympathise with miserable men, whom they see rushing headlong into destruction, and to bewail their madness and to interpose with God as much as is in them; in such a way, however, that their compassion render them not slothful or indifferent, so as to be indulgent to the sins of men (Calvin, *Twelve Minor Prophets*, Vol. 2, pp. 329, 330).

At the time Sennacherib besieged Jerusalem (II Kings 19:1-7; Is. 37:1-7), Hezekiah's response is to initiate a public fast. He also sends some of his palace administrators to the prophet Isaiah specifically asking him to "pray for the remnant that still survives" (Is. 37:4b). Rhodes believes that "such an appeal recalls the long and continuing tradition of the intercessory role of Israel's earlier prophets" (A. Rhodes, "Israel's Prophets as Intercessors," in *Scripture in History and Theology*, A. L. Merrill and T. Overholt, editors, 1977, p. 117).

In the seventh century two prophets in particular remind us of the ministry of prayer that is a part of a prophet's calling. Habakkuk is frustrated that God is not responding to his prayers (Hab. 1:2-4). Then in one of the briefest, yet most moving prayers, he asks the Lord, "In wrath remember mercy" (Hab. 3:2).

The prayers of Jeremiah provide us with exceptionally important material for study. It is notable that on four occasions Jeremiah is forbidden by the Lord to pray (Jer. 7:16; 11:14; 14:11; 15:1). The last incident is particularly interesting because of the Lord's insistence that even if the great prayer warriors Moses and Samuel who functioned as prophets and interceded with God in remarkable ways (Ex. 32:31, 32; 34:9; I Sam. 12:23) were to stand before him, they would not prevail (Jer. 15:1-4). These four occasions surely indicate that Jeremiah, like Amos, is a person who combined denunciatory prophetic preaching with compassionate and serious pleading before God.

The confessions of Jeremiah (4:19-21; 8:18-9:1; 15:10, 15-21; 20:7-18), have been the subject of intensive study and need to be addressed separately, but they surely provide us with evidence of a man who stormed the gates of heaven in prayer for his own spiritual and physical well-being. In one passage in which Jeremiah reminds the Lord of the charges of his accusers he says, "Remember that I *stood before you* and spoke in their behalf to turn your wrath away from them" (Jer. 18:20).

Two incidents are recorded in which specific requests for prayer are made to Jeremiah (cf. Jer. 37:1-17, particularly v. 3, and 42:1-6).

False prophets were telling the people that the exile would last only a few years and that the vessels taken by Nebuchadnezzar would be speedily returned. Jeremiah accused these prophets of speaking lies. His argument was: "If they are prophets and have the word of the Lord, let them *plead* with the Lord Almighty that the furnishings remaining in the house of the Lord and in the palace of the king of Judah and in Jerusalem not be taken to Babylon" (Jer. 27:18).

Three passages in Ezekiel remind us of the ministry of prayer and intercession in which prophets engaged.

Ezekiel sees a vision of the glory of God departing from the temple (cf. 9:3). The scene that follows is one of devastation and ruin because of the detestable things done within the city (9:4b). As the slaughter continues the prophet is in anguish and pleads, "Ah, Sovereign Lord! Are you going to destroy the entire remnant of Israel in this outpouring of your wrath on Jerusalem?" (Ez. 9:8).

Ezekiel 11 contains the record of a meeting of leaders in Jerusalem. Evidently these leaders are responsible for the deaths of innocent people. The narrative records the name of one individual, Pelatiah, who suddenly dies. His death seems to represent for Ezekiel the tragic situation involving the whole people, and again the prophet cries out in intercessory anguish, "Ah, Sovereign Lord! Will you completely destroy the remnant of Israel?" (Ez. 11:13).

Ezekiel is very critical of the false prophets who "have not gone up to the breaks in the wall to repair it for the house of Israel so that it will stand firm in the battle on the day of the Lord" (13:5). Their not building a wall refers to the protection of God's people through intercessory prayer. "Without question Ezekiel is thinking of omission to plead for the nation in prayer, though perhaps he may also have had some other form of intercessory work in mind" (von Rad, *Old Testament Theology*, Vol. 2, p. 275)

One of the great prayers for revival in the Bible may be found in the 64th chapter of Isaiah. Here we are reminded of how fervently the prophets sought the face of God for renewal and blessing:

> Oh, that you would rend the heavens and come down, that the mountains would tremble before you!
> As when fire sets twigs ablaze and causes water to boil, come down to make your name known to your enemies and cause the nations to quake before you! (Is. 64:1, 2)

This prayer for the living presence of God contains a moving confession:

> No one calls on your name or strives to lay hold of you; for you have hidden your face from us and made us waste away because of our sins. Yet, O Lord, you are our Father. We are the clay, you are the potter; we are the work of your hand. Do not be angry beyond measure, O Lord; do not remember our sins forever. Oh, look upon us, we pray for we are all your people. (Is. 64:7-9)

As we study the prayers of the apostles in the New Testament so we will profit from listening to the prophets as they engage in the ministry of prayer for those to whom they proclaim the word of God.

2. Prophets and Suffering

The prophets often encounter fierce opposition. Their messages were resisted (Amos 2:11, 12; Micah 2:6), leading to persecution. As he is about to die, Stephen puts this question to his audience, "Was there ever a prophet your fathers did not persecute?" (Acts 7:52). Jesus' words in the Sermon on the Mount address the issue of suffering quite pointedly:

> Blessed are you when people insult you, persecute you and falsely say all kinds of evil against you because of me. Rejoice and be glad, because great is your reward in heaven, for in the same way they persecuted the prophets who were before you. (Mt. 5:11, 12; cf. Luke 11:50, 51)

Jesus' words, of course, are not directed exclusively to prophets. *But he draws a principle from the lives of the prophets* and *applies it across the board to all of God's people.* God's servants, the prophets, are called upon to experience hardship and suffering, sometimes to an extreme. Hints of that suffering may be found in the calls of the prophets: "What if they do not believe me or listen to me?" (Ex. 4:1) suggests a degree of discomfort based upon personal rejection. The warnings to Ezekiel and Jeremiah, at the time of their call, to disregard the faces of their audiences, suggest some degree of hostility that the prophets will experience. (Jer. 1:8, 17 literally says "Do not fear their faces." Cf. also Ez. 2:6.) False prophets who proclaim peace will be acclaimed but true prophets require supernatural power from the Spirit of God to be able to "declare to Jacob his transgression, to Israel his sin" (Micah 3:5, 8).

> The visions of your prophets were false and worthless; they did not expose your sin to ward off your captivity. (Lam. 2:14)

False prophets will receive the applause of the crowds who are unwilling to listen to the Lord's instruction. They are anxious to align with the wishes of the majority and prophesy "pleasant things and illusions" (Is. 30:9,10). The true prophet's ministry will require "confronting people with the Holy One of Israel" (Is. 30:11b). Sooner or later such a ministry takes its toll because psychological and emotional persecution is as real as physical persecution.

One prophet stands out above all others as someone who is called upon by the Lord to pay a heavy price for the privilege of ministry and service. That prophet is Jeremiah. Perhaps his story reminds us that while all who seek to serve God are called upon to suffer (I Peter 4:12,13), some experience suffering and persecution to a much greater degree than others.

From the beginning of his call Jeremiah is given a difficult message to convey. He was appointed to "uproot, and tear down, to destroy and overthrow" and then to "build and plant" (Jer. 1:10). He is to proclaim a message that is often against his own temperament and personality. His message is unpopular, which makes him unpopular. His life is threatened on more than one occasion. He refers to the people of his own village plotting to take his life (Jer. 11:18-23) and even members of his own family are implicated in the plot (Jer. 12:6). He is often in conflict with the false prophets of his day (Jer. 23:9-40). He publicly confronts Hananiah, who was saying the exile would last only 2 years (Jer. 28) while he himself anounces that it would last 70 years (Jer. 25:12), a much less popular position.

Jeremiah's writings are cut up and thrown into the fire by Jehoiakim. On this occasion he is seized and imprisoned with Baruch (Jer. 36:26).

He is regarded by his contemporaries as a traitor, and after preaching that the presence of the temple would not prevent the judgment of God, he is threatened with death. On this occasion when death was imminent (Jer. 26:14, 15) some officials intervene to remind the authorities that Jeremiah's message is no different from Micah's a century earlier (Jer. 26:18).

In addition to hostility and fierce opposition, physical abuse and persecution, Jeremiah suffers an emotional separation and loneliness that periodically plagues him. He remains unmarried at the direction of the Lord (Jer. 16:2). His loneliness is a measure of his identification with the Lord, who had set him apart. He speaks of himself as being "full of the wrath of the Lord" (Jer. 6:11). He not only proclaims it; he feels it and lives it, and thus he says, "I never sat in the company of revelers, never made merry with them; I sat alone, because your hand was on me, and you had filled me with indignation" (Jer. 15:17).

> God feels anguish for his people . . . but he also feels anger for them . . . The remarkable tension felt by Jeremiah is attributed also to God himself (J. Goldingay, *God's Prophet, God's Servant,* 1984, p. 41).

For Jeremiah, identification with God means identification with the word of the Lord. "I am ridiculed all day long, everyone mocks me . . . the word of the Lord has brought me insult and reproach all day long" (Jer. 20:7b, 8b).

"Concerning the prophets: My heart is broken within me, all my bones tremble; I am like a drunken man, like a man overcome by wine, because of the Lord and his holy words" (Jer. 23:9). Heschel writes concerning this verse, "What convulsed the prophet's whole being was God. His condition was a state of suffering in sympathy with the divine pathos" (A. Heschel, *The Prophets,* 1962, p. 118). Jeremiah's conflict, which leads to his being hated, cursed, ostracized and rejected, is with public leaders, royalty (Jer. 22:13–30), prophets (Jer. 23:9–22, 27, 28), priests (8:10), family (11:21) and the people (18:11, 12).

Jeremiah's conflict and suffering are

> not accidental or incidental because of wrong strategy or insen-

sitivity, nor is the conflict about marginal matters on which Jeremiah might as well have compromised. As we have it, conflict is definitional of Jeremiah's call . . . The conflict occurs because Jeremiah has been given a vision of reality and a word about reality that is deeply at odds with the vision of reality held by his contemporaries, and these two visions can in no way be accommodated to each other (W. Brueggemann, "The Book of Jeremiah: Portrait of a Prophet," in *Interpreting the Prophets*, J. Mays, P. Achtemeier, editors, p. 125).

Jeremiah suffered for the cause of God and truth in a world of falsehood and self-deception. In terms of New Testament revelation he was being persecuted because of righteousness (Mt. 5:10) and for the sake of Christ (Mt. 5:11b).

Jeremiah's suffering must also be understood in terms of his identification with God's people. Prophets are always called to function with a dual identification:

Jeremiah is torn apart not merely because of his own affliction, nor only because of Israel's affliction, but because of the affliction of God, which God allows him to share (Goldingay, *God's Prophet, God's Servant*, p. 39).

God's servant suffers anguish over the spiritual blindness and stubbornness of his people. His preaching of God's divine justice is with tears. He is not a stern moralist but one who reminds us of him who wept over Jerusalem (Luke 13:34; 19:41):

Since my people are crushed, I am crushed;
I mourn, and horror grips me.
Is there no balm in Gilead? Is there no physician there?
Why then is there no healing for the wound of my people?
Oh, that my head were a spring of water
and my eyes a fountain of tears!
I would weep day and night for the slain of my people.
(Jer. 8:21–9:1)

The prophet Jeremiah identifies with the people by means of his prayers. He is an intercessor and his task is to pray, even when his prayers are not answered and the Lord says "no" (Jer. 14:11; 15:11). He not only intercedes for them but in some sense sees himself implicated in the collective morass of blindness caused by sin.

Although our sins testify against us,
O Lord, do something for the sake of your name.
For our backsliding is great;
we have sinned against you
(Jer. 14:7)

Why then is there so much emphasis in the book of Jeremiah on the affliction and suffering of the prophet? What are we to learn from it? It is a strong reminder that all ministry involves suffering (Phil. 1:29), more particularly that prophetic suffering results from the two-fold identification with God and with his people. We will see in the following section that the tension Jeremiah experienced leads him almost to the breaking point. Certainly, in one case, he is commanded to repent from having blasphemously referred to the Lord as a "deceptive brook, like a spring that fails" (Jer. 15:18b, 19).

The paradox of ministry is that in aligning with God we will find ourselves "out of sync" with men:

He who is totally turned toward God is consequently turned away from men; it is just this inclination toward God that has isolated him from men. The simplicity of this truth is striking: those who are turned toward God are removed from human community; and this position has nothing to do with pride vis-a-vis other men (G. von Rad, "The Confessions of Jeremiah" in *A Prophet to the Nations*, L. Perdue, B. Kovacs, editors, 1984, p. 340).

Isolation from the human community is the cause of much of the prophets' suffering.

In the suffering of Jeremiah we are confronted with a wide spectrum of human distress impinging on every facet of the human personality. We meet:

Fear of shame, fear of failure, loss of strength, doubting of faith, loneliness, pity, disappointment turning to hostility towards God . . . With Jeremiah a new element is announced in God's dealings with his prophets: Jeremiah serves God not only with the harsh proclamation of his mouth, but also with his person; his life becomes unexpectedly involved in the cause of God on earth (von Rad, "The Confessions of Jeremiah," p. 346).

In the case of the parallels between Jeremiah and the people of God today we need to be reminded that Jesus drew a principle from the lives of the prophets and applied it not merely to leaders but to all of God's people (cf. Mt. 5:11, 12). Thus we are compelled to say that the extensive accounts of Jeremiah's suffering suggest that he represents all of the people of God who "bind themselves to the Lord to serve him, to love the name of the Lord and to worship him . . ." (Is. 56:6).

"What happens to Jeremiah *is* what happens to the true Israel of God, and if we wish to be associated with the Israel of God then this is what we must accept. Being a prophet involves that identification" (Goldingay, *God's Prophet, God's Servant*, p. 37).

In the famous question that Jesus asked his disciples (Who do people say the Son of Man is?) it is not surprising that some have compared Christ to Jeremiah. Some parallels may be drawn between them. "Both experienced isolation and betrayal by those nearest to them; the loss of family and home and a permanent place to lay one's head; being inwardly torn apart (in Gethsemane in Jesus' case) even while they were hard as a rock outside (in the temple or on trial)" (Goldingay, *God's Prophet, God's Servant*, p. 30).

3. Prophets and Spiritual Honesty

Prophecy is essentially a ministry of disclosure, a stripping bare. Israel's great prophets do not merely lift the veil of the future in order to destroy false expectations; at the same time, they expose the conduct of their contemporaries. They do so in a way that brings into full view the secret motivations and concealed intentions behind what these people are doing. Prophets tear the masks away and show the true face of the people behind them (H.W. Wolff, *Confrontations with Prophets*, 1983, p. 35).

Perhaps this isn't a very inviting or exhilarating task but it is a necessary one: to tear away the masks. Was this part of what God meant when he told Jeremiah he would have to uproot, tear down, destroy and overthrow? (Jer. 1:10). Jeremiah points to the core of the human problem with a diagnosis of the human condition that makes prophetic criticism necessary. "The heart is deceitful above all things and beyond cure. Who can understand it?" (Jer. 17:9). Some "prophets" are raised up by God to criticize secular society. Old Testament prophets had to criticize those who claimed to know God in order to remove "the mask of unshakeable piety" (Wolff, *Confronta-*

tions, p. 46). The people of God are not immune to the danger of self-deception. Prophets are one important means of awakening people to this danger:

> A prophet wakes us up from our sleepy complacency so that we see the great and stunning drama that is our existence, and then pushes us onto the stage playing our parts whether we think we are ready or not. A prophet angers us by rejecting our euphemisms and ripping off our disguises, then dragging our heartless attitudes and selfish motives out into the open where everyone sees them for what they are (E. Pederson, *Run with Horses*, 1983, p. 48).

Think of the self-deception that gripped David at one point in his life. The story is well-known. David momentarily succumbed to the temptation to pattern his life after other Near Eastern kings whose accountability went no further than themselves. David saw and took a woman whom he lusted after. The big problem developed when she became pregnant. Now what! Thus a cover-up operation began that included bringing Bathsheba's husband home from the front lines to cohabit with his wife so that the child could be palmed off as belonging to him. Unfortunately for David, that didn't work. Uriah's reasons for sexual abstinence were very noble (II Sam. 11:11), yet one also wonders, in light of the normal sexual drives of a man deprived of his wife's company because of war, if God was the reason behind his unnatural decision.

The second step was David's attempt and success in getting Uriah drunk (II Sam. 11:13b). But that didn't work either! Finally, David plotted to have him killed and sent word to Joab by letter, "Put Uriah in the front line where the fighting is fiercest. Then withdraw from him so he will be struck down and die" (II Sam. 11:15).

When word was sent back to David about Uriah's death the narrative gives no indication of even the slightest remorse or regret on his part. The deceitfulness of sin was in full force. The cover-up was apparently successful.

David continued his business-as-usual approach to his rule and kingdom. One wonders how "the man after God's own heart" (Acts 13:22) could live with himself in light of what he had done. But the big lie was at work. The human mind has an amazing capacity for self-deception and for rationalizing sin. What can avail against such a state of mind? The Scripture says two things: "But the thing David had done *displeased the*

Lord. The Lord *sent Nathan* to David" (II Sam. 11:27b, 12:1a).

God sent a prophet to unmask the big lie of David's life, and the prophet's story penetrated it. David convicted himself when, in responding to Nathan's story about the rich man with many sheep and the poor man with one little ewe lamb, David burned with anger and said to Nathan, "As surely as the Lord lives, the man who did this deserves to die! . . . Then Nathan said to David, You are the man!" (II Sam. 12:5, 7).

David's self-deception had ended and his pious mask was removed by the prophet's simple story and powerful, direct application. What would have happened to David were it not for Nathan's ministry of removing the mask?

Some masks, however, are a lot less obvious than David's. After all, confronting adultery is confronting a sin that is rather bare-faced and blatantly opposed to God. Other prophets engaged in the ministry of unmasking were faced with much more subtle forms of sin and of hiding from God.

Micah, the eighth-century compatriot of Isaiah, confronted hypocrisy among the religious leaders and power brokers of the day. One group he addresses are those who lie awake scheming how to take property from the smaller landowners. "They covet fields and seize them, and houses and take them. They defraud a man of his home, a fellowman of his inheritance" (Micah 2:2). Since coveting is clearly in violation of the commandment and a person's land has sacred significance, being an inheritance from the Lord, such behavior should have been seen as wrong-doing. Coveting, of course, can be covered up to some extent. Or it could be that these people were operating with the common mask that business and the church are not related!

The prophet believes that business ethics and God do go together. His word provokes a reaction from a group of opposing prophets who say, "Do not prophesy about these things" (Micah 2:6). False prophets are unwilling to put roadblocks in the way of sin. They will prophesy of sweet nothings and the people love to have it so (2:11). They even ask the question, "Is the Spirit of the Lord angry?" (2:6b). Micah unmasks their behavior by comparing it and testing it with the holy requirements of God's law.

The intensity of the unmasking increases in the oracle in 3:1–4. The prophet's language is strongly confrontational and extreme. He addresses the leaders in such a way as to make it clear there is a great gulf between their duties ("Should you not know justice . . .") and their performance level ("you who hate good and love evil") (3:1, 2). They are financial cannibals as well as butchers of people's lives.

The unmasking must penetrate even deeper. All the while they are involved in their subtle business of oppression their lives continue unaltered. They continue to "cry out" to the Lord, but God is not impressed with their prayers under these circumstances (cf. Is. 1:15) and he is not about to listen "because of the evil they have done" (3:4b). "If a man shuts his ears to the cry of the poor, he too will cry out and not be answered" (Prov. 21:13).

The religious hierarchy is the most difficult case to expose. Micah deals with them in the oracle in 3:5–12. The first part refers to some prophets as "seducers" who lead people astray. Their messages are based upon money, not truth. What they preach depends on how they are fed (3:5). Such deception eventually leads to exile. "The visions of your prophets were false and worthless; they did not expose your sin to ward off your captivity" (Lam. 2:14). People are free to believe the lie. Self-deception reigns supreme. Wolff points to a frightening scenario. People who

> were able to really hear God's word will not be able to hear it any more. Anyone who falsifies the word, who distorts it, will have the word taken away from him. He will open the Scriptures, but they will no longer say anything to him . . . The person who no longer takes his bearings from the word of the Lord will find it impossible to find his bearings at all (*Confrontations*, p. 43).

The final point of Micah's attempt at unmasking the hypocrisy of the religious establishment comes with the oracle in 3:9–12. Judges, priests and prophets will be exposed (3:11). Judges despise justice and twist all that is right (3:9b). The prophets sometimes describe the problem of injustice by saying people "do not *know* how to do right" (Amos 3:10). With such a statement the evaluation of the social fabric of society is carried to its deepest and darkest level. Sin has blinded to the point where the truth is no longer *known*. "Woe to those who call evil good and good evil, who put darkness for light and light for darkness" (Is. 5:20). Knowledge of truth, of course, does not guarantee its observance. Where the truth is no longer *known*, however, it's an absolute certainty that it cannot be lived and followed.

The prophets do not merely uphold an abstract principle of justice:

> It is more accurate to see them as proclaimers of God's pathos, speaking not for the idea of justice, but for the God of justice, for God's concern, for justice . . . Prophetic morality rests upon both a divine command and a divine concern (A. Heschel, *The Prophets*, p. 219).

Micah mentions three acts of injustice, three blatant violations of the law.

First, the leaders and rulers are building "Zion with bloodshed and Jerusalem with wickedness" (3:10). During the reign of Hezekiah tremendous building projects are undertaken (II Chron. 32:27–31), and it is possible that in the interests of progress and military security the lives of the lower classes suffer.

The second thing Micah mentions is the corruption and bribery rampant among the various religious leaders (3:11a). It is the old story, that "when money speaks truth is silent." Micah demonstrates that the perversion of justice is connected to the lure and deceitfulness of riches, and his prophetic words are directed at unmasking this hidden reality.

The ultimate deception is not with money, however, but with religion. The most disastrous act of deception is to be seeking to use and manipulate God for one's own purposes. Micah tells us that in the midst of this scene of bloodshed, corruption, bribery and oppression, "they lean upon the Lord and say, 'Is not the Lord among us? No disaster will come upon us' " (3:11b). They are wearing the mask of religious orthodoxy with its statements of faith and its absolute certainty of having the truth. Faith becomes totally privatized with no public dimension to it. The Bible is appealed to by these people (cf. "Is not the Lord among us" with Ps. 46:11). The prophets want their listeners to know that "statements of faith may become the slogans of religious self-security . . . That is why trust in God of this kind is a dreadful mask. Micah testifies that God himself rips off this mask" (Wolff, *Confrontations*, pp. 46–47).

Micah's admonition is little different from that of Jesus who says, "Not everyone who says to me, Lord, Lord will enter the kingdom of heaven, but only he who does the will of my Father who is in heaven" (Mt. 7:21).

Amos announces that the Lord is going to use a sieve to differentiate between the godly and the ungodly. "As grain is shaken in a sieve, and not a pebble will reach the ground," so "all the sinners among my people will die by the sword, all those who say, 'Disaster will not overtake or meet us' " (Amos 9:9b, 10). These are the ones who hear the prophet's words (which are designed to unveil the secrets of their hearts and to remove the mask of religious hypocrisy) but do not listen and so continue with the mask of piety. Amos' words, directed against the northern kingdom, find fulfillment in the exile that occurs in 722 B.C.

Micah's words are directed against the southern kingdom, which is granted a reprieve from the Assyrian devastation when Sennacherib's siege of Jerusalem is thwarted by the miraculous intervention of the Angel of the Lord (II Kings 19:35, 36). The reprieve lasts for about 120 years. Near the end of this stay of execution Jeremiah is also called upon to engage in the prophetic ministry of unmasking.

Jeremiah is the prophet par excellence whose *ministry* and *life* are a call to spiritual honesty and to the removal of the masks that prevent the hearing of the word of the Lord. Sin has the deceptive power to prevent us from facing the true reality, the true picture of our lives. As a part of their ministry, prophets have to disturb us and cause us to see more of this true picture of the human heart, to penetrate the self-deception.

The true vision of God alone can expose the deception. Isaiah experiences this when he receives the vision of God enabling him to see that the "real" king was neither the dead Uzziah (Is. 6:1) nor the new king, Uzziah's son Jothan, but the Lord himself. "My eyes have seen the king, the Lord Almighty" (Is. 6:5b).

Brueggemann makes the interesting suggestion that the "language of grief" is the key medium for bringing the divine vision of reality to a community in the throes of deception. Jeremiah is a paradigm for the prophetic attempt to address those who are unwilling to listen. Certainly his writings center on the confrontation of truth with falsehood and self-deception:

> He grieves the grief of Judah because he knows what the king refuses to know. It is clear that Jeremiah did not in anger heap scorn on Judah but rather articulated what was in fact present in the community whether they acknowledged it or not. He articulated what the community had to deny in order to continue the

self-deception of achievable satiation. . . . Jeremiah knew long before the others that the end was coming and that God had had enough of indifferent affluence, cynical oppression, and presumptive religion (*The Prophetic Imagination*, 1978, p. 51).

No portion of Jeremiah's writings better captures his conflict with self-deception and his ministry of unmasking than his temple sermon found in chapter seven.

Pederson reminds us of the importance of Jeremiah's sermon, delivered right outside the temple:

> It is especially important in times of success, when everything is going well, when the church is admired and church attendance swells. We think everything is fine because the appearances are fine and the statistics are impressive. The church is never in so much danger as when it is popular and millions of people are saying "I'm born again, born again, born again" *(Run with Horses*, p. 65).

The temple sermon is delivered shortly after Josiah's death in 609 at the beginning of Jehoiakim's ascension to the throne (cf. Jer. 26:1). It is found in 7:1–15 and can be divided into three sections — 7:1–7, 8–11, 12–15.

In 7:1–7 Jeremiah seeks to unmask the organized hypocrisy of establishment religion centering upon the temple.

In 7:8–11 he presents the disparity between true covenant religion with its emphasis on the Ten Words and the establishment-sponsored religion in which ritual preempts ethics and sincerity overrides truth, or, as Brueggemann comments, "The Torah violators attempt to hide in the sanctity of the ritual" (W. Brueggemann, *Jer. 1–25, To Pluck Up, To Tear Down*, 1988, p. 76). The simile of the robbers' den is used to depict the charge.

In 7:12–15 Jeremiah attempts to draw a lesson from the past by comparison of what transpired at Shiloh (a religious center located in the northern kingdom) and what is about to happen to Jerusalem.

In 7:3, 4 Jeremiah urges the people to reform their ways and their actions. This change of behavior can be effected only if the people do not trust in the deceptive words, the temple of the Lord, the temple of the Lord, the temple of the Lord.

Jeremiah is referring to their interpretation of the unconditional promises made to the nation in the covenant with

David; i.e., the external presence of the temple serves to guarantee Jerusalem's inviolability. It does so even when the moral requirements of the covenant law are being flagrantly disregarded. Verses 5, 6 and 9 show that for Jeremiah the moral stipulations of the covenant are not to be ignored and overshadowed by liturgy. Jeremiah attacks Judah's massive disobedience to the moral law (7:9, cf. Hos. 4:1–4). More than that he rejects the temple as a "place of refuge, hiding, and safety for those who violate torah through their life in the world" (Brueggemann, *Jer. 1–25*, p. 76).

The image of the robbers' cave is quite apropos:

> Robbers and bandits who sally forth for robbery and plunder secure for themselves a hideout in some secluded area, to which they retire for protection and safety away from the eyes of the authorities until the hue and cry dies down, only to issue forth again when the pursuit ceases, to commit fresh robberies (J.A. Thompson, *The Book of Jeremiah*, New International Commentary, 1980, p. 281).

Thus they are able to say, despite their denial of the covenant laws (7:9), "we are safe, safe to do all these detestable things" (7:10). Twice, then, Jeremiah pleads with them not to "trust in deceptive words" (7:4, 8). "Their religious performance was impeccable; their everyday life was rotten" (Pederson, *Run with Horses*, p. 66).

To unmask the hypocrisy Jeremiah resorts to an appeal to history. He has already challenged this temple theology through the use of an alternative theology found in the little words, "if . . . then" in 7:5–7. "Now *if* you obey me fully and keep my covenant, *then* out of all nations you will be my treasured possession" (Ex. 19:5).* He shows through the use of prophetic imagination that the people are acting just as common thieves who make use of the robbers' den or cave to conceal themselves between pillaging forays into the countryside. Now in 7:12–15 he invites them to take a pilgrimage to Shiloh. The historical symbol of Shiloh provides

a way in which the coverup and the stonewalling can be ended

---

* For a helpful discussion of the tension between the unconditional promises of the Davidic covenant and the conditional promises of the Mosaic covenant see J. Bright, *Covenant & Promise*, 1976.

> . . . It means that the prophet is to reactivate out of our historical
> past symbols that always have been vehicles for redemptive hon-
> esty (Brueggemann, *The Prophetic Imagination*, p. 49).

The exodus functions commonly in this manner as a positive
symbol of hope, and Shiloh is used here as a negative symbol
or pointer in the direction of redemptive honesty; i.e., seeing
the true picture so that it can be changed. Worship at the time
of Eli was centered at Shiloh where people flocked to sacrifice
and pray to the Lord (I Sam. 1:3). The sanctuary of the Lord is
there (I Sam. 1:9, 24). The ark of the covenant is kept there and
it is at Shiloh that the Philistines defeat Israel (I Sam. 4). What
happens at Shiloh can and will happen to Jerusalem. Jerusalem is

> just like Shiloh in that it must obey to survive. It is just like Shiloh
> in its profound disobedience. And therefore, it is just like Shiloh in
> that it must be destroyed . . . The Jerusalem temple is under death
> sentence, and a whole world of religious and political self-interest
> with it. Jerusalem enjoys no 'safe conduct' in the midst of its poli-
> cies, faith, and decision-making (Brueggemann, *Jer. 1-25*, p. 77).

When Jeremiah's sermon ends its repercussions follow him
just as they follow us today. He pays a price for attempting to
unmask the ingrained, systemic hypocrisy of the religious
establishment. In Jer. 26:1–6 his sermon is repeated and the
consequences for him are severe, so severe that he barely
escapes with his life (cf. 26:7–24). It's to his credit and part of
the record of his history that "the soggy religious mush of the
masses never dulled his perceptions nor muted his insistent
witness" (Pederson, *Run with Horses*, p. 59). Jeremiah's sermon
is a pointer to the warnings of the New Testament against
"having a form of godliness but denying its power" (II Tim. 3:5).

Jeremiah's "prophetic criticizing" is by way of his ministry
of "articulated grief." His preaching and passion are the passion of God himself. His grief is both public and private (the
so-called confessions of the prophet are found in 11:18–23;
12:1–6; 15:10–12; 15:15–21; 17:14–18; 18:18–23; 20:7–18). The
depth of his emotional anguish does not emanate from self-
pity but from his perception of a reality that is being ignored
by the people. "Jeremiah had seen what was there for all to see
if only they would look, but the others refused to look, simply

denied, and were unable to see" (Brueggemann, *The Prophetic Imagination*, p. 52).

By his life and ministry, Jeremiah vividly identifies with the pain of God. He is no mere doomsday prophet. His God is a wounded lover (Jer. 2:1–3; 3:1–10), a disconsolate parent. As grieving parent he rebukes and unmasks through his pain:

> Is not Ephraim, my dear son, the child in whom I delight? Though I often speak against him, I still remember him. Therefore my heart yearns for him; I have great compassion for him, declares the Lord. (Jer. 31:20)

It is difficult at times to distinguish Jeremiah's pain from the Lord's pain. His is no heartless, painless, tearless preaching of the divine anger. Jeremiah is in extreme anguish over the suffering, stupidity, stubbornness and spiritual insensitivity of the people, who are living in a fool's paradise and in their own fantasy land. He seeks to rescue them from their delusion, to unmask their vain and futile pretensions and to persuade them to turn to the Lord in "true and earnest" repentance.

The prophetic record of "unmasking" continues beyond Jeremiah and into the post-exilic period. The prophet Haggai is engaged in two unmasking operations.

The people return with the clear command to rebuild the temple. But when they meet opposition they withdraw in fear from the task committed to them. They remain inactive for nineteen years. The process of rationalization inevitably sets in. They convince themselves that "it is not yet time for the house of the Lord to be rebuilt" (Haggai 1:3b). The prophet Haggai employs sarcasm to unmask their hypocrisy and to show the people that their justification of their disobedient inactivity is a sham! "Is it a time for you yourselves to be living in your paneled houses, while this house remains a ruin?" (Haggai 1:4). Timing is not the issue. The unwillingness to rebuild is the result of a priority problem. The prophet's incisive word unmasks the people's deceptive words.

The second incident of stripping bare the thoughts and intents of the people comes in Haggai 2. The people are discouraged in the work of rebuilding but for the wrong reasons. The prophet discerns this discouragement. "Who of you is left who saw this house in its former glory? How does it look to you now? Does it not seem to you like nothing?" (Haggai 2:3)

He encourages them to continue the work of rebuilding by getting them to focus on the promises of God's presence (2:4), Spirit (2:5), and the glorious hope of the future (2:6–9).

The book of Malachi contains six disputation dialogues in which the prophet engages in the ministry of self-disclosure. The prophet makes a probing diagnosis of the people's heart condition. His initial remarks are stringently challenged. The people are saying, No way! That's not true of us (Mal. 1:2, 6b; 2:17b; 3:7b, 8b; 3:13). The prophet then probes deeper and gives more detail to buttress his case and to penetrate their religious masks.*

This concludes our examination of the prophetic ministry of unmasking hypocrisy and self-deception. The prophets call the people of God to spiritual reality and honesty. But they do so in their personal lives as well as in their prophetic function.

We said earlier that Jeremiah was the prophet par excellence whose *ministry* and *life* are a testimony to spiritual reality and honesty. We must now briefly examine the complaints or confessions of Jeremiah that have been the subject of much study. They are a unique part of the entire book. In a sense they are unique to the whole Bible because of the intensity of feeling to which the prophet gives expression. Their only possible rival in depth of feeling and honesty of expression would be found in the psalms of individual lament. Scholars differ, however, over whether Jeremiah's confessions are expressions of personal feelings related to his own experiences or liturgical compositions uttered in worship, by the prophet as cultic mediator of the people. Bright examines this issue and argues persuasively for the former position which we accept (cf. "Jeremiah's Complaint: Liturgy or Expressions of Personal Distress," in *Proclamation and Presence*, H. Durham and J.R. Porter, editors, 1976, pp. 189–204).

Jeremiah employs the forms of speech used in the lament psalms to bring his personal complaints to the Lord. The persecutions of the prophet Jeremiah (see section III C.2) are the basis for his complaints, though we cannot connect individual complaints with individual circumstances. The abuse the prophet experiences is the result of the faithful execution of his prophetic calling. However, circumstances do not seem to be verifying what the Lord had promised at the time of his call

---

* For details see chapters 6 & 7.

(Jer. 1). In the extremity of his despair he cries out to God. As Bright remarks:

> The confessions do indeed show us a weak and angry mortal. But they also let us see a man utterly dependent upon God, utterly obedient to his calling and perplexed at its outcome, at the end of his resources, who with utter honesty lays himself bare before God, who alone can help — if help there is at all. And if at times his complaints heighten into angry accusations, it was always to God that he returned: He had nowhere else to go ("A Prophet's Lament and its Answer: Jer. 15:10–21," in *A Prophet to the Nations*, p. 334).

Jeremiah is a prophet of the word (1:9; 15:16; 23:9–36) and God promises two things at his call: First, "I have put my words in your mouth" (1:9). Second, "I am watching to see that my word is fulfilled" (1:12). Everything in Jeremiah's experience seems to go counter to that promise. His plea is for God to vindicate His word but it doesn't seem to be happening. Instead, as Jeremiah says, "The word of the Lord has brought me insult and reproach all day long" (20:8b). Such is the unbearable tension with which this prophet lives.

His intense desire to see the word of God obeyed is at least part of the reason why he accuses God of overpowering him in his prophetic call (20:7). The polarity of his emotions reflects both the compassion and anger of God toward his people. "The tension of being caught, heart and soul, in two opposing currents of violent emotion, was more than a human being could bear" (Heschel, p. 125). It causes him to curse the day of his birth (20:14–18) and to accuse God of being a deceitful brook (15:18) which, to be sure, takes him beyond the boundary of acceptable complaint. In this case, the prophet, who preaches repentance, is called upon by God to repent. "If you repent, I will restore you that you may serve me; if you utter worthy, not worthless words, you will be my spokesman" (15:19). There is no word of rebuke in all the other complaints, until Jeremiah reaches the point of seeking to go back on his call and refers to God as a deceptive brook and a dried-up spring.

God is not threatened by most of Jeremiah's complaints. In response to the complaint in 12:1–4, the prophet is told by the Lord to prepare for more difficult times! In other words, the worst is yet to come (12:5). The worst seems to refer to a plot

hatched by Jeremiah's own family members and revealed to
him by the Lord (12:6). Jeremiah proves himself not to be a
quitter. He may feel like it (9:2) and talk about quitting (20:9)
but even at the lowest ebb of his life he remains true to his calling. When the raw nerve of his emotions is finally touched and
he threatens to leave his prophetic calling and he is told to
repent of his worthless words, he does so, and the evidence for
this is that the Lord uses the same images of a fortified wall of
bronze to reconfirm to Jeremiah his renewed call to service
(Jer. 15:20; cf. 1:18):

> Jeremiah may have spoken in weakness, but he acted in strength.
> His "confessions" show him at his lowest moment; but they must
> be read in the context of the whole book in which they are found,
> for here we learn of the message he proclaimed and continued to
> proclaim, of the suffering he endured and continued to endure,
> and of the steadfast loyalty to his calling which he exhibited to the
> very end. In that context, the "confessions" remain the words of a
> weak mortal; but they may also be read as the words of a brave
> and devoted man (Bright, "A Prophet's Lament," p. 335).

James tells us that "Elijah was a man just like us" (Jas. 5:17).
The Old Testament perhaps is telling us the same thing about
Jeremiah. Fortunately the record of Jeremiah's internal struggles to continue faithful is preserved and included among his
messages. Is he the only prophet who bombards the Lord with
his agonizing thoughts and feelings and doubts?

For what purpose then are these "documents of self-revela-
tion" (S. Blank, *Jeremiah, Man and Prophet*, 1961, p. 65) preserved? Are they just part of the larger biographical and auto-
biographical material included in the book? Surely, even without this material Jeremiah is the best known of the prophets.
We know what message he preaches and we know what it costs
him to persevere in doing so. His humanness becomes prominent in his confessions:

> We would have thought that one who could preach such an obvi-
> ously unpopular message, and do so unremittingly over a period
> of more than forty years in the face of persecution, must have been
> a man of iron courage and unshakable faith. But we learn from
> his own words that he was not. Jeremiah was a weak mortal . . .
> His faith was neither serene nor unshakable; on the contrary,
> there were times when it crumbled beneath him and spilled him

into the pit of despair. He addressed his God with utter honesty, yes, but it was an honesty that at times trod perilously close to blasphemy (Bright, *A Prophet's Lament*, p. 333).

Why does Jeremiah leave an account of his prayers? We agree with Blank who argues that they are paradigmatic or, in the words of Paul, they are written for our learning (S. Blank, "Prophet as Paradigm," in *Essays in Old Testament Ethics*, J. Crenshaw and J. Willis, editors, 1974, pp. 113–130).

Is it surprising that this kind of spiritual honesty should be a spur to service and a refreshing wind to the soul? Does not the Biblical record indicate that God's "power is made perfect in weakness"? (II Cor. 12:9). Isn't it encouraging that God continues to use mortals even when their faith is weak? God places the treasures of his word "in jars of clay to show that this all-surpassing power is from God and not from us" (II Cor. 4:7). God uses jars of clay that are easily cracked!

We can be most grateful to God that this record of spiritual struggle and spiritual honesty has been left to us. It's a record of weakness and of the divine response to that weakness. Does Jeremiah ever get complete victory over his emotions, his doubts and turmoils? One can't be dogmatic but this much is sure — in the tenth year of Zedekiah (32:1), at the very end of Jeremiah's 40-year ministry, an incident is recorded in which Jeremiah receives a directive from the Lord to buy his relative's property at Anatoth (32:7). Surely that is not a very good business deal during war time! Jeremiah leaves the deed of purchase with Baruch and then prays to the Lord. At the end of his prayer he lapses into the same perplexity, fear and doubt as found in the so-called confessions. He wonders out loud, What sense does it make to purchase this property, since the city is about to be handed over to the Babylonians?

And though the city will be handed over to the Babylonians, you, O Sovereign Lord, say to me, "Buy the field with silver and have the transaction witnessed." (Jer. 32:25)

The evidence thus seems to indicate that he continued to be troubled by the ways of God and remained both a weak mortal and God's chosen and called prophet.

Are there depressed servants of God struggling with ministry? Let them go to the prophet Jeremiah for instruction, though not for imitation. Jeremiah may bring hope and comfort to those whose anger is also directed toward their God:

> In the furnace of the afflictions of our ministries, blasphemous thoughts do sometimes arise in our hearts against God. We, however, conceal what Jeremiah revealed. He is disgusted with his office and dissatisfied with his God. He wants to escape from the constant pressure upon him and so he cries with passionate intensity against God (D.Kingdom, "Ministerial Depression," *Banner of Truth* [Dec. 1982], p. 20).

So what is the comfort? Is it just that an Old Testament prophet's experience of depression has points of similarity with our own? That is some comfort, yet the real comfort to those who identify with Jeremiah's doubt, depression and despair is that "such is the mercy of God that he made him the prophet par excellence of the new covenant! (31:31–34). The prophet who knew such depression is the messenger of the God of hope" (D. Kingdom, "Ministerial Depression," p. 20).

IV.   How to Preach From the Prophets

There are many *specialized* questions in interpreting the prophets. Understanding the *predictive component* of their biblical message requires some special hermeneutical procedures. The literature on this is vast but two of the best introductions to the understanding of predictive prophecy are A. Mickelson, *Interpreting the Bible*, 1983, chapter 13 and W. Kaiser, *Back Toward the Future*, 1989.

There are a host of questions concerning the *literary characteristics* of the prophetic literature. These arise because the prophets are both speakers as well as writers. "Through a complex process we can no longer trace, the spoken prophecies eventually became the literature we find in our Bibles today" (Greidanus, p. 238).

It is sometimes difficult to see whether the order of a book is chronological or topical. Some books give evidence of a precise chronological approach (Haggai 1:1, 15; 2:1, 10, 20), and others such as Jeremiah, are best understood as an anthology of his messages.

The juxtaposition in many prophetic books between oracles of judgment and oracles of hope is intentional. It is a constant reminder that the prophets announce the end of the old order as a prelude to the introduction of the new. Judgment then becomes the prelude to grace. "The spoken prophecies of judgment must now be read in the literary context of promised salvation" (Greidanus, p. 240). Grace is God's last word as both the Law (Deut. 30:1–10) and the Prophets indicate (Hos. 14:4).

Recent study of the prophets has concentrated on two lines of approach to their messages. First is the study of the prophetic forms of speech. The purpose of such study is to move from the form of the prophet's message to an analysis of the content of the message. The style and structure of their writings bear on the understanding of what they were saying. In recent times, C. Westermann's book, *Basic Forms of Prophetic Speech*, 1967, has pioneered the way and others have subjected his ideas to scrutiny and further refinement.*

In addition to this approach, which examines the prophetic style and structure, one finds another emphasis in the prophetic literature. Here, special attention is given to the theological foundation for understanding the messages of the prophets, or what John Bright calls "theological exegesis":

> By theological exegesis is meant an exegesis of the text in theological depth, an exegesis that is not content merely to bring out the precise verbal meaning of the text but that goes on to lay bare the theology that informs the text . . . All biblical texts are expressive of theology in that all are animated, if at times indirectly, by some theological concern. It is incumbent upon the interpreter to seek to discover what that theological concern is. To do so is no violation of sound exegetical principles. Rather, it is the completion of the exegetical task (J. Bright, *The Authority of the Old Testament*, 1967, p. 170).

A. Pay Attention to Prophetic Forms of Speech

"Viewing the prophetic books as a whole, virtually all of their genres of literature and discourse fall into one of three general categories: reports, speeches, or prayers" (G. Tucker, "Prophetic Speech," in *Interpreting the Prophets*, J. Mays and P. Achtemeier, editors, p. 29). Reports may include the narratives documenting prophetic conflict (Amos 7:10–17; Jer. 27, 28), the accounts of the calls of the prophets (Jer. 1; Is. 6; Ez. 1–3), or the symbolic activities that are a part of their ministry (Jer. 13:1–11; Is. 20). Their prayers take the form of personal statements of praise (Amos 4:13; 5:8; Is. 25:1–8), intercession (see Jer. 14:7, 9, 21–24; Amos 7:2, 4; Hab. 3:2) or lament (Jer. 11:18–23; 12:1–6; 17:14–18; 20:7–18).

In the broadest sense the speeches that make up the preponderance of material consist of oracles of judgment and oracles of salvation. Of these the oracles of judgment predominate. In preaching their messages of judgment the prophets often employ what may be called covenant "lawsuit" terms. God is

---

* See articles in the bibliography at the end of this chapter under D.

portrayed as a judge and prosecuting attorney in a court of law in which his people are arraigned and called to offer a defense if they can.

In the popular theology of the day Yahweh was to decide in favor of his people and against the nations. With startling newness the prophets see Yahweh as summoning, accusing, threatening and deciding not in favor of his chosen ones but against them. The employment of this form of argument is common among the prophets (cf. Hos. 2:4ff; 4:1, 12:3–15; Is. 3:13–17; 5:1–7; Micah 1:2–9; Jer. 2–4:4).

The prophets employ another common literary form that may be called the "woe oracle." It is believed that the life context behind the prophetic woe oracle was a lament uttered by mourners at a funeral. A woe oracle takes the following form: first, an announcement of doom; next, a reason for the pronouncement of doom. When the prophets employ this literary form they are giving advance notice of the death of Israel. They adopt the form and employ it in the case of the soon-to-be-deceased Israel (cf. Amos 5:1, 2; Is. 5:8–30; 10:1–3; 28:1–4; Hab. 2:6–8; Micah 2:1–5; Zeph. 2:5–7).

In Isaiah 5:8–30 there is a six-fold repetition of the woe oracle. In employing a woe oracle the prophet indicts the hearers for their reprehensible behavior. Paying attention to the literary structure provides clues as to how best to preach from a passage.*

Another example of how the recognition of a prophetic form of discourse will enable the reader to teach and preach the prophet's message is in the use of the *disputation* oracle. The disputants are the prophet and his opponents. In a most recent study of this genre the author argues that "the name 'disputation speech' can worthily be given to those texts where an opinion of the speakers is explicitly reported by the prophet and refuted by him" (Adrian Graffy, *A Prophet Confronts His People; The Disputation Speech in the Prophets*, 1984, p. 23). The book of Malachi consists of six such dialogues. God, by means of his prophet, remonstrates with his people for their failure to live and worship as his people. The prophetic charges are denied by the people's statements, "How is what you say true?" (cf. Mal. 1:2, 6b; 2:17b; 3:7b, 8b, 13). The charges are then reiterated with further amplification and clarification. Rather than

---

* See R. Chisholm, "Structure, Style and the Prophetic Message: An Analysis of Isaiah 5:8–20" *Bibliotheca Sacra* 143 (1986), pp. 46–60.

following the chapter divisions, which disguise these dialogues, it is much preferable to teach the book by means of
these six disputation dialogues. *Review and Expositor*, Vol. 34,
No. 3, entirely devoted to Malachi, contains many excellent
suggestions on preaching from the book based on an understanding of its structure:

> Sermons based on the oracles of Malachi might adopt a structure
> similar to that of the oracles themselves, consisting of three basic
> moves: (1) a statement of the basic affirmation of the oracle trans-
> lated into contemporary idiom, (2) a consideration of common
> objections to the affirmation as those might be forming in the
> minds of your listeners, and (3) a response to these objections
> emphasizing the content and message of the biblical text. The dia-
> lectic form of the text would lend itself well to the use of the dia-
> logue sermon involving other persons or even the whole congrega-
> tion in the interaction reflected in the text (W. H. Gloer, "Preach-
> ing from Malachi," *Review and Expositor* 34, 1987, p. 458).

Our understanding of the prophet Habakkuk will sharpen if
we see the stylistic similarities between this book and the
lament psalms. The lament psalms have the structure of a
complaint followed by divine response (cf. Ps. 10, 12). This pattern is seen in the book of Habakkuk where the prophet's complaint (1:2–4) is followed by God's response (1:5). A second
complaint (1:12–17) is followed by the divine response (2:2–5)
which culminates in a series of woes pronounced against evil-
doers both within and outside the nation (2:6–20):

> The book of Habakkuk partakes of much that is common to the
> lament psalms. It begins with lament over corruption in the land,
> the response to which leads to another questioning lament. The
> full response to this lament on how a holy and righteous God can
> allow the evil and ruthless Chaldeans to serve his purpose is con-
> firmed with the psalm in chapter 3 . . . The prophet uses the
> lament tradition, originally cultic, to express his prophecy which
> has the function of proclaiming that salvation and protection are
> coming for the people of God (W.H. Bellinger Jr., *Psalmody and
> Prophecy*, 1984, pp. 84, 85).

There is merit in paying attention to the *whole* structure of a
literary text as well as the parts. The book of Amos provides
another interesting example of how analyzing structure and

form provides help in interpreting the message. The macro-structure of the book would seem to be:

I.   1:1   Introduction   *Amos*
II.   1:2–2:16   Judgment oracles against the foreign nations
                   followed by two judgment oracles against
                   Judah and Israel
      1:3–5   Judgment oracle against Damascus
      1:6–8   Judgment oracle against Gaza
      1:9–10   Judgment oracle against Tyre
      1:11–12   Judgment oracle against Edom
      1:13–15   Judgment oracle against Ammon
      2:1–3   Judgment oracle against Moab
      2:4–5   Judgment oracle against Judah
      2:6–16   Judgment oracle against Israel

In each instance the oracle is introduced by a wisdom for-mula. "For three sins . . . even for four." It is followed by the specific accusation and indictment and concludes with a pro-nouncement of punishment. The whole purpose of the oracles against foreign nations has recently come under investigation. They may well be connected with the holy war and God-as-warrior tradition within Israel. Amos uses this tradition in a unique way when he portrays God as judging not only Israel's enemies but his own people.

III. 3:1–15   The section is introduced with the form "Hear
                   this word." The substance of the oracle is
                   directed against the people of Israel.

IV.   4:1–13   Again the section begins, "Hear this word."
                   This time the accused are the cows of Bashan,
                   the wealthy women in Israel. (4:3)

                   The remainder of the chapter consists of an
                   oracle against the religious sins being
                   perpetuated at Gilgal and Bethel. (4:4–5)

                   A first-person-singular divine pronouncement
                   of the covenant curses goes from 4:6–12 and is
                   concluded with a piece of doxology in 4:13.

V.   5:1–6:14   "Hear this Word, O house of Israel." This section begins with a funeral dirge in 5:1, 2 followed by three introductory phrases; "This is what the Sovereign Lord says" (5:3), or "This is what the Lord says to the house of Israel" (5:4), or "Therefore this is what the Lord, the Lord God Almighty, says." (5:16)

In 5:18–27 we have a prophetic woe passage concerning the day of the Lord.

Amos 6:1–7 contains a prophetic woe directed against the notable men (rulers) of the nation. The final oracle begins with the Sovereign Lord swearing by himself and declaring that he abhors the pride of Jacob. It goes from 6:8–14.

VI. 7:1–9:10 Five Visions of Judgment interrupted by a prophetic call narrative in 7:10–17.
     7:1–3   Vision of Swarm of Locusts
     7:4–6   Vision of Fire
     7:7–9   Vision of the Plumb Line
     8:1–3   Vision of the Ripened Fruit

The vision of the ripened fruit is followed by several messages introduced by varying formulas.

     8:4–6   Hear this
     8:7–8   The Lord has sworn
     8:9–10   In that day
     8:11–12   The days are coming
     8:13–14   In that day

     9:1–10   Vision of the Smiting of the Altar

VII. 9:11–15   Final Eschatological Message

This message is divided into two sections:

     9:11, 12 Introduced by the statement "in

that day" referring to the
indefinite messianic future.

9:13–15   Introduced by a similar indefinite
messianic future statement, "the
days are coming."

When it becomes clear how the individual oracles are constructed into a whole, it provides us with a way of approaching
the material in preaching. It is not that one must of necessity
handle every smaller unit, though "when one comes to the
actual study or exegetically informed reading of the prophetical books, the first thing one must learn to do is THINK
ORACLES (Stuart and Fee, *How to Read the Bible for All Its
Worth*, p. 158). What a recognition of the structure of the book
can do is provide us with additional options for preaching.
One might choose to preach from the book *consecutively*,
choosing the larger sections, and thus the book could be
preached in six or seven sermons. Since the preponderance of
the book contains oracles of judgment, it might be thought
that the consecutive approach leads to an imbalance of judgment over grace. In that case, one could preach three or four
messages.

Message one: Prophet, Preacher, and Prayer — Amos 7
Message two: History and Moral Accountability — Amos 1
and 2
Message three: The Prophet's Words of Judgment and
Repentance — Amos 3–6
Message four: The Triumph of Grace — Amos 9:11–15
If we want to preach only one message from the whole of the
book we need to be aware of the smaller units as a handle for
coming at the whole. There is much to be said for this "one
message from a book" approach. Sometimes in examining the
trees the forest becomes obscured. But the whole is best seen
by knowing what the parts are. The church today would be
better served by hearing expositions of *all* the prophets, rather
than becoming more expert on a *single* prophetic book. If we
deem it wise to go into more detailed messages we must pay
attention to the seams that make up the whole garment.

B. Pay Attention to Theological Exegesis

It is easier to say what we are not talking about, in using the expression "theological interpretation," than what we are referring to. Theological interpretation is not forcing a text to say what your theology knows it must be saying, even though it doesn't appear from the text to be saying that!

There may be no such thing as pure exegesis but it is the biblical text that needs to inform our theology and not the other way around. To pass all texts through our theological grid is to start with the wrong assumptions.

According to Kaiser, theological exegesis involves

> the comparison of the teachings and sentiments found in one book with (1) those that preceded it in time (the analogy of ante-cedent Scripture) and (2) those that followed it in the progress of revelation (the analogy of faith) (Kaiser, *Malachi*, p. 148).

For Greidanus the importance of theological interpretation is that it

> reminds us that the primary concern of Scripture is to acquaint us with God, his word, his will, his acts . . . Theological interpreta-tion serves a useful function if it reminds preachers of the central concern of the prophets — the concern to reveal God at work in history for the purpose of reestablishing his kingdom on earth (Greidanus, *The Modern Preacher and the Ancient Text*, p. 256).

J. Bright was one of the earliest to call attention to the signifi-cance of theological exegesis. He argues:

> The preacher needs to understand not only what the text says, but also the concerns that caused it to be said, and said as it was. His exegetical labors are, therefore, not complete until he has grasped the text's theological intention (Bright, *The Authority of the Old Testament*, pp. 171, 172).

Some examples of the value and importance of theological interpretation may help. In Isaiah 1:2 God speaks: "I reared children and brought them up, but they have rebelled against me." The full significance of this statement is best understood by knowing the background law of the rebellious son as found in Deuteronomy 21:18–21. Isaiah's statement on the remnant (in 1:9) must be understood in light of an antecedent theology of the remnant found in texts such as I Kings 19:18.

The prophets accuse Israel of legal violations of the covenant and sometimes specify those charges in the Ten Commandments. Both Hosea (4:1–3) and Jeremiah (7:9) cite transgressions of these laws as evidence that Israel does not really *know* God. Yet it is this covenant law they say they will obey when they respond to the reading of the book of the covenant. "We will do everything the Lord has said; we will obey" (Ex. 24:7b).

The covenant curses of Deut. 28 and Lev. 26 are the background for the five first-person-singular divine pronouncements of judgment in Amos 4:6–12. Jeremiah's attack against those hiding behind the false security of the temple presupposes some understanding of the statement of Exodus 19:5 (cf. the if-then statement in Jer. 7:5,7 with Exodus 19:5). It would be possible to trace the employment of the Davidic covenant concept (II Sam. 7) right through from the eighth century to the post-exilic period to show the extensive usage of this key theological idea. An understanding of this important covenant will certainly aid us when it comes to interpreting these prophetic messages concerning the future messianic kingdom. (Cf. Hos. 3:5; Amos 9:11, 12; Is. 9:6,7; Jer. 23:5, 6; Ez. 34:23.)

Kaiser's definition of theological exegesis has two components. The theological ideas of one book are compared with those ideas that *preceded* it and those that *followed* it. Kaiser lists four ways to help identify an antecedent theology for a text:

1. The use of certain *terms* which have already acquired a special meaning in the history of salvation and have begun to take on a technical status (e.g., "seed," "servant," "rest," "inheritance").
2. A direct reference or an indirect allusion to a previous *event* in the progress of revelation (e.g., the exodus, the epiphany on Sinai) with a view to making a related theological statement.
3. Direct or indirect citation of *quotations* so as to appropriate them for a similar theological point in the new situation (e.g., "Be fruitful and multiply . . ."; "I am the God of your fathers").
4. Reference to the *covenant(s)*, its *contents* of accumulating promises, or its formulae (e.g., "I am the Lord your God, who brought you up out of the land of Egypt [Ur of the Chaldees]"; "I will be your God; you shall be my people, and I will dwell in the midst of you.") (*Toward an Exegetical Theology*, 1981, p. 137).

It is important, then, to be familiar with the historical periods in which scriptural revelation is given if the principle is to be followed of determining the meaning of a text by paying attention to its antecedent theology.

But the other consideration in the theological interpretation of the prophets is to give attention to those parts of scriptural revelation that *follow* the text being interpreted. It's important in summarizing the content of prophetic revelation to see how later revelation has developed an earlier concept and to trace that process of development. This needs to be done *both within the Old Testament and between Old and New Testament*. As an example of the former we believe that before we can adequately understand the New Testament imagery of the church as God's temple (Eph. 2:21, 22; I Cor. 6:19), it would be a most useful exercise to trace the development of the temple terminology throughout the Old Testament. Such a study has been done by E. Clowney, which opens up the riches of this Old Testament idea, allowing us to see more clearly what is involved in the New Testament usage of the term (cf. "The Final Temple," *Westminster Theological Journal*, 35, (1972), pp. 156–189). F.F. Bruce's book, *The New Testament Development of Old Testament Themes*, contains an illuminating discussion on the progress of teaching between the testaments.

A list of Old Testament themes to be studied in their Old Testament context and then integrated into their New Testament fullness would include the election of Israel, the covenants with Abraham, Moses and David, the law, the land, the people of God, the kingship of God, the word of God, the presence of God, and the various representations of the messianic figure; i.e., the divine King, the Righteous Branch, the servant of the Lord, the Son of Man.

Since the message of the prophets concerns itself to a considerable extent with the "new thing" God is going to be doing, it becomes an indispensable part of teaching and preaching from these books to relate them to new covenant realities. In concluding this section we would call attention to H.W. Wolff's three rules for preaching from the Old Testament:

> First, to enquire as carefully as possible into the historical meaning of the text, so that the situation of the witness and his listeners and, above all, the intention of his message may be exactly and distinctly grasped; second, to compare the Old Testament text with corresponding New Testament passages and the center of their

kerygma, so as to show how far the Old Testament message eluci-
dates the message of the New, and how far the one has been super-
seded by the other; third, to seek out, with the message of the text,
those people to whom that text speaks, among the listeners to the
sermon, so that the original kerygmatic intention of the text — and
thus the will of the living God today — is not buried, either under
history or under philosophy. (*Old Testament & Christian Preaching*,
1986, p. 105).*

C. Pay Attention to Application

Perhaps the most challenging thing about preaching from
the prophets is not the difficulty in understanding the historical and cultural background of the prophet or even the theological antecedents that undergird his message. Rather, the
most vexing issue is that of application. To understand the
"then" of the prophet's word is one thing. To move from the
past to the present is quite another. Yet without proper application the prophets' message will have merely an academic
and an antiquarian interest. "Exegesis without application is
academic, exposition that is not grounded in exegesis is either
superficial or misleading and even both" (B. Ramm, *Baker's
Dictionary of Practical Theology*, E. Harrison, editor, 1960,
p. 101).

Exegesis that does not eventuate in application is inade-
quate. Stuart gives three reasons why exegesis can't be the end
of the task involved in preaching, but must lead to application:

First, it ignores the ultimate reason why the vast majority of people
engage in exegesis or are interested in the results of exegesis: they
desire to hear and obey God's word as it is found in the passage.
Exegesis, in other words, is an empty intellectual entertainment
when divorced from application. Second, it addresses only one
aspect of meaning — the historical — as if God's words were
intended only for individual generations and not also for us and,
indeed, for those who will follow us in time. The Scriptures are *our*
Scriptures, not just the Scriptures of the ancients. Finally, it leaves
the actual personal or corporate existential interpretation and use
of the passage to subjectivity. The exegete, who has come to know

---

* For a more detailed approach to theological exegesis, see D. Stuart, *Old
Testament Exegesis*, 1984, pp. 37, 38, 82; Kaiser, *Toward an Exegetical Theology*, pp. 131–147; Greidanus, *The Modern Preacher and the Ancient Text*,
1988, pp. 102–121, 228–262; E. Achtemeier, *Preaching from the Old Testament*, 1989.

the passage best, refuses to help the reader or hearer of the passage at the very point where the reader's or hearer's interest is keenest. The exegete leaves the key function — response — completely to the subjective sensibilities of the reader or hearer, who knows the passage least (*Old Testament Exegesis*, p. 40).

In the face of the vast difference between then and now it is no small matter to apply the text:

Application, then, in Bible preaching and teaching and in personal Bible study involves determining how the relevance of a passage for hearers/readers today may or may not differ from its relevance for its original hearers/readers (Zuck,"Application in Biblical Hermeneutics and Exposition," in *Walvoord: A Tribute*, D. Campbell, editor, 1982, p. 17).

There are several guidelines that will help in the task of application.

Application can happen only once the passage has been understood:

Only after the Bible student has accurately determined the meaning of the passage for the initial hearers in the "then and there" can he accurately apply that meaning to himself and others "now and here" (Zuck, p. 26).

Undoubtedly this is a failing in much preaching. There must be serious wrestling with the meaning of the text before one can begin to think about application. Daane issues a warning to preachers concerning a subtle temptation which needs to be overcome. He writes:

The primary concern with which preachers often approach a text is a concern for "what it means for the hearer today." Eager to discover relevance, the minister never takes time to hear what the text really says. The desire to apply it takes precedence over hearing what it declares. Application dominates interpretation. Students are particularly prone to this folly — and folly it is, for how can one apply what one has not yet heard or understood? (J. Daane, *Preaching with Confidence*, 1980, p. 61).

Application must be based on principles that provide the bridge between then and now:

> To principlize is to discover in any narrative the basic spiritual, moral, or theological principles. These principles are latent in the text and it is the process of deduction which brings them to the surface. It is not an imposition on the text (B. Ramm, *Protestant Biblical Interpretation*, 1970, pp. 199, 200).

To illustrate that application must be based on principlizing, consider the call narratives of the prophets Isaiah, Jeremiah and Ezekiel. In each case the prophets are told by God that their messages would receive an overwhelmingly negative and hostile reaction. From the point of view of listeners or converts, the prophets would be failures (Is. 6:9–13; Jer. 1:8–10, 17–19; Ez. 2:3–8; 3:7–9). When it comes to the application of those call narratives are we forced to say that ordination sermons today ought to contain similar warnings that very few people will believe? Must today's servant of God be told that his/her words will meet with the same hostile reaction as the words of the prophets? If we say this, we are not doing justice to the specific historical redemptive moment in which these prophets were operating. We cannot and must not transfer these dire and painful words, which reveal that hardly any one will believe their words, into our contemporary situation.

The principle that can be deduced from the Lord's constant warnings not to be afraid (Jer. 1:7; Ez. 2:6, 7; 3:9), and the persistent reminders that their audiences were stubborn and rebellious and therefore wouldn't listen (Ez. 2:4), is that God requires faithfulness to himself rather than spectacular results. The same principle is central to Paul's philosophy of ministry:

> On the contrary, we speak as men approved by God to be entrusted with the gospel. We are not trying to please men but God, who tests our hearts . . . We were not looking for praise from men. (I Thess. 2:4–6)

The prophets were not abrasive individualists looking for a fight. Yet in Jeremiah's case, he experiences conflict with the leaders shaping and directing the affairs of state (cf. Jer. 36), with his fellow prophets (Jer. 23:9–22; 27; 28), with his family (Jer. 11:21) and with the general population. The application of the above circumstances must take into account the uniqueness and particularity of the redemptive historical moment. The extent, degree and intensity of the conflict need not be duplicated with extreme literalness.

What does seem clear is that preaching the truth will inevitably lead to some conflict and that the minister of the gospel today must choose for the fear of God over the fear of man (Prov. 29:25). The application of the call narratives, which stress the inevitability of conflict in the ministry of the prophets, would then concentrate on (a) faithfulness to the Lord whatever the cost and (b) a passionate contending for the truth. The prophetic call brings one into collision with alternative world views which cannot be avoided (I Kings 18:21; Jer. 9:3). Jesus speaks similarly:

> If the world hates you, keep in mind that it hated me first. If you belonged to the world, it would love you as its own. As it is, you do not belong to the world, but I have chosen you out of the world. That is why the world hates you. (John 15:18, 19)

Another principle from the call narratives would be that ministry will involve suffering. Ministry involves identification *with God* and with *those to whom we minister*. God suffers and so must his servants. Jeremiah's suffering involves his feeling of extreme aloneness (Jer. 15:17):

> Jeremiah embodies what it means to be Israel . . . What happens to Jeremiah is what happens to the true Israel of God, and if we wish to be associated with the Israel of God, then this is what we must accept (Goldingay, *God's Prophet, God's Servant*, p. 37).

Another thing to keep in mind in applying the prophetic message is to determine what aspects of the original message are similar to our contemporary circumstances. This means we have to search for the "dynamic equivalent" between then and now (See W. Brueggemann, "As the Text Makes Sense," *Christian Ministry*, [Nov. 1983], pp. 7–10). Amos directed some stringent words against the religiosity of his day. In one such oracle he said:

> Go to Bethel and sin;
> go to Gilgal and sin yet more.
> Bring your sacrifices every morning,
> your tithes every three years. (Amos 4:4)

The principle is rather obvious. Bethel and Gilgal were centers of worship with a venerable history. What Amos is attacking is a religion that has lost its punch. He rejects a religion of orthodoxy at the expense of orthopraxis. Belief must be verified by practice. He is making the point that it is possible to sin in the very act of offering to the Lord what would be understood by the worshiper as sincere worship. Amos says to the people, "You not only sin during the week in your commercial and business transactions and in your marketing techniques when you defraud the gullible by skimping the measure, boosting the price and cheating with dishonest scales" (Amos 8:5). He tells the people that their very acts of worship are sin because they are a means of *hiding* from God rather than approaching him. Jesus announced the same principle in the Sermon on the Mount (Mt. 5:23, 24).

Stuart gives many detailed and helpful suggestions and procedural steps for moving from exegesis to application; the reader is urged to consult his book, *Old Testament Exegesis*, pp. 41–43, 136.

Bibliography on Preaching From The Prophets

A. Justice in the Prophets

Limburg, J. *The Prophets and the Powerless*. Atlanta: John Knox Press, 1977.
Mays, J. "Justice: Perspectives from the Prophetic Tradition." *Interpretation* 37 (1983): pp. 5–17.
Rooy, S. "Righteousness and Justice." *Evangelical Review of Theology* 6 (1982): pp. 260–271.
Stek, J. "Salvation, Justice and Liberation." *Calvin Theological Journal* 13 (1978): pp. 133–165.

B. Application in Preaching

Brueggemann, W. *The Prophetic Imagination*. Philadelphia: Fortress Press, 1978.
———. "As the Text Makes Sense." *Christian Ministry* (Nov. 1983): pp. 11–13.
———. *Jeremiah 1–25. To Pluck Up, to Tear Down*, Grand Rapids: William B. Eerdmans Publishing, 1968.
Clines, D.J.A. "Notes for an Old Testament Hermeneutic." *Theology News and Notes* (March 1975): pp. 8–10.
Marty, M. "The World in Front of the Text." *Christian Ministry* (Nov. 1983): pp. 11–13.
Zuck, R. "Application in Biblical Hermeneutics and Exposition." In *Walvoord, A Tribute*, D. Campbell, editor. Chicago: Moody Press, 1982.

C. Theological Background for Preaching From the Prophets

Bruce, F.F. *This is That: New Testament Development of Old Testament Themes*. Exeter: Paternoster Press, 1968.
Goldingay, J. *God's Prophet, God's Servant*. Exeter: Paternoster Press, 1984.
Heschel, A. *The Prophets*. New York: Harper & Row, 1962.
Kaiser, W. *Toward Rediscovering the Old Testament*. Grand Rapids: Zondervan Publishing, 1987.
———. *Toward an Old Testament Theology*. Grand Rapids: Zondervan Publishing, 1978.
———. *The Uses of the Old Testament in the New*. Chicago: Moody Press, 1985.

Stuart, D., and G. Fee. "The Prophets — Enforcing the Covenant in Israel." In *How to read the Bible For All Its Worth*. Grand Rapids: Zondervan Publishing, 1982.

von Rad, G. *The Message of the Prophets*. New York: Harper & Row, 1962.

Wolff, H.W. *Confrontations With Prophets*. Philadelphia: Fortress Press, 1983.

Wright, C. *An Eye for An Eye: The Place of Old Testament Ethics Today*. Downers Grove: Inter Varsity Press, 1983.

D.   Prophetic Forms of Speech

Chisholm, R. "Structure, Style and the Prophetic Message: An Analysis of Isaiah 5:8–20." *Bibliotheca Sacra* 143 (1986): pp. 46–60.

Clements, R. "Patterns in the Prophetic Canon." In *Canon and Authority*, G. Coats and B.O. Long, editors, Philadelphia: Fortress Press, 1977.

March, W.E. "Prophecy." In *Old Testament Form Criticism*, John H. Hayes, editor, San Antonio: Trinity University Press, 1974.

Tucker, G. "Prophecy and the Prophetic Literature." In *The Hebrew Bible and its Modern Interpreters*, G. Tucker and D. Knight, editors, Philadelphia: Fortress Press, 1985.

———. "Prophetic Speech." In *Interpreting the Prophets*, J. Mays and P. Achtemeier, editors. Philadelphia: Fortress Press, 1987.

Westermann, C. *Basic Forms of Prophetic Speech*. Philadelphia: Westminster Press, 1967.

E.   Preaching From the Prophets

Achtemeier, E. *The Old Testament and the Proclamation of the Gospel*. Philadelphia: Westminster Press, 1973.

———. "Preaching From Isaiah, Jeremiah, and Ezekiel." In *Biblical Preaching*, J. Cox, editor. Philadelphia: Westminster Press, 1983.

Bright, J. *The Authority of the Old Testament*. London: SCM Press, 1967.

———. "Haggai Among the Prophets: Reflections on

Preaching from the Old Testament." In *Faith to Faith*, D.Y. Hadidian, editor. Pittsburgh: Pickwick Press, 1979.

Gowan, D. "Preaching From the Prophets." In *Reclaiming the Old Testament for the Christian Pulpit*. Atlanta: John Knox Press, 1980.

Longman, T. "The Form and Message of Nahum: Preaching from a Prophet of Doom." *Reformed Theological Journal* (Nov. 1985): pp. 13–24.

Rust, E. "Preaching From the Minor Prophets." In *Biblical Preaching*, J. Cox, editor. Philadelphia: Westminster Press, 1983.

F.   Exegesis of the Old Testament

Achtemeier, E. *Preaching From the Old Testament*. Philadelphia: Westminster Press, 1989.

———. "The Artful Dialogue: Some Thoughts on the Relation of Biblical Studies and Homiletics." *Interpretation* 35 (1981): pp. 18–31.

Chisholm, R. "Wordplay in the Eighth-Century Prophets." *Bibliotheca Sacra* 144 (1987): pp. 44–52.

✸Greidanus, S. *The Modern Preacher and the Ancient Text*. Grand Rapids: William B. Eerdmans Publishing, 1988.

Hayes, J. and C. Holladay. *Biblical Exegesis*. Atlanta: John Knox Press, 1982.

Kaiser, W. *Toward an Exegetical Theology*. Grand Rapids: Baker Book House, 1981.

———. "Inner Biblical Exegesis as a Model for Bridging the 'then' and 'now' Gap; Hosea 12:1–6." *Journal of the Evangelical Theological Society* 28 (1985): pp. 33–46.

La Sor, W.S. "The Sensus Plenior and Biblical Interpretation." In *A Guide To Contemporary Hermeneutics*, D. McKim, editor. Grand Rapids: William B. Eerdmans Publishing, 1986.

Michelson, A.B. *Interpreting the Bible*. Grand Rapids: William B. Eerdmans Publishing, 1963.

Stuart, D. *Old Testament Exegesis*. 2nd edition. Philadelphia: Westminster Press, 1984.

von Rad, G. "About Exegesis and Preaching." *Biblical In-*

terpretation in Preaching. Nashville: Abingdon, 1977.

Wolff, H.W. *Old Testament and Christian Preaching*. Philadelphia: Fortress Press, 1986.

V. The Message of Habakkuk

I.   The Prophet and His Times

II. General Overview of His Message

III. The Dialogue Between The Prophet and His God 1:1–2:1
   A.   The Prophet's First Complaint   1:2–4
   B.   The Divine Response   1:5–11
   C.   The Prophet's Second Complaint   1:12–17
   D.   The Waiting Prophet   2:1

IV. The Disclosure of the Divine Purpose   2:2–20
   A.   The Divine Vision   2:2, 3
   B.   The Righteous Contrasted With The Proud   2:4, 5
   C.   Five Woes Directed Against the Oppressor   2:6–20
   D.   Summons to Silence

V.   The Prophet's Response   3:1–19
   A.   Prayer   3:2
   B.   Theophany   3:3–15
   C.   Confession of Faith   3:16–19

VI. Application
   A.   The Prophet and Evil
   B.   Nature of Faith
   C.   The Prophet and Evil
   D.   God and History
   E.   Habakkuk and the Cross

Violence is a regular part of the diet of the media in today's world. We are treated to a TV version of the Vietnam war in the '60s and to the assassination of the alleged murderer of President Kennedy. Our TV screens give us nightly coverage of the latest horrors in Lebanon, the violence in Northern Ireland and in Israel and the latest atrocities of world-wide terrorism. Planes are now blown up over matters of political ideology. Class struggle erupts into violence as management and labor go at each other's throats. Even religionists are getting into the act and books are now written on the morality of violence or the theology of revolution. It wasn't too long ago that a young radical, Abbie Hoffman, wrote a book called *Revolution for the Hell of It*. It is easy to become conditioned to a passive acceptance or an unverbalized despair over the inroads of violence within our society.

Violence also permeates the fabric of Jewish society in the late seventh century B.C. Jeremiah portrays Jerusalem as pouring out her wickedness and violence as a well pours out its water (6:7).

The book of Habakkuk forms part of the literature of the Old Testament dealing with theodicy. Theodicy may be defined as "the attempt to pronounce a verdict of 'Not Guilty' over God for whatever seems to destroy the order of society and the universe" (J. Crenshaw, *Theodicy in the Old Testament*, 1983, p. 1). Such defences of God were not unique to the Old Testament. The literature of Mesopotamia contained works such as *I Will Praise the Lord of Wisdom*, sometimes known as the *Poem of the Righteous Sufferer*, which dates back to the period between 1200 and 800 B.C. In this poem the unfortunate victim can find no relief from his tragedies either through prayer, sacrifice, priest or magician:

Misfortune is multiplied; I cannot find justice
I cried to the god, but he would not look at me
I cried to the goddess, but she would not raise her head.
The seer could not determine my future by divination
The oracle-priest could not elucidate my case through sacrifice.   ANET, p. 434

He reluctantly concludes that the will and ways of the gods are inexplicable:

What is good in one's sight is evil for a god
What is bad in one's mind is good for his god.

Who can understand the counsel of the gods in the midst of heaven?
The plan of a god is deep waters, who can comprehend it?
Where has befuddled mankind ever learned what a god's conduct
is?   ANET, p. 435

The mood of contemporary man on this problem is noticeably different from that of previous generations, or of ancient times, whether in Israel or Mesopotamia. C.S. Lewis, with characteristic insight, points to the contrasting attitudes between ancient and modern man.

The ancient man approached God (or even the gods) as the accused person approaches his judge. For the modern man the roles are reversed. He is the judge: God is in the dock. He is quite a kindly judge: if God should have a reasonable defense for being the god who permits war, poverty and disease, he is ready to listen to it. The trial may even end in God's acquittal. But the important thing is that Man is on the bench and God in the dock (C. S. Lewis, *God in the Dock*, 1970, p. 244).

Is God on trial for Habakkuk? In a certain sense he is, yet the Old Testament presents many of its godly heroes querying, scolding, and complaining against God. Abraham has his problems with divine justice, chiding God for not being just in his treatment of the righteous and the wicked (Gen. 18:23–25). The Psalmist is so shaken by the "injustice" involved in the prosperity of the wicked that before his moment of enlightenment (Ps. 73:17) he is reduced to despair and considers the possibility of giving up his faith (73:2,13). Jeremiah raises the same question about the ways of God and even at one point accuses God of deceit (cf. 8:18–9:1; 12:1–5; 15:16–20; 20:7–9). But in these and other examples the godly people of faith in Old Testament times are not putting God on trial *in the same way* that he is put in the dock by modern man. We will attempt to demonstrate the difference in attitudes by a consideration of this Old Testament prophet.*

I.   The Prophet and His Times

Little can be said about the man Habakkuk. While we

---

*   See under VI Application, B, The Nature of Faith.

would prefer to know some of the details of the prophet's personal life, our curiosity must remain unsatisfied. The Hebrew root for "Habakkuk" means "to embrace." Some suggest he is the son of the Shunammite woman, since she is told she would embrace a son (II Kings 4:16). The Greek version of Bel and the Dragon, the apocryphal addition to Daniel, contains a rather bizarre account of Habakkuk's being instructed by the Angel of the Lord to take some boiled pottage to Daniel in the lions' den! Such a story is quite obviously legend since Daniel lived considerably later. Because of the mention of musical instruments in 3:1, some believe the prophet is a Levite and cultic prophet associated with the temple. Others identify him with the watchman referred to in Isaiah 21:6 because of his statement in 2:1, "I will stand at my watch and station myself on the ramparts . . ."

The absence of any certain knowledge of the externals of his life should cause us to focus more intently on his inner life and the issues of faith and doubt with which he wrestles.

The clearest evidence for dating the book is the reference to the Chaldeans in 1:6. The Chaldeans became a world power by destroying Nineveh in 612 and then scored a decisive victory over Pharaoh Necho of Egypt in 605 at Carchemish. It is likely that the book is to be dated between the decisive victory in 605 and the final destruction of the temple in 587. Since King Josiah died in 609, while a religious reformation of some kind was going on, the picture of rampant sin within Judah given by Habakkuk fits the period after his death better than before.

The general picture of the times in which this prophet wrestled with God is clear. Judah has been under the domination of Assyria for many years and survives only by paying tribute. A glimmer of relief appears on the horizon when the Chaldeans, who live in the vicinity of Babylon, in southern Mesopotamia, combine with the Medes to end Assyria's domination of the whole region. With the fall of Nineveh in 612, new hope springs up in Judah that life will be different and genuine independence might again be a reality. Then Josiah is tragically killed in his attempt to resist Pharaoh Necho of Egypt. His untimely death is mourned by Jeremiah (II Chron. 35:25). Not long after, Nebuchadnezzar comes to power in Babylon and soon addresses his attention to Judah. It is the beginning of the end.

In these times of turmoil, terror and tragedy, this prophet
agonizes over what is happening. He is like the Psalmist who
cannot reconcile God's promise to David of an everlasting
covenant with the historical realities present after the tragic
death of Josiah (Ps. 89:46–49).

Such seems to be the broad historical picture that elicits the
disputation dialogue between the prophet and God. There is a
timelessness to the prophet's message, however, that makes its
understanding critical for our own generation. The more the
awareness of the reality of evil by any generation, the greater
the need for believing people to come to terms with the lessons
from this timeless little book.

II. General Overview of His Message

Before looking at some of the details it will be well to look at
the whole. The book reveals the perplexities and struggles of a
servant of God with the ways of God. The prophet complains
and scolds God for his inactivity in the face of wickedness
within the covenant nation. He paints a picture of sin out of
control and a disintegrating society. People are not listening to
God; his law is ineffective and powerless, and furthermore,
God is not listening to the prophet who passionately and persistently seeks his face over these concerns.

The first answer the prophet receives from God is, I am doing something! I am raising up the Chaldeans to serve as my
instrument of correction and judgment. God's answer creates
a more severe problem for the prophet. In the light of divine
holiness, the new question becomes, "Why are you silent while
the wicked swallow up those more righteous than themselves?"
(1:13). The wicked here are the Chaldeans; earlier they were the
wicked within the covenant nation (1:4b). Those who are more
righteous are the people of Judah or possibly the remnant. The
prophet's new complaint arises over his inability to understand the justice of God in using a wicked instrument to punish wickedness (though less wicked) within the covenant nation.

Habakkuk decides to seek the Lord for an answer to his
complaint. The divine response comes in the form of a revelation to come in the future and for which the prophet must wait.
It centers on the contrast between the proud (2:4a) and those
who are righteous — by faith (2:4b). The prophet is informed
of two additional things. The wickedness of the Chaldean na-

tion will eventually be judged (2:1–19). God is in control, he is sovereign and before the mystery of his ways, the earth must be silent (2:20).

Chapter three contains the prophet's response to God's revelation to him in chapter two. He prays and stands in awe of his God. He reminds himself of past encounters with him, and then makes confession of his determination to wait patiently: to trust, to rejoice and to draw upon the strength that comes from the Lord (3:16–19).

III. The Dialogue Between the Prophet and His God 1:1–2:1

A. The Prophet's First Complaint   1:2–4

The lament psalms sometimes begin with the question "why" and at other times with "how long." There are three parties involved in such laments. There is the one who complains, there is God and there are those against whom the complaint is directed. God himself is sometimes the subject of the complaint. Why has God rejected (Ps. 74:10), abandoned or forgotten (Lam. 5:20) his people? Why does he hide his face? (Ps. 44:24). "How long, O Lord? Will you be angry forever?" (Ps. 79:5; 80:4; 85:5; 89:46). "How long, O Lord, will you hide yourself?" (Ps. 89:46). When the prophet asks "How long," he is not complaining about something that has *suddenly* transpired; it is the duration of the disturbance which evokes his agony of spirit.

The prophet Habakkuk laments that violence and injustice are part of the fabric of society. The term violence occurs many times in the book (1:2, 3, 9; 2:8, 17). It refers to flagrant offences against fellowmen. It speaks of the intentional and malicious design to injure and harm another. It is used to describe society at the time of Noah (Gen. 6:11). Combined with the word "destruction" in 1:3b, it refers to the unjust and self-regarding behavior toward the weaker elements of society (cf. Amos 3:10; Jer. 6:7). God the Holy One sees this behavior and allows it to go on without punishment. God causes the prophet to see the depths and the extent of the evil but he himself, while seeing it, does nothing about it!

The two word pairs in the final clause of verse 3, "strife and conflict," point to the hostility and anger generated by the clash of independent wills when God's standards (his law and his justice) are flagrantly disregarded.

Verse 4 introduces the law of God for the first time. "Therefore the law is paralyzed and justice (MISHPAT) never prevails." As Calvin remarks, the prophet "was not made indignant through a private feeling, but because he could not bear the profanation of God's worship and the violation of His holy law" (*Twelve Minor Prophets*, Vol. 4, p. 21). Justice, which often has reference to the specific applications of the law in everyday life, is more likely used here in parallelism to law and should be understood to indicate a prophetic utterance. Law and justice both point to God's divine revelation. The usage would be similar to Hosea 6:5:

> Therefore I cut you in pieces with my prophets;
> I killed you with the words of my mouth;
> My judgments (mishpatim) flashed like lightning upon you.

The prophet complains that the truth of God was being rendered ineffective, the assumption being that such was the result of the extensive corruption of the religious and civil leadership.

B. The Divine Response   1:5–11

This section consists of three main thoughts. First, the revelation to the prophet of what God is actually doing. Second, the effect of this on the prophet and his people (1:5, 6a). Third, a description of the Chaldeans as a ruthless and dreaded people (1:6a–11).

1. *The Revelation of What God is Actually Doing:*
"I am raising up the Chaldeans."

In the previous century the prophets began to speak of instruments of judgment whom the Lord would use in the accomplishment of his purposes. Amos speaks in general terms, "I will stir up a nation against you, O house of Israel" (6:13). For him, nature and history are avenues whereby God is seeking to get the attention of his people (Amos 4:6–11). The Lord would give the command to shake the house of Israel among all the nations as grain is shaken in a sieve and "all the sinners among my people will die by the sword" (Amos 9:10). Being sovereign and in control of history, he brings Israel out of Egypt, the Philistines from Captor and the Arameans from Kir (Amos 9:7). Isaiah speaks in terms remarkably similar to those of Habakkuk. The Assyrian king is God's razor hired from beyond the river to shave their heads, legs and beards (Is. 7:20) and is the rod of God's anger and the club of his wrath, dispatched against a godless people (Is. 10:5, 6; cf. Deut. 28:49, 50).

2. *The Effect of the Revelation*

The prophet is told to become a keen observer of what is happening within the horizons of world politics and history. The revelation is not merely addressed to him, however, but to a group, presumably his countrymen, since the imperatives "look, watch and be utterly amazed" are plural. It will be "in your days," which in all likelihood means within a relatively short period of time, certainly within the lifetime of the existing generation. The response to raising up the Chaldeans will be amazement and disbelief (1:5b, 1:6b). The NIV "utterly amazed" translates two identical verbs that are emphatic. The amazement may be connected with the degree of the devastation coming, as described in 1:11, or with the sudden emergence of Babylon under Nabopolassar and his son Nebuchadnezzar.

The downfall of Assyria and resurgence of Babylon are attributed to the Lord who controls the destiny of nations. The popular theology that Jeremiah and Habukkuk encounter speaks of Zion's impregnable position. The promises to David are understood as an ironclad guarantee of her security regardless of her conduct. The people are confirmed in this fools' paradise by the religious leaders who "lied and said, 'No harm can come to us, we will never see the sword or famine' " (Jer. 5:12; cf. Jer. 7). It is likely then that the amazement referred to Babylon's approaching destruction of Judah:

'To be amazed' is man's response to an event that utterly confounds all previous expectations (cf. Gen. 43:33; Ps. 48:5; Is. 13:8; 29:9; Jer. 4:9); it runs counter to what the listeners 'believe.' The destruction of Jerusalem is such an event, creating both a national crisis and a theological crisis among God's people (C. Armerding, *The Expositors Bible Commentary*, Vol. 7, F. Gaebelein, editor. 1985, p. 502).

The work in which God is engaged is his work of judgment and grace. The phrase in the NIV, "I am going to do something," is in the KJV translated, "I am working a work." It's composed of two words in Hebrew of the same root. The noun form is used primarily in the Psalms to refer to God's saving deeds on behalf of his people, whether in judgment of their enemies or in deliverance of his people (Ps. 44:2; 64:9; 77:12; 92:4; 143:5; cf. also Is. 5:12).

3. *Description of the Chaldean Nation*   1:6–11

The description is extremely graphic. Their cavalry is compared to wolves and leopards — animals unrivaled in speed and power. Jeremiah also uses the lion, the leopard and the wolf as symbols of divine judgment (5:6). The violence of which the prophet complained in his opening lament (1:2a) is now going to be visited on Judah by the Chaldean hordes (1:9). Their military exploits and methods are not all that is in view. Several phrases describe their motives and their character. "They are a law to themselves and promote their own honor" (1:7). They make a god of their own unaided strength (1:11b). "Their character was rooted in self-sufficiency that acknowledged no superior authority and no dependency, which was tantamount to self-deification" (Armerding, *The Expositors Bible Commentary*, p. 503). They were ruthlessly arrogant with no higher law to answer to than their own.

C.   The Prophet's Second Complaint   1:12–17

1.   *The Prophet's Certainties*   1:12, 13a

Before the prophet comes to the heart of his new complaint he begins with some things that are bedrocks of his faith. He refers to the *eternality* of God (1:12a) Before attempting to sort out his problems, which arise from the actions of men *within* history, he begins by reminding himself of the high and holy one who inhabits eternity (Is. 57:15) and who is *before* history. Habakkuk also refers to God as *my* God. The perplexities of his soul are those of one cleaving to the Lord with personal trust and confidence (cf. Ps. 18:12). He speaks of the Lord as *my Holy One*. As such, he is unutterably opposed to evil. His eyes are too pure to countenance wrongdoing. He is all *power-*

ful. He is the Rock who appoints and ordains the Chaldeans to execute judgment. He is the covenant-keeping *faithful* One. Such is implied in the statement, "we shall not die."

2. *The Prophet's Perplexities*   1:13a–17

His specific problem is, How can God be just and still use as an instrument of judgment a nation whose own shirts were not clean. Compared to Judah, the Chaldeans are worse scoundrels and deserving of more punishment, so how is it just for the Lord to be silent in the face of the Chaldean wickedness. The prophet sees that Judah's sins require correction but now he voices his doubts about the propriety of an evil instrument. The nations are as helpless before such a tyrant as fish are in the net of the fisherman. The net is the symbol and instrument of Chaldean power (1:15). The Chaldeans are guilty of sacrificing to the net, i.e., worshiping power.

D.   The Waiting Prophet   2:1

Having voiced his complaints to the Lord the prophet waits for his response. He is portrayed as a watchman on a lookout high above the city who is in a position to see the approaching enemy (II Kings 9:17; II Sam. 18:24). The language is not to be understood literally but expresses the prophet's need to hear what the Lord will say to him and in him. The lookout symbolizes spiritual preparation and mediation, withdrawal and detachment from his previous state of mind, and represents his attempt to remove himself from his own human thoughts.* Habakkuk draws a deliberate distinction between his thoughts and those of God.

The prophets are often called watchmen, who are to observe the Lord's purposes and sometimes warn of impending danger

---

* G.A. Smith, *The Book of the Twelve Prophets*, Vol. 2, 1899, p. 138, remarks "This verse is not to be passed over, as if its metaphors were merely of literary effect. They express rather the moral temper in which the prophet carries his doubt . . . Nor is this temper patience only and a certain elevation of mind, nor only a fixed attention and sincere willingness to be answered. Through the chosen words there breathes a noble sense of responsibility. The prophet feels he has a post to hold, a rampart to guard. He knows the heritage of truth, won by the great minds of the past; and in a world seething with disorder, he will take his stand upon that and see what more his God will send him."

(Is. 21:6–8; Hos. 9:8; Is. 56:10; Ez. 3:17). Habakkuk wanted to hear of these purposes both for the faithful people of God and for the nations who attempt to build their empires on blood (Hab. 2:4, 14). Such hearing requires watching:

> It is not enough to open our eyes once, and by one look to observe what happens to us; but it is necessary to continue our attention. This constant attention is, then, what the prophet means by watching; for we are not so clear sighted as immediately to comprehend what is useful to be known. And then, though we may once see what is necessary, yet a new temptation can obliterate that view (Calvin, *Twelve Minor Prophets*, Vol. 4, p. 60).

> Morning by morning, O Lord, *you hear my voice*;
> morning by morning I lay my request before you and *wait* in expectation. (Ps. 5:3)

We must assume that the Psalmist's waiting in expectation is for the Lord's response. Yet for that response to be received by the Psalmist it is necessary for him to affirm, "I will listen to what God the Lord will say" (Ps. 85:8). So Habakkuk speaks of "waiting to see" what the Lord will say just as the Psalmist speaks of listening to what the Lord would say. How important this attitude of soul is in a world in which Satan is active (I Peter 5:8), sin is deceptive (Heb. 3:13), and where the mind of the flesh is at enmity with God! (Rom. 8:7):

> It is hence no wonder that many fall away under trials, yea, almost the whole world; for few there are who ascend into the citadel of which the prophet speaks, and who are willing to hear God speaking to them (Calvin, *Twelve Minor Prophets*, Vol. 4, p. 63).

The prophet boldly prepares a response to God's rebuke (2:1b). Such a stance may appear to be a challenge to God and betray anything but a listening attitude, for how can he be planning in advance how to respond to the Almighty? The word for complaint in 2:1b, "What answer I am to give to this complaint," is used in Job in the disputation dialogues between Job and God (13:3, 6; 23:4). Job seeks clarification of his problem by the question and answer method common in disputes. The rebuke in wisdom literature is one means of imparting wisdom. God himself imparts wisdom by means of rebuking. The prophet wishes to be corrected by the Lord, but such

correction would come through the discussion that the prophet was to have with God.

IV. The Disclosure of the Divine Purpose   (2:2–20)

A. The Divine Vision   2:2,3

1. *Written on Tablets*

The prophet has rejected human wisdom as the answer to
his perplexing question and seeks an answer from the Lord.
He receives a revelation that is to be written upon tablets. The
purpose of the written form is to preserve it for the future. The
fulfillment will await the future. The vision is certain to come;
there is an appointed time for it; it is speaking (panting in
haste) of the end. It will not be one of the deceiving visions of
the false prophets. It will certainly come.

Its transcription on tablets identifies its importance for future generations. Jeremiah and Isaiah are also instructed to
write but on a scroll and in a book (Is. 8:1; 30:8; Jer. 30:2). The
plural "tablets" on which the revelation is to be written would
recall to mind the tablets of the covenant at Sinai (Ex. 24:12;
31:18; Deut. 9:2; 10:2, 4) thereby confirming the critical nature
of this new revelation to the prophet. In Jewish tradition the
613 laws of Moses are said to be summarized in David's eleven
commandments in Psalm 15, Isaiah's six in 33:15–16, Micah's
3 in 6:8 and Habakkuk's one in 2:4.

2. *The Purpose of the Vision*

The importance of the vision is seen in the statement, "so
that a herald may run with it" (2:2). The Authorized Version
reads, "so that he who reads it may run." The message is to be
taken to others and proclaimed. Running is a term used by the
prophets as they announce God's message. "I have not sent
these prophets, yet they ran. I have not spoken to them, yet
they prophesied" (Jer. 23:21). Running and prophesying are
clearly a case of synonymous parallelism (cf. Zech. 2:4). This
surely is a crucial message which is being given. It is to be proclaimed throughout the ages.

There is a metaphorical meaning of the verb "to run" which
should also be considered here. The sun runs its course, fulfill-

ing its divine appointment (Ps. 19:6). "I run in the path of your commands" (Ps. 119:32). Isaiah used the verbs to walk and to run in speaking of obedient service to God (40:31).

Walking and running portray life as either in obedience or disobedience, depending on context. We may say then that the statement, "he who reads it may run with it," might accordingly be understood as: he who reads it may follow its directions diligently and obediently. Whoever reads it will be shown the right way of thinking and living if they follow the direction in life for which the vision calls.

3. *The Time Frame of the Vision*

The vision has some eschatological terminus. It speaks (yearns for) of the end (2:3). In light of 2:6–20 the end may refer to the destruction of the Chaldean nation which will eventually receive its due reward. In Daniel the end and the appointed time have future eschatological significance (11:35; 12:9; 8:19). The Greek translation of the Old Testament focuses on the coming of a person. "If he tarry, wait for him." The writer of Hebrews implies a messianic reference when he exhorts his audience to persevere in trust and confidence despite not seeing the promises of God immediately realized. They are to wait, "for in just a very little while he who is coming will come and will not delay" (Heb. 10:37a).

B. The Righteous Contrasted with the Proud 2:4,5

The substance of the vision is given in these two verses. The Chaldean tyrant is not mentioned by name, either here or in the following woes. The vision is intentionally general in order to describe ungodly oppressors at any point in history. In this section we should note two things: (1) the proud are not upright, and (2) the righteous live by faith, which is expressed in persevering faithfulness.

1. *The Proud Are Not Upright.*

The universal testimony of the Bible is that God resists the proud. From Babel (Gen. 9) to Babylon (Rev. 18) the message is that pride precedes a fall. Pride excludes from salvation because it and self-reliance go together. "The soul, being swollen with pride, shuts out faith and with it the presence of God" (E. Pusey, *Minor Prophets*, vol. 6, 1885, p. 77). The proud locate all goodness and power within themselves. They see no need for God or his righteousness. God hates pride because it is a blatant challenge to his authority. God always eventually punishes the proud. "The eyes of the arrogant man will be humbled and the pride of men brought low, and the Lord alone will be exalted in that day" (Is. 2:11; cf. also 2:12–17). The Assyrian was judged for "the willful pride of his heart and the haughty look in his eyes" (Is. 10:12; cf. 10:13–19). Babylon received similar treatment (Is. 13:19).

The Chaldean proud one is not upright. He is a law to himself (Hab. 1:7). He makes a god of his strength (Hab. 1:11) and sacrifices to the net, the symbol of his strength (Hab. 1:16). He is greedy and arrogant and his appetite for his helpless victims is as voracious as the grave. Habakkuk is informed that the proud one will continue in his evil ways *for a time* and this means that the prophet must continue to live with the tension between good and evil.

This blind continuance in evil by the proud one is provoked by the deceptive influence of wine (2:5a). Habakkuk is not to be understood as suggesting a direct influence between strong drink and pride. "But strong drink serves as an agent by which the latent pride of person comes forth in all its ugliness. Strong drink evokes expressions of bloated self-esteem inherent in the sinful mind and heart" (O. Palmer Robertson, "The Justified Shall Live by His Steadfast Trust," *Presbyterian*, 9, 1983, p. 71). In the downfall of the Babylonian King Belshazzar, son of Nebuchadnezzar, there is some connection implied between wine and the pride involved in false worship. It is while drinking wine from the silver and gold goblets taken from the temple in Jerusalem that his entourage "praised the gods of gold and silver, of bronze, wood and stone" (Dan. 5:4). Daniel pronounces the destruction of the Babylonian empire at the hands of the Medes and Persians as due to the fact that "you did not honor the God who holds in his hand your life and all your ways" (Dan. 5:24). Wine is often mentioned in the Old Testament in connection with pride, unbridled greed and injustice (Is. 5:11,12, 22–23; Prov. 31:4,5; Amos 6:6).

It is a principle of divine revelation that "moral tyranny is suicide"; that nations which build cities on bloodshed will be laboring for the fire and will wind up on the scrapheap of history (Hab. 2:13). This revealed outlook is based on the long view of history. The history of the Babylonian nation is short-lived, lasting only from 612 to 539 B.C., when Cyrus enters Babylonia virtually uncontested.

2. *The Righteous Live by Faith*

The proud are not upright and will therefore not survive; they will *die*. The righteous, on the contrary, will *live* by their faithfulness. There are continuing debates over whether the Hebrew word should be translated as "faithfulness" or "faith." It is undisputed that the *word* may be used of the legal standing of a person; the forensic background is unmistakable in Deut. 25:1. Judges are to acquit the righteous (both the noun and the verb in Hebrew are the same root and are commonly translated, to "justify the righteous"). The word has reference to one's legal standing of guilt or innocence before the court (e.g., Ex. 23:7).

Isaiah 5:23 is instructive in that it pronounces against taking away the righteousness of the righteous. This is not referring to the removal of the moral character of a person but giving a false legal verdict to the wicked and depriving the innocent (the righteous) of their rightful acquittal. "Righteous" comes quite naturally to have an ethical meaning, but the righteousness of character and conduct develop out of the idea of a just legal standing before God. The righteous one, who has been given this standing by faith, lives his life in faithfulness before the Lord. The two key Hebrew roots in 2:4b, "The *righteous* shall live by his *faith*" (faithfulness) are found in the well-known statement, "Abraham *believed* God and it was reckoned to him for *righteousness*" (Gen. 15:6). The Old Testament doctrine of justification by faith is indeed less developed than in the New Testament but the essence of it is present there. The saints of God in the Old Testament look to the mercy of God as the basis for forgiveness (cf. Is. 55:6; Micah 7:18; Ps. 130:3–5; Dan. 9:9,18). "I trust in your unfailing love; my heart rejoices in your salvation" (Ps. 13:5). "This conception almost carries with it the other point that man's right attitude to God is one of trust, for if acceptance is due to God's mercy, then man obviously cannot rely on what he himself does and must rest his faith elsewhere" (L. Morris, *Apostolic Preaching of the Cross*, 1955, p. 239).

The Old Testament does not conceive of faithfulness to God apart from trust and reliance upon God (Ps. 64:10). The righteous (those who know God by faith) will live by their trustful commitment to God. They will continue to trust and obey; they will not be destroyed or swallowed up by the evil times.

In 1:5 faith is weak, and will not believe that God will dislodge Assyria from the pinnacle of her power and use the Chaldeans as his instrument of judgment upon his people. The remainder of the book will develop the new theme begun in 2:4; viz., the blossoming of faith that culminates in the prophet's great statement of 3:17. God's promise is that he will deal with evil at the proper moment and that in the meantime the righteous will live by their faithful trust in him. The trust is "not so much an abstract quality of 'reliability,' but a way of acting which grows out of inner stability . . . It seems more to emphasize one's own inner attitude and the conduct it produces" (A. Jepson, *Theological Dictionary of the Old Testament*, G.J. Botterweck & H. Ringren, editors, Vol. 1, 1974, p. 317). Such an attitude of entrustment is the heart's response to that irrevocable stability that comes from knowing that Yahweh remains who he is, the faithful covenant-keeping God (cf. Hos. 2:20).

The New Testament elaborates on the text of 2:4 in two directions, both of which are consistent with the original context. Paul cites it in connection with faith as the source of righteousness (Rom. 1:17). The writer to the Hebrews cites it in the course of his argument on the need for trustful perseverance in the face of severe testing (Heb. 10:37–39). The book of Hebrews makes the connection between faithful trust and life and gives a catalogue of those attitudes and actions produced by faith in the face of the crises experienced within the world (Heb. 11).

C. Five Woes Directed Against the Oppressor   2:6–20

A series of "woe" pronouncements makes up the next unit of thought. They are referred to as a taunt song (2:6). The use of the "woe" form has been identified with a cry of mourning. We know from Jeremiah of the existence of professional mourners, who sing appropriate songs of grief (Jer. 9:12–18). In his song of mourning at the decease of Jonathan, David speaks movingly of his love for Jonathan (II Sam. 1:19–27). Isaiah parodies the normal funeral dirge when he presents a mock

funeral song and gloats over the death of the tyrant king of
Babylon instead of mourning him (Is. 14:4–21).

Habakkuk's woes are an advance pronouncement of the
death of the tyrant and a condemnation of the sinful principles by which he perpetuates his rule and kingdom. In response to the revelation of the triumph of faith and the ultimate downfall of the proud, the prophet celebrates in advance
the doom of evil and final triumph of God in the world. This
he does by condemning the sinful principles of life common to
oppressors in every generation. The absence of specific historical references confirms this, though in the context an application to the Babylonian oppressors is reasonable.

He pronounces doom against all who are overcome by unholy ambition, greed and covetousness, who build their kingdom by violence, cruelty and bloodshed, taking advantage of
the weak. He attacks drunkenness and immorality and ends
with a polemic against idolatry (2:18–20).* The despair of the
prophet in chapter one has obviously given way to a new courage. This new courage arises from his new perspective. The
realities confronting him are the same, but faith is now mobil-
ized for action.

D.   Summons to Silence   2:20

Three eternal principles have come into focus in chapter
two, to buttress the faith of God's people. The first is that the
righteous *live* by faithful trust in the Lord, but the proud who
defy God will perish. The second is found in the important
section 2:12–14, and is the principle that history is moving toward the full revelation of the divine glory. This truth, of
course, cannot be known apart from faith because appearances are deceiving!

The cup of wrath from the Lord's right hand will come to
the oppressors of this world (Hab. 2:16b). There is a moral or-

---

* R. Davidson, *The Courage to Doubt*, 1983, p. 118 comments:
In all cases in the Old Testament such attacks have one primary purpose,
to underline the essential character of Israel's God, as a living, active God,
in contrast to the powerless nonentities whom other nations worship.
Such gods are always satirized as being utterly devoid of life or breath
(Heb. *ruah*), the dynamic, life-giving energy which called creation into being and characterizes the control that Israel's God exercises over all history (cf. Gen. 1:2; Isa. 40:7).

der operating in history and the nations will exhaust themselves for nothing because the Lord Almighty has determined that their labor, their empire-building, will eventually go up in flames. "When a nation is committed to self-aggrandizement through oppression of others, it has written its own obituary. There is a self-destroying power in evil that time always reveals" (F. Gaebelein, *Four Minor Prophets*, 1970, p. 167). "The earth will be filled with the knowledge of the glory of the Lord, as the waters cover the sea" (Hab. 2:14). The glory of the Lord will be seen in the display of His wrath against the Chaldeans. The glory of the Lord in the Old Testament refers to his visible presence, by which the preeminent value of his character and actions are revealed both in the exercise of his mercy and grace and in the display of his justice (Prov. 16:4). The kingdoms of this world which are hostile to God will be destroyed for he will not give his glory to another (Is. 42:8). Habakkuk 2:14 is similar to but not identical with Isaiah 11:9:

> "The earth will be full of the knowledge of the Lord as the waters cover the sea." In Isaiah, for example, this thought closes the description of the glory and blessedness of the Messianic Kingdom in its perfected state. The earth is then full of the knowledge of the Lord, and the peace throughout all nature which has already been promised is one fruit of that knowledge. In Habakkuk, on the other hand, this knowledge is only secured through the overthrow of the kingdoms of the world and consequently only thereby will the earth be filled with it and not with the knowledge of Jehovah (as in Isaiah) but with the knowledge of His glory which is manifested in the judgment and overthrow of all ungodly powers (C. F. Keil and F. Delitzsch, *Commentary on Minor Prophets*, Vol. 2, 1949, p. 86).

The third principle that emerges in chapter two is that of Divine Sovereignty. Heathen idols are nothing. They are lifeless. The Lord is the living God who is in his holy temple (2:20). He is not a dumb idol covered with gold and silver, rather he is the creator of heaven and earth. The temple refers then, to heaven. "The Lord is in his holy temple; the Lord is on his heavenly throne" (Ps. 11:4). From heaven He, as the enthroned Sovereign, observes the conduct of men and women. The call for silence is a call for reverent submission to his mysterious purposes: "Be still and know that I am God; I will be exalted among the nations" (Ps. 46:10; cf. Zech. 2:13).

Zephaniah counsels a similar silence in the light of the impending day of the Lord (1:8).

The prophet sees the Lord as sovereign in history, in charge of the nations; he is not at a loss to know what to do, to control and counteract the evil operating within the world. "The king's heart is in the hand of the Lord; He directs it like a watercourse wherever he pleases" (Prov. 21:1). Even when that evil comes to expression in the strongest possible way by means of the absolute will of an ancient monarch, God still exerts his sovereign and unrivaled dominion. The prophet recommends a different kind of silence in the face of this sovereign God; i.e., the silence of voluntary submission.

> We submit to God when we bring not our own inventions and imaginations, but suffer ourselves to be taught by his word. We also submit to him, when we murmur not against the power of his judgements, when we humble ourselves under his powerful hand, and do not fiercely resist him, as those do who indulge their own lusts (Calvin, *Twelve Minor Prophets*, Vol. 4, p. 132).

V. The Prophet's Response

God's revelation to the prophet evokes a response. He complains bitterly to the Lord and announces his intention to wait, to listen to what God will say. In chapter three we have the grand finale to the dramatic encounter between the prophet and God. The superscription (a prayer) and the postscript bring the dialogue between the Lord and his prophet to a fitting conclusion, for the setting of chapter three is one of formal worship. As such, the form of the chapter indicates that the prophet's personal response functions as a model for all the godly within the nation.

A. His Prayer 3:2

1. *God's Work* 3:2a

God is now the all-consuming reality for the prophet, whose problem has faded into the background. Habakkuk begins:

I have heard of your fame;
I stand in awe of your deeds, O Lord.

To what is the prophet referring as the Lord's "deeds"? The singular form of the noun was used in 1:5 to refer to the *work* of God in raising up the Chaldeans. The NIV "I am going to do something" in 1:5 is more literally "I am performing a work or a deed," which work is identified in 1:6 as the raising up of the Chaldeans. Since chapter two is more immediately contextual to the prophet's prayer it is possible that the deeds that Habakkuk is in awe of are those righteous actions of the sovereign Lord mentioned in 2:6–20 and, in particular, 2:14.

Since the Lord is in control of history and it is moving toward the manifestation of the divine glory, the prophet may be expressing his awe at the forthcoming manifestation of God's righteous anger against all vain and proud pretenders to the divine throne. It may also be that the deeds in view are those alluded to in 3:3–15, i.e., the mighty acts of the victorious warrior God of Israel over Pharaoh and his hosts. The remembrance of such deeds in the past buttresses Habakkuk's faith that the covenant God will similarly vindicate his people in the future. The latter view is the least likely as the prayer is offered before the theophany described in 3:3–15. Based on a passage like Psalm 77:9,11, however, it can't be entirely ruled out. There is no reason why the Lord's deeds cannot refer both to his work of raising up the Chaldeans as his disciplining agent as well as his subsequent work of bringing them before the bar of his divine justice.

By saying that he had heard the divine voice (NIV "fame" is taken by some to mean speech or report):

He makes a confession and gives evidence of repentance . . . He prescribes for the faithful the way by which they were to obtain favor from God, and turn him to mercy and that is by dreading his threatenings, and by acknowledging that whatever God threatened was near at hand (Calvin, *Twelve Minor Prophets*, Vol. 4, p. 136).

The prophet stands in awe of the goodness and severity of God just as the Psalmist who confessed:

If you, O Lord, kept a record of sins
O Lord, who could stand?
But with you there is forgiveness;
Therefore you are feared. (130:2)

2. *God's Work Renewed*   3:2b

"Renew them in the midst of the years; in the midst of the years make them known." The suffix on the Hebrew verb "renew" is best understood as applying to the nearest antecedent, "deeds or works." What then is meant by the phrase "renew them" (your deeds or works)? The basic meaning of the verb is to call to life, to revive. The work of God most likely refers to his deeds in raising up the Chaldeans as his disciplinary agent and his later work of governing history for the ultimate display of his glory. God will act to overthrow all nations and kingdoms that ignore him and to establish his righteous kingdom. To this end then, the prophet prays for that work of God to take place. What had previously been a source of perplexity to him is now the content of his prayer! The disciplinary activity of God against his people would be a prelude to this grace. He accepts in principle the need for God's strange work of judgment (Is. 28:21) but prays that it may soon give way to God's saving work of renewal within the covenant nation.

Calvin interprets the prayer, "renew or revive your work," in a somewhat different way, though the end result is the same. He views the work as the nation whom God has formed and created. "Your love, O Lord, endures forever — do not abandon the works of your hand" (Ps. 128:6b). Even more relevant would be the statement:

Yet, O Lord, you are our Father;
We are the clay, you are the potter;
We are all the work of your hand.
(Is. 64:8)

As such it is a prayer that the remnant will be kept alive, preserved from extinction, supported and comforted in time of trouble. In this view, the prophet is simply praying for the ultimate preservation and good of God's true people without any specific focus on judgment as a means to this end. The prayer is similar to that of the Psalmist: "Will you not revive us again, that your people may rejoice in you?" (85:6).

The final phrase, "in the midst of the years make known," has no object. Whether it is "make yourself known" or "make known your works," the prophet prays for the Lord's power, pity, promise and providence to be clearly seen in the world in the preservation of his people.

3. *In the Midst of the Years*   3:2b

He prays that God's work will continue in the "midst of the years." (NIV translates 'in our day' in our time.) The phrase, repeated twice, is of considerable importance. Calvin referred it to the "middle course of the people's life," believing that the prophet was praying that the Lord would not take away the life of his people prematurely, i.e., before Christ was to come in the flesh. Others take it to mean "within a short period of time," or ascribe it merely to the difficult times.

The phrase is best understood in connection with the promise of the coming of the vision "at the appointed time" (2:3). The interval between the appointed time and the present time seems to Habakkuk to be long series of years. The oracle poses a tension between the reality and certainty of its fulfillment at the appointed time and the *appearance* of delay and lingering (2:3b). At the end of the period of waiting, there will be relief from this tension because the justice of God will then be clearly revealed in the punishment of evil in all its manifestations. The prophet prays that the Lord will not unduly delay the outworking of his purposes but bring them to pass in the period between the present distress and his appointed time when his promise shall have its full and final fulfillment. The years then have specific reference to years of distress.

4. *The Balancing of Divine Anger and Compassion*   3:2b

One of the best-known and most eloquent prayers in the Bible is Habakkuk's plea: "In wrath remember mercy." Some suggest a meaning of turmoil and distress instead of wrath, but the identical root is used by Isaiah in his reference to the Lord's rousing himself in anger to perform his strange and alien work of judgment (Is. 28:21). The prophet's plea for mercy is grounded upon the nature of God and his covenantal commitment to his people (Ex. 34:6; Ps. 51:1; 86:15; 145:8). "The Lord your God is a merciful God; he will not abandon or destroy you or forget the covenant with your forefathers, which he confirmed to them by oath" (Deut. 4:31). Mercy in the midst of wrath would mean alleviating and mitigating the cruelty of the Chaldeans toward Judah and accelerating their demise and destruction. In the exercise of his anger and wrath toward his children, God disciplines them, and such chastisement is a testimony to his love:

> When therefore we provoke God's wrath, by our sins, we feel him to be angry with us; but yet the Prophet connects together things which seem wholly contrary — even that God *would remember mercy in wrath*; that is, that he would show himself displeased with them in such a way as to afford to the faithful at the same time some taste of his favour and mercy by finding him to be propitious to them (Calvin, *Twelve Minor Prophets*, Vol. 4, p. 139).

When God comes to judge his people, they are not to give in to despair but to flee to the God of mercy as their only refuge. Such counsel was given by the writer of Lamentations to those suffering in exile. "Because of the Lord's great love we are not consumed, for his compassions never fail . . . for men are not cast off by the Lord forever, though he brings grief, he will show compassion, so great is his unfailing love" (Lam. 3:22, 31–32). Judgment is his strange work (Is. 28:21) for "he does not willingly bring affliction or grief to the children of men" (Lam. 3:33). "His compassions are new," i.e., never exhausted (Lam. 3:23).

When David becomes aware of the gravity of his sin with Bathsheba his plea for forgiveness is based on the mercy of God (Ps. 51:1a). No matter how much progress we have made in the life of faith we can never approach God on the basis of our attainments in faith and sanctification. Habakkuk teaches us not to "plead our merit, but his mercy" (*Matthew Henry's Commentary: Isaiah to Malachi*, p. 1366).

B.   Theophany   3:3–15

This section may be divided into two parts.* In 3:3–7 there is a theophany reminiscent of the Sinai theophany. References to Mt. Paran in verse 3 and Teman, which was located in Edom or Seir, clearly connect this section with Deut. 33:2–4 which speaks of the revelation of God's law at Sinai. The Sinai theophany serves as an analogy for the new revelation of the

---

* R. Davidson, *The Courage to Doubt*, p. 118 remarks,

  To take it out of its context in worship is to rob it of its power. It is the language of devotion clothed in evocative poetry. It is the language of a great mediaeval cathedral soaring heaven-wards, pointing to the transcendent God.

divine presence alluded to in Habakkuk 2:14 and prayed for by the prophet in 3:2.

The prophet sees God's *glory* covering the heavens and his praise filling the earth (3:3b); terminology that calls attention to the universal extent of his sovereign rule. His praise filling the earth connects with Habakkuk's earlier statement that the earth will be filled with the knowledge of the glory of the Lord (2:14). Habakkuk sees God's "splendor" and compares it to the sunrise (3:4a). Here again the imagery ties in with the splendor and radiance from the divine presence manifested at Sinai (Ps. 18:8–12) and the Lord is perceived as illuminating the world, not with the "delicate light of sunrise, but with the awe-inspiring radiance that characterized his descent on Mount Sinai, a light as brilliant as the lightning that accompanied that event, incandescent with his glory" (Armerding, *Expositors Bible Commentary*, Vol. 7, p. 526).

The prophet sees the *power* of God. Rays flash from his hand (3:4b); i.e., flashes of light emanate from his hand, the symbol of divine power (Deut. 3:24; 4:34). His power is revealed in the operations of nature; e.g., "Sun and moon stood still in the heavens at the glint of your flying arrows, at the lightning of your flashing spear" (3:11). God is seen in his role of judge and brings with him plague and pestilence (3:5), a grim reminder of his judgments against Egypt (Ex. 9:3) and the covenant nation when they rebelled against him (Deut. 28:21; 32:24). There is a universal scope to the display of his power, for he shakes the earth and makes the nations tremble (3:6a). Mountains crumble and are shattered because, though they may seem to be ancient (*olam* 3:6a), he alone is eternal (*olam* 3:6b).

In the second section of 3:3–15, from verses 8–15, the Lord is directly addressed and there is great prominence given to the imagery of conflict. The Old Testament sometimes makes use of mythological imagery to portray the Lord's conflict with his enemies. The enemy is the watery chaos, which is given considerable emphasis in the whole section and refers to the nations (3:12). The divine *anger and wrath* are vividly revealed to the prophet (3:12). God's anger is directed against the sea (3:15), which calls to mind his victory over the Egyptian enemies (Ex. 14:28), when he as the Lord of Hosts with his horses and victorious chariots came to deliver his people (3:13).

Though his anger is unleashed against the nations (3:12b) he comes to "save and deliver" his people (3:13a), terms that contrast with Habakkuk's criticism of the divine inactivity in 1:1–4. Such saving activity is based upon his covenantal faithfulness to his people and to their anointed one (3:13a). The latter may refer to a king (I Sam. 20; II Sam. 23:1) or a priest (Ex. 40:13). Here, because of the background of the exodus, it likely refers to Moses who incorporated the various Messianic functions of prophet (Deut. 18:15), shepherd (Num. 27:17) and servant of God (Num. 17:7; Heb. 3:5, 6). The anointed one is contrasted with "the leader of the land of wickedness" (3:13b), a likely reference to the Egyptian pharoah. In all these allusions there is a double reference:

> The oppression in Egypt foreshadows subsequent oppression, and the deliverance at the Red Sea embodies the promise of subsequent deliverance . . . In the present chapter, set against the background of imminent danger preceding the Exile (vv. 2, 16–17; cf. 1:5–11), and also fraught with eschatological undertones of judgment and salvation, the "anointed" will therefore represent both the king in Habakkuk's own time and the Christ whose sufferings and glory the prophets predicted (Armerding, *Expositors Bible Commentary* Vol. 7, p. 531).

The prophet's act of remembering and recounting the past saving actions of God provides a context for trusting in the covenant Lord to be gracious in the present and for the faithful to cleave to his promises. Like the words of a popular song during World War II, "we did it before and we can do it again," God's people were reminded of his saving acts in their past history so as to provide them with hope for the future.

C.   Confession of Faith   3:16–19

In 3:2 the prophet spoke of hearing the Lord's voice, the message spoken to him in chapter two. In chapter three he has heard (3:16a) and encountered the Living God, the God of Glory, Power, Wrath and Salvation. The prophet responds to the vision of the Lord's coming to judge the nations and to rescue his people (3:13a). Four words delineate and describe his new attitude.

1. *Fear of God* 3:16a

The description in 3:16a is of the overwhelming physical response to the vision, a feature in prophetic visions (Dan. 8:17, 27). The prophet has had an immensely powerful and physically overwhelming encounter with God. The bodily sensation of weakness and trembling reflects as well the internal response of fear spoken of before his encounter (3:2a). It is a mark of the godly to tremble at God's word (Is. 66:2b; Ps. 119–120):

> Whosoever therefore securely slumbers will be confounded in the day of affliction; but he who in time anticipates the wrath of God and is touched with fear as soon as he hears that God the judge is at hand, provides for himself the most secure rest in the day of affliction (Calvin, *Twelve Minor Prophets*, Vol. 4, p. 172).

2. *Quiet Confidence* 3:16b

I will "wait patiently" for the day of calamity to come. Fear has given way to faith, agitation and unrest to patience. The prophet of the "whys" and the "how longs" has now become willing to trust God with the future in quiet and submissive confidence. He has seen beyond the calamity to the Holy One's working out his mysterious providence and has thereby gained the strength to wait patiently:

> Ye fearful Saints, fresh courage take
> The clouds ye so much dread
> Are big with mercy, and shall break
> in blessings on your head.
>
> Judge not the Lord by feeble sense
> But trust him for His grace
> Behind a frowning providence
> He hides a smiling face.
>
> His purposes will ripen fast
> Unfolding every hour
> The bud may have a bitter taste
> But sweet will be the flower.
> W. Cowper (1731–1800)

3. *Rejoicing Trust* 3:16,18

The prophet's initial trembling before God gives way to a

spirit of triumph. In the absence of the normal observable signs of God's blessing the prophet still cleaves to God and rejoices in him. In the Old Testament prosperity was linked to covenant obedience and blessing. Habakkuk acknowledges the justness of God in depriving the people of the outward, external signs of blessing. The Lord gives and he takes away (Hos. 2:8,9; Job 1:21). He now admits that the nation is worthy of judgment. But he will yet trust God and rejoice in him.

To be able to rejoice in God even in the face of great affliction is to attain the pinnacle of faith. It is interesting to compare Habakkuk's confession of faith with the Psalmist's in Ps. 144 (a wisdom Psalm), particularly verses 13–15:

Our barns will be filled with every kind of provision.
Our sheep will increase by thousands,
   by tens of thousands in our fields,
Our oxen will draw heavy loads.
There will be no breaching of walls
No going into captivity
No cry of distress in our streets.
Blessed are the people of whom this is true
Blessed are the people whose God is the Lord.

In contrast with this perspective, Habakkuk is able to confess from his heart, "Blessed are those who when the roof caves in are still able to rejoice because even then they have God as their God."

This statement takes its place along with others, e.g., Job 1:21 or Ps. 27:1–4, as one of the supreme utterances of confidence in God. To be able to experience joy with storm clouds threatening outside is truly a precious and rare gift. Inner joy is the source of all true strength, for it's the joy of the Lord alone that is our strength (Neh. 8:10). Hence, as Calvin remarks, this doctrine is extremely useful, for it reminds us:

that whenever signs of God's wrath meet us in outward things, this remedy remains to us, to consider what God is to us inwardly; for the inward joy which faith brings to us can overcome all fears, terrors, sorrows and anxieties (Calvin, *Twelve Minor Prophets*, Vol. 4, p. 175).

It is important to note that the form of the verbs "to rejoice" and "to be joyful" expresses a determination and intention of the strongest degree. Faith means that our love for and service to our God will be independent of our circumstances. Like the Psalmist who initially struggled with doubt (Ps. 73:2–16), we must aspire to confess:

> Whom have I in heaven but you? And earth has nothing I desire besides you. My flesh and my heart may fail, but God is the strength of my heart and my portion forever. (Ps. 73:25, 26)

4. *Renewed Strength* 3:19

By referring to the sovereign Lord as his strength, the prophet draws a contrast between God and all other supports. His confident assurance is in God, and finding strength in God under such depressing circumstances, he models a persevering hope in the Lord. David experiences severe affliction from Saul who sought to kill him: "Day after day Saul searched for him, but God did not give David into his hands" (I Sam. 23:14). It is Jonathan who becomes a source of strength for his friend, when he comes to David in the desert of Ziph and "helped him find strength in God" (I Sam. 23:16).

In Psalm 18, from which the prophet likely drew some of his ideas (cf. vs. 33 with Hab. 3:19), the Psalmist personalizes this thought by referring to God as the Lord, my strength. His circumstances are so extreme that he speaks of himself as being entangled in the cords of death and confronted with the snares of death (Ps. 18:4,5). Like the Psalmist, Habakkuk testifies to faith's stability, resilience and vigor even in the face of adversity (3:19).

Strength is needed to overcome obstacles and opposition from *within* and from *without*. Strength is given by the Lord to the weary to serve him with the full vigor that surpasses that of youth, so that all who draw on his strength soar on wings like eagles, run and will not be weary, walk and will not grow faint (Is. 40:23–31).

The secret of drawing strength from the Lord is given in the New Testament in several places. Our Lord said, "Apart from me, you can do nothing" (John 15:5b). If we can do nothing without Christ we can do everything through him who gives us strength (Phil. 4:13). The key to strength is in that true humility which knows itself and boasts in weakness so that Christ's power may be exchanged for human weakness. "I will boast all the more gladly about my weaknesses, so that Christ's power may rest on me" (II Cor. 12:9). "He that is the God of our salvation in another world, will be our strength in this world" (*Matthew Henry's Commentary: Isaiah to Malachi*, p. 1371). We need his strength to engage in our spiritual warfare (Eph. 6:10–18). We need his strength "to run with perseverance the race marked out for us" (Heb. 12:16).

VI. Application

A. The Prophet and Evil

The problem of evil is existential rather than theoretical. This is obvious from the intensity of the feelings implied in the verbs "call for help" and "cry out to you." The query "how long" implies that the issue exercises his soul for a considerable period of time. The prophetic spirit will often be engaged in seeking answers for questions which those of lesser spiritual perception are not even asking!

There is much to be commended in this prophet in his attitude toward sin and its effects on society. He has often prayed to the Lord to correct the people for their evil, and it was an important part of the office of a prophet to intercede. A century earlier Amos cries out to God with the poignant words, "Sovereign Lord, forgive! How can Jacob survive? He is so small" (Amos 7:2, 5; cf. Gen. 20:7). Jeremiah, Habakkuk's contemporary, prays much for the tide of wickedness to be reversed only to be told on four occasions to stop praying! It is too late (7:16; 11:14; 1411; 15:1). Calvin reminds us that

> all who really serve and love God, according to the prophet's example, ought to burn with holy indignation whenever they see wickedness reigning without restraint among men and especially in the church of God. There is indeed nothing which ought to cause us more grief than to see men raging with profane contempt for God, and having no regard for his law and for divine truth (Calvin, *Twelve Minor Prophets*, Vol. 4, p. 18).

The prophet exemplifies one who has a balanced concern for the well-being of his people and a burning zeal for the divine glory.

B. Nature of Faith

Faith is not without its questions. It is not blind, unintelligent belief. Doubt isn't the same as unbelief. Doubt and questioning are part of normal Christian experience, and there is a rich legacy of biblical material in which God is confronted by his people regarding his ways within the world (Gen. 18:13; Jer. 11:18–23; 15:10–21; Ps. 73). We should not be living emotionally and intellectually anaesthetized lives. By our involvement with and understanding of the issues of our world we affirm the true nature of faith (I Chron. 12:32).

True faith in God's word never detaches us from life in this world but attaches us to it in a new way. We must weep and pray and ask "why" and "how long." When we do so we learn that part of revealed truth concerns the hiddenness of God and his ways (Prov. 25:1; Ps. 97:2; 1 Tim. 6:16; Is. 55:4, 5). In the Bible this isn't a problem or an excuse but a source of praise. "Oh, the depth of the riches of the wisdom and knowledge of God! How unsearchable his judgments, and his paths beyond tracing out! (Rom. 11:33, cf. Is. 45:15). Jesus joins the chorus of praise to the Father that chose to hide certain things from the worldly wise and learned and to reveal the same things to little children (Mt. 11:25, 26). There are times when God "pulls rank"! This is exactly what is implied in the statement, "The Lord is in his holy temple. Let all the earth keep silence" (2:20).

On one hand, questions of faith brought to God are welcomed. Any loving parent welcomes honest enquiries about why things are done a certain way. On the other hand, the way children ask their questions indicates whether they come in a spirit of willingness to hear what the parent is saying or with a spirit of combat to challenge parental authority.

Why does God sometimes pull rank and remind us to whom we are talking? Why does he call for the silence of submission? Why are we given in the Bible a doctrine of the hiddenness of God? There is, according to the Bible, a *foolish* wisdom and a *wise* ignorance. A foolish wisdom majors on problems and questions that God has not chosen to answer. It arrogantly assumes that it knows and asks the right questions. It begins with the autonomous human intellect rather than the revelation of God. The wise ignorance leaves God's secrets (Deut. 29:29) to himself and cleaves to the blessed knowledge of what he has revealed and is content to admire the divine wisdom in what has not been revealed. People of faith *live* with some unsolved problems but also with their quota of God-taught certainties. The true child of God is willing to live with some mystery because he is willing to allow God to be God!

People assume that they must be able to fathom everything done in the world. How presumptuous! God must conform to our ideas. God is in the dock! Such an attitude fails to see who God is and who we are. We, to whom Jesus said, "you cannot add one cubit to your stature" (Mt. 10:27), venture to measure God by our creaturely and sinful ideas. The whole starting point is wrong and contrary to Biblical thought.

Faith enables a man to transcend his present situation and live in the light of unexplained events. Does this mean that true faith is not consistent with struggles and perplexities? Hardly, or stalwarts like Abraham, Habakkuk, Job, Jeremiah and the Psalmist would be disqualified.

What is the difference then between the ungodly and godly as they react to and are confronted with this hiddenness of God and His ways? The difference is in the spirit in which questions are asked. Do we approach the Lord arrogantly or with a recognition of our creatureliness and sinfulness? Discussions with God in the Bible are never between two equal participants! God is in heaven; we are on earth. He is holy; we are sinful. He knows all; we are ignorant and sinful. "Stop trusting in man, who has but a breath in his nostrils. Of what account is he?" (Is. 2:22). God educates his children in mystery, that he might exercise them in the life of faith. Let this not be interpreted as a put-down on searching for truth or answers. Rather, it is a *caution* to search with a proper attitude, one that gives recognition to the vast gulf that exists between the sinner and a holy God.

Habakkuk's problems were created by his faith in a God who was both holy and righteous, powerful and good. With whom can one get angry in a world governed by chance? Certainly not God. The answer to suffering given in Harold Kushner's recent best-seller, *Why Bad Things Happen to Good People*, is to posit a God who is himself developing and to jettison his sovereignty and power and allow him to retain his goodness. In this view, God would like to do more to overcome suffering but his hands are tied; he can't because he is not omnipotent. By such reasoning we can extricate the Lord from his problem, but at what a cost!

Habakkuk was convinced of the reality of a righteous and holy God and he learned to trust God's goodness. After 2:4 his questions fall into the background and faith takes control. Complaints fall by the wayside, replaced by confidence. The prophet learns that obedience is not always immediately rewarded, nor is evil always instantly judged (Eccl. 8:11):

> Blind unbelief is sure to err, and scan His work in vain; God is His own interpreter and He will make it plain. (W. Cowper, 1731–1800)

At any point in history the scales of divine justice may not appear to be balanced. We must be willing to walk in the obedience of faith when things around us allow for a different understanding of life. This is simply to say that true faith *produces* faithfulness. One is the root and the other the fruit, and what the Lord has joined together should not be put asunder. Faithfulness is the outgrowth of faith, and faith is oriented to the revealed picture of God.

C.   The Prophet's Doctrine of God

Habakkuk believes in a God who reveals himself and speaks in contrast to the idol gods of the surrounding nations who cannot speak (2:18). This God is the eternal God (1:12a) whose ways are eternal (3:6b). Though he is the High and Holy One who inhabits eternity (Is. 57:15), he enters into personal relationship with his people. Therefore he is addressed by the prophet as *my* God, *my* Holy One (1:12a). He is faithful and trustworthy in his convenantal commitments; therefore, the prophet proclaims, "We will not die" (1:12b). His holiness and righteousness require that sin be punished in whatever quarter it is found (1:13). In the exercise of his justice in the punishment of evil he acts mysteriously and sovereignly, employing different instruments such as the Chaldeans. His mysterious ways sometimes give the impression that evil-doers will be able to put God to the test and succeed in challenging him (Mal. 3:15). Habakkuk's God is the sovereign ruler who is enthroned in heaven and before whom the earth is to bow in silent and believing submission (2:20). Infinitely glorious, he is determined to display his glory in the entire earth (even as he did at the giving of the law at Sinai and through the revelation of his august presence in the tabernacle and temple, 2:14, 3:3b).

All who brazenly oppose him will become monuments to the display of his righteous and holy anger (3:2, 8, 12). He acts in covenant mercy toward his own (3:2b,13a).

This summary of his teaching concerning God is immensely relevant to the issue of *how* Habakkuk handled his problem and, by implication, how we handle our own problems of faith. He openly and honestly acknowledges his problem. He sincerely and persistently seeks the Lord for an answer. He cries out to the Lord and is willing to *wait* upon God for what he would say. Would that all who claim to love God and believe his word would bring their perplexities and distresses to him in this way! Faith doesn't look exclusively at the world (the facts) and draw its conclusions. Faith brings God, as he has revealed himself, into the picture along with the facts.* It commits problems to him and looks for answers from him, and it *perseveres* in doing so. This is what is meant when Scripture calls upon God's people to seek God with all their heart (cf. Jer. 29:13).

Many dabble in the things of God and in matters of faith. For such, religion is a means of manipulating God for one's *own ends*. When he refuses to give to them all they ask, they turn against him assuming that they have tried the Christian faith and it hasn't worked! Of course, the whole perspective is radically wrong, because it starts with man rather than God and it degrades God into someone we use for our own purposes.

This view of religion has infected the church today so that the focus of our preaching and teaching is on what we can achieve and how we may feel better if we will only decide to be born again! God will solve all our psychological problems overnight if we trust him. If we commit some of our money to him, he will certainly give us much more, for hasn't he promised this? If God is first, our families second and we are third, won't we be successful business men and women? Hasn't he promised to heal all our diseases, and if he doesn't, that must be because of our lack of faith. Then too, doesn't faith bring with it a scintillating sex life?

The distortions in all of these modern gospels are subtle and therefore dangerous because they contain partial truths, and a partial truth made out to be the complete truth becomes an un-

---

* This point is developed at length in the messages on Ps. 73 in D.M. Lloyd-Jones, *Faith on Trial*, 1965.

truth. The focus of the Old Testament prophet Habakkuk, like that of all the other prophets, is the covenant God, who in infinite and condescending grace calls a people to himself to show forth his praise, by humble trust and obedience to him. They are his "treasured possession" (Ex. 19:4–6), not because of their blood line but because through his grace they fear the Lord, honor his name, and serve him. These are the distinguishing characteristics which mark them as the people of true faith who know the Lord (Mal. 3:16–18; Hos. 2:19, 20).

God himself is the supreme gift to his people. Gaining some true glimpse of his glory and greatness is our highest calling in life (Ps. 27:4), which will put a proper perspective on our problems and perplexities. He who has God has everything, and this perspective allows the person of faith to view the events of the *present* against the backdrop of *eternity*.

D.   God and History

M. Lloyd-Jones, in his helpful little book, *From Fear to Faith*, succinctly summarizes the lessons in this area.

(1) History is under divine control. This is so much a part of the Old Testament that in our generation we tend to lose sight of the uniqueness of such a perspective. There are so many texts that teach and imply this that one hardly knows where to begin: Gen. 20:6; 45:5; 50:20; Ruth 2:3; II Sam. 17:14; II Chron. 36:17; Is. 7:18–20; 10:5–19; 37:26; Jer. 25:9; Amos 4:6–11; Hab. 1:6.

(2) History is following a divine plan (Hab. 3:13a; Dan. 2:44, 45; Deut. 32:8).

(3) History progresses under a divine timetable (Dan. 9:24–27; Gal. 4:4). Here is where extreme tension enters, because as creatures living in time, we take the short view of history and God is not in a hurry, and he takes the long view of history.

(4) Events within our world are connected with the divine purpose for the people of God. Cyrus' decree, allowing the Jews to return from exile, is a prudent and strategic political move on his part, but it is part of the divine purpose as well. In the Cyrus Cylinder his political polytheism is clear. "May all the gods whom I have brought into their cities pray daily before Bel and Nabu for long life for me" (ANET, p. 316).

The biblical statements on the exile demonstrate a fascinating interplay between a sovereign God working out his purposes and the freely chosen activities of those agents through whom these purposes are worked. The exile is the result of the anger of the Lord being directed against his people. God's people have "mocked his messengers, despised his words and scoffed at his prophets until the wrath of the Lord was aroused against them and there was no remedy. He brought up against them the king of the Babylonians" (II Chron. 36:16,17a). Jeremiah adds one fascinating note to the picture. He too refers to the anger of the Lord as the cause of their banishment from his presence (Jer. 52:3), but follows it with the little remark, "Now Zedekiah rebelled against the king of Babylon" (52:3b). It was Zedekiah's rebellion against the king of Babylon that brought the king of Babylon against the covenant nation. "Men's own free decisions are the means by which God works out his purpose. It is thus He who controls history" (Goldingay, *God's Prophet, God's Servant*, p. 71).

It is not true, of course, that we can know *how* this is happening; *how* God works good out of evil in our personal lives, or *how* history is bound up with the divine purpose of salvation for the church of Christ. We have been warned against pretending that we have inside information on how God works within history (Eccl. 11:5). But it surely is of immense comfort and motivation to be assured by the Lord that he is building his church and that the gates of hell will not prevail against it (Mt. 16:18), and that in his inscrutable wisdom history is moving toward the consummation of all things.

This we know by divine revelation, and as George Adam Smith pointed out a long time ago, there is a two-edged prong to this knowledge. To nations and world powers and their leaders it is a warning against the atheism of force. Power becomes an alternate god when those who *wield* it do so without any moral controls on its exercise. The Chaldeans are judged because their own strength is their god and they sacrifice to the net, the instrument used in the exercise of their power (1:11b and 1:16a). Smith also pointed to the atheism of fear, which affects those *against* whom power is wielded, who cower in the face of it and respond as if it were the only kind of strength that mattered.*

When the prophets speak and direct their oracles against the

---

* Smith discusses the atheism of fear and force in *The Book of Isaiah*, Expositor's Bible, W.R. Nicoll, editor, chapter nine.

foreign nations it is unlikely that such were personally delivered. Their purpose is to assure God's people who are suffering under the heel of the oppressors of the ultimate historical judgment which will eventually catch up with power-hungry evil-doers.

Such a view of history may tend at times to go against the grain of our sophisticated realism:

> The process of life and the course of history by no means always reveal signs of God's rule but frequently conceal it so that man loses confidence in God. The root cause of the problem is to be found not in God's character but in man's shortcomings, his wanting to force God's providential rule to adapt itself to his own standards and to worship him according to the image which man has made for himself (A. Weiser, *The Psalms*, 1962, p. 314).

Faith, however, trusts in the promise, and the promise is that kingdoms established on violence and bloodshed will eventually crumble under the holy determination of Almighty God to root evil out of the world and to display his own glory and righteousness within the created order (Hab. 2:14; II Peter 3:13).

The Psalmist in Psalm 73 serves as our example in this struggle between faith and sight:

> He no longer squeezes God and the interpretation of everything that happens into the narrow compass of his own egocentric trains of thought, but conversely seeks to understand and evaluate the realities of human life in the light of the reality of God . . . It signifies a radical change in man's attitude of mind when he abandons the ground of visible data as the starting point of his thinking and relies on the invisible reality of God to such a degree that it becomes by faith the unshakable foundation of his seeing and thinking (Weiser, *The Psalms*, p. 512).

E.   Habakkuk and the Cross

Habakkuk faces the mystery of the silence of God in the face of human evil within Judah and the Chaldean nation. There is no doubt but that his disturbing "whys" (1:3,13) are important. However, they pale into comparative insignificance before the great mystery of the "why" that Jesus uttered from the cross. "My God, my God, *why* have you forsaken me?" (Mt.

27:46). God spares not his own Son and in the process answers not his own Son, who himself "cries out" to the Father over his silence.

Jesus suffers in silence, but by the silence of the cross, when it seems as though the Father doesn't care or that things are out of control, the powers of darkness, which make their final assault against him, are destroyed. That cross, where God is silent in the face of his Son's cry, becomes our salvation. The seed of the woman has crushed the serpent's head (Gen. 3:15), and Christ, the Son of God, having disarmed the powers and authorities, makes a public spectacle of them, triumphing over them (Col. 2:15).

We conclude with J. Calvin's prayer with which he ended his commentary on this great prophet of God in the hope that its sentiments will indeed be ours:

Grant, Almighty God, that as we cease not daily to provoke thy wrath against us, and as the hardness and obstinacy of our flesh is so great, that it is necessary for us to be in various ways afflicted, — O grant, that we may patiently bear thy chastisements, and under a deep feeling of sorrow flee to thy mercy; and may we in the meantime persevere in the hope of that mercy, which thou has promised, and which has been once exhibited towards us in Christ, so that we may not depend on the earthly blessings of this perishable life, but relying on thy word may proceed in the course of our calling, until we shall at length be gathered into that blessed rest, which is laid up for us in heaven, through Christ our Lord.   Amen.

(Calvin, *Twelve Minor Prophets*, Vol. 4, pp. 177, 178)

Bibliography on Habakkuk

Achtemeier, E. *Nahum — Malachi: Interpretation* — A Bible Commentary for Teaching and Preaching. Atlanta: John Knox Press, 1986.

Armerding, C. *Nahum, Habakkuk,* Vol. 7: The Expositor's Bible Commentary. Grand Rapids: Zondervan Publishing, 1976.

Baker, D. *Nahum, Habakkuk and Zephaniah.* Tyndale Bible Commentaries. Downers Grove: Inter Varsity Press, 1988.

Barber, C. *Habakkuk and Zephaniah.* Chicago: Moody Press, 1985.

Calvin, J. *Twelve Minor Prophets*, Vol. 4. Grand Rapids: William B. Eerdmans Publishing, 1950.

Craigie, P. *Twelve Prophets*, Vol. 2. Daily Study Bible. Philadelphia: Westminster Press, 1985.

Crenshaw, J. *Theodicy in the Old Testament.* Philadelphia: Fortress Press, 1983.

Gaebelein, F. *Four Minor Prophets: Obadiah, Jonah, Habakkuk and Haggai.* Chicago: Moody Press, 1970.

Gowan, D. *The Triumph of Faith in Habakkuk.* Atlanta: John Knox Press, 1976.

Keil, C.F., and F. Delitzsch. *The Twelve Minor Prophets*, Vol. 2. Grand Rapids: William B. Eerdmans Publishing, 1949.

Laetsch, T. *The Minor Prophets.* St. Louis: Concordia Publishing Co., 1956.

Lloyd-Jones, D.M. *From Fear to Faith.* London: Inter Varsity Press, 1953.

Lewis, C.S. *God in the Dock.* Grand Rapids: William B. Eerdmans Publishing, 1970.

Pusey, E. *The Minor Prophets*, Vol. 2. Grand Rapids: William B. Eerdmans Publishing, 1950.

Robertson, O.P. "The Justified Shall Live by his Steadfast Trust." *Presbyterion* 9 (1983): pp. 52–72.

Smith, R.L. *Micah-Malachi,* Vol. 32: Word Biblical Commentary. Waco: Word Books, 1984.

Smith, G.A. *The Book of the Twelve Prophets*, Vol. 2. London: Hodder & Stoughton, 1898.

Bibliography on Themes Within Habakkuk

Violence

Hengel, M. *Victory Over Violence*. Philadelphia: Fortress Press, 1973.

Sider, R. *Christ and Violence*. Kitchener: Herald Press, 1979.

Tournier, P. *The Violence Within*. San Francisco: Harper & Row, 1982.

Faith

Blamires, H. *The Faith and Modern Error*. London: S.P.C.K., 1965.

Davidson, R. *The Courage to Doubt*. London: SCM Press, 1983.

Ellul, J. *Living Faith: Belief and Doubt in a Perilous World*. San Francisco: Harper & Row, 1983.

Evans, C.S. *Quest for Faith*. Downers Grove: Inter Varsity Press, 1976.

Guinness, O. *In Two Minds: The Dilemma of Doubt*. Downers Grove: Inter Varsity Press, 1976.

Hals, R. *Grace and Faith in the Old Testament*. Minneapolis: Augsburg Publishing, 1980.

Holmes, A. *Faith Seeks Understanding*. Grand Rapids: William B. Eerdmans Publishing, 1971.

Taylor, D. *The Myth of Certainty: The Reflective Christian and the Risk of Commitment*. Waco: Word Books, 1986.

Questions on Habakkuk

Chapter One

The prophet Habakkuk prophesied some time during the period between 605 and 587 B.C. The general picture of the times is clear. Judah had been under the domination of Assyria for many years and had survived only by paying tribute. A glimmer of relief appeared to be coming when the Chaldeans, who lived in the vicinity of Babylon, in southern Mesopotamia, combined with the Medes to end Assyria's domination of the entire region. With the fall of Nineveh in 612, new hope sprang up in Judah that life would be different and genuine independence might again be a reality. Just around the same time, King Josiah, a godly king during whose reign some kind of religious reformation took place, was tragically killed in his attempt to resist Pharaoh Necho of Egypt. His untimely death was mourned by Jeremiah (II Chron. 35:25). Not long after his death, Nebuchadnezzar came to power in Babylon, and that was the beginning of the end as far as Judah's independence was concerned. In these times of turmoil and tragedy, the prophet agonized over what was happening.

Read the book through and look for the divisions within the book. After reading through the book give a *general* overview of the book's message.

Study chapter one in detail. How unique was this prophet in complaining to the Lord? Look up in a concordance the *phrase* "how long" to see how it was used, particularly by the Psalmist. What does the phrase "how long" say concerning the depth or duration of his problem? Summarize as exactly as you can the *exact nature* of his complaint in 1:2–4.

Read 1:5–11. What is God's response in 1:5, 6? What does he say will be the effect of this revelation on prophet and people? Why would they have been utterly amazed over the Lord's use of foreign nations to discipline Judah and Jerusalem? What was the popular theology of the day in Jerusalem? (cf. Jeremiah 7).

Read Habakkuk 1:12–17. How does this passage take one step further in the evolution of the prophet's complaint against God? What are the prophet's *certainties*? What are the prophet's *perplexities*?

Chapter Two

1. The prophet is portrayed as a watchman (cf. Is. 21:6-8, 56:10 and Ez. 3:17, which describe the task of a watchman). In the case of Habakkuk, what is the purpose of his watching? Are watching and waiting the same? cf. Ps. 5:3. What practical lesson can be learned from the way the prophet attempts to handle *his* problem?

2. The content of the revelation was inscribed on tablets (cf. Ex. 24:12, 31:18; Deut. 9:2, 10:2, 4.) What does the fact of the vision being written on tablets say about its importance? The purpose of the vision is stated in the words, "That the one who reads it may run" (2:2). What do you think is meant by "run"? (cf. Ps. 119:32, Is. 40:31)

3. For what time frame is the vision given?

4. Chapter 2:4,5 contains a contrast. Who is being contrasted in these verses? What is said about the two groups being contrasted in these verses? What are godly people called to do in every generation, according to 2:4? Why is it both difficult and necessary to have this attitude in order to deal with life's ups and downs? (Rom. 3:21-28; 8:26-39).

5. In chapter 2:6-19 five woes (2:6b, 9, 12, 15, 19) are pronounced against the "him" referred to in 2:6a. Notice that they are referred to as a taunt song (cf. Is. 14:4). Habakkuk's woes are a pronouncement in advance of the death of the Chaldean tyrant and a condemnation of the sinful principles by which he perpetuates his rule and kingdom. What are those sinful principles?

6. Study in more detail the third woe in 2:12-14. Paraphrase the thought in your own words. What philosophy of history is being put forth in these brief words? Is there any difference between 2:14 and Isaiah 11:9? What truth about God is taught in 2:20? What does it mean "to be silent" before him?

Chapter Three

God's revelation to the prophet evokes a *response*. He had complained bitterly to the Lord and had announced his intention to listen to what God had to say. The chapter can be divided into A. The Prophet's Prayer 3:2; B. The Theophany 3:3-15; C. The Prophet's Personal Confession 3:16-19.

1. Isolate the various components of his prayer and study the key words in the prayer. What is the "work" (NIV "deed") referred to in 3:2? What is meant by "the midst of the years"? What is meant by God's fame (3:2a)? Discuss the phrase "in wrath remember mercy." Why would the prophet have to remind God of His need to display mercy?

2. The Theophany: What attributes of God are featured in the theophany?

3. The Prophet's Confession: Specifically isolate and discuss the *prophet's personal reaction* to the revelation of God.

4. In drawing the study of this book to a conclusion and applying it, discuss the teaching and application in relation to four areas:
   A. The Prophet and Evil
   B. The Nature of Faith
   C. The Prophet's Doctrine of God
   D. The Book's View of God and History

VI. The Message of Haggai

I. Introduction

Haggai is not a well-known prophet. In spite of the "desire of the nations" passage in 2:7, the book has been neglected in the recent teaching ministry of the church. It might surprise those in the church today who hardly know where to find the book in the Bible that it played a vital role in the ministry of that morning star of the reformation, Savonarola, who in November 1494 preached a challenging series of messages from this prophet. Later Scotland's most powerful preacher, John Knox, also found it to be a very relevant book in his ministry of renewal and reformation.

Haggai differs noticeably from the other prophetic books. The other prophets criticize the covenant nation for overt and flagrant sins such as idolatry or superstitious worship, social injustice or spiritual and physical adultery, violence, and rejection of God's law. Haggai has to contend with a much more subtle but no less soul-damaging attitude on the part of the people of God; that of apathy and indifference in service and worship. Thus Haggai confronts us with the call to examine our priorities in life.

A. Historical Background

Israel goes into captivity in 605, 597 and 586 B.C. Jehoiachin, the king (with 10,000 of the choicest soldiers and craftsmen) is taken captive to Babylon in 597 and a puppet king Zedekiah, the uncle of Jehoiachin, is set up as king. Eleven years later in 586, Zedekiah's rebellion prompts Nebuchadnezzar to return and set fire to the temple and the royal palace, and the people of God are taken into exile. It isn't long, however, until the Babylonian nation crumbles before the power of the Persian nation. Eventually in 539, Cyrus, the Persian king, gives a decree allowing the Jews to return to Jerusalem (Ezra 1:1-4). As the exile has taken place in three stages, so also does the return, and a group of the faithful remnant led by Joshua, the high priest, and Zerubbabel, the governor, return to Jerusalem in obedience to the word of God and in accordance with Cyrus' decree. The two Old Testament prophets, Haggai and Zechariah, are part of the first return. These prophets of God are with Joshua and Zerubbabel, encouraging them in their work of rebuilding the temple (Ezra 5:2). The temple serves as the external sign of the covenant. The rebuilding of the temple indicates to the people that the covenant promise of salvation is still in the process of coming to fulfillment.

B.   The Remnant

The people who return are called the remnant (Hag. 1:14). They are the spiritual elite. What do we know about them according to Scripture? First of all, they are obedient to the word of God. They leave a very happy and comfortable existence in Babylon to come back to a land that is devastated by a foreign power. So they are a *faithful* people. Second, they assemble "as one man" (Ezra 3:1), so that when they first come back they are a people *united*, in outlook and purpose. Third, they are a *worshiping* community, for despite their fear of "the peoples around them" (Ezra 3:3), they build an altar and on its foundation they offer the various sacrifices of the Old Testament including free will offerings. So they are a worshiping people (Ezra 3:2–6). Fourth, they are a *serving* people. Their work of service begins impressively so that within a year after their arrival they hold a ceremony of praise celebrating the completion of the foundation of the temple. "And all the people gave a great shout of praise to the Lord, because the foundation of the house of the Lord was laid" (Ezra 3:11).

God is at work in his people in the opening stages of this post-exilic period. Whenever God is at work in the lives of his people, however, Satan is also actively seeking to counteract that work, that resolve, that spiritual activity of the people of God. Ezra 4:1 mentions enemies of the people of God who begin to agitate and foment trouble. Initially they try to press for an unholy alliance (Ezra 4:2): "Let us help you build because, like you, we seek your God." And then when this offer is rejected, they seek to discourage the people of Judah and to make them afraid to continue their building project (Ezra 4:4). Unfortunately, they succeed. So the work of rebuilding stops for 19 years until the reign of Darius, which is where the book of Haggai begins (Ezra 4:5).

II.   False Contentment — Chapter One

A.   The Problem Confronted   1:3

In chapter one, the prophet probes the hearts of the people

regarding the long delay. The initial reason for the work stopping was opposition — *opposition to the cause of God by the enemies of the people of God*. But whereas opposition may be the factor that initially causes them to stop rebuilding, it is not the real reason that they are not serving God at the moment when the prophet comes on the scene. In response to their excuse, "It is not yet time to rebuild the temple," he asks them, "Is it a time for you yourselves to be living in your paneled houses, while this house remains a ruin?" (Hag. 1:4).

There is a deeper underlying reason for their failure to serve God. It is the problem of priorities. They are saying it isn't time to do the work of God, but why isn't it time? Because they have more important things to do. They have become preoccupied with their standard of living. Perhaps they reasoned, "We tried to do what the Lord said and we ran into opposition and so we stopped." How long does the work cease? At least 18 years (Ezra 4:5). That is a long time to stop, and moreover, when is it ever true that opposition to the work of God is a sufficient reason to discontinue doing the will of God?

There is another factor at work. They become entangled in the business of living — buying and selling and marrying and giving in marriage and all the rest of it. The prophet has to challenge them to think more seriously about the work to which God calls them. Can't you just imagine the surprise and disbelief on their faces and on their lips as they listen to what the prophet has to say? "Don't we have a right — having returned to a devastated land — don't we have a right to build our businesses up again and to build our homes? Have we not this right?"

Those who claim to belong to God and who name the name of Christ and are redeemed by the blood of Christ must not allow their own desires and their own interests to crowd out the interests of the gospel. When Jesus warns those who listen to the preaching of the word to be careful how they hear, he doesn't list a group of high profile sins in people's lives that keep them from obeying the gospel. He doesn't name the big sins. He talks about the cares of this world and the deceitfulness of riches and the legitimate pleasures as things that choke the word and keep people from responding to the gospel in a meaningful way (Mt. 13:22; Luke 8:14).

To His disciples Jesus says, "Seek first the Kingdom of God and his righteousness and all these things shall be added to you" (Mt. 6:33). Life is not to be a game of trivial pursuits. Sometimes even the good may be the enemy of the best. Isaiah's question needs to be asked from time to time: "Why spend money on what is not bread, and your labor on what does not satisfy? Listen, listen to me, and eat what is good" (Is. 55:2).

B. The Prophet's Pastoral Care   1:4–11

All who teach and preach the word of God must be concerned to motivate people to serve God. Are we merely to confront them with God's commands and say, "Go and work, do it — do what God says"? Shouldn't we give them biblical *motives* for obedience in addition to telling them what the Lord requires? After confronting the people of God with the true nature of their disobedience, the first thing Haggai does is to urge them to look seriously within. Attempts to promote their own material well-being are not paying off. Their obsession with affluence is not producing dividends. Their hard work to upgrade their standard of living is not working. Their eating and drinking do not lead to satisfaction and their wages are being swallowed up by inflation. Little wonder that their efforts toward becoming prosperous are not successful, because prosperity in the Old Testament is not something to be sought directly; it is a by-product of God-centered living. It is not something that is meant to be the all-encompassing goal of human society. Prosperity is a gift from the Lord, and his people find it by pursuing God himself rather than the gift.

We too would do well to consider the question, "Am I really receiving the full blessing that God intends for me as a child of God and a believer in his covenant promise?" It is so easy because of all kinds of legitimate pressures to neglect to take a proper look at ourselves and ask whether our priorities, our values and our ambitions are really godly or whether the world has set our agenda. The call to examine oneself is, of course, fraught with danger. Too much introspection is paralyzing; too little introspection is problematic because we need occasional spiritual check ups!

Disciplined self-examination before God, in order to learn what one's weaknesses, blind spots, and deepest needs are, is an ongoing necessity. In this we need divine help. We need to pray with the Psalmist: "Search me, O God . . . test me . . . see if there is any offensive way in me, and lead me in the way everlasting" (Ps. 139:23–24). Self-examination brings the self-knowledge that spiritual realism requires (J.I. Packer, *Hot Tub Religion*, 1987, p. 180).

Covenant renewal ceremonies play an important role in the Old Testament (Joshua 24:19–27). At such times people are called to examine their commitment to Yahweh. We must give thought to our ways lest we unconsciously absorb the values and the mentality that are in conflict with the gospel.

The second thing he does is to appeal to them, on the basis of God's glory, to begin again to serve God: "Go up into the mountains and bring down timber and build the house, so that I may take pleasure in it and be glorified" (1:8). How critical it is to come to a biblical understanding of what it means to glorify God! Question one of the Westminster Larger Catechism asks, "What is the chief and highest end of man?" The answer can hardly be improved: "Man's chief and highest end is to glorify God, and fully to enjoy him forever."

The appeal to "the glory of God" as the motive for service is pervasive in the Scriptures. The glory of God has to do with the "displayed excellence" of God. The people of God are privileged to give visibility to their God. "Let your light so shine before men that they may see your good works and glorify your Father who is in heaven" (Mt. 5:16). Jesus said, "It is my Father's glory that you should bear much fruit" (John 15:8). Paul prays that the people of God might "be filled with the fruits of righteousness that come through Jesus Christ and are unto the glory and praise of God" (Phil. 1:11). To what higher motive can the prophet appeal than that of the glory of God? He says to them, "Now look, get busy and serve the Lord and do what he said because he will take pleasure in what you're doing and he will be glorified in what you're doing."

In the New Testament this appeal to act and live in obedience to God and for his glory centers on Christ's redemptive accomplishment. "You are not your own. You were bought with a price. Therefore honor (glorify) God with your body" (I Cor. 6:20).*

C. The People's Response   1:12

They "obeyed the voice of the Lord their God and the mes-

---

* See the useful study by J. Dwight Pentecost, *The Glory of God*, 1978.

sage of the prophet Haggai." Where is the voice of the Lord to be heard? There is a clear identification between obeying the voice of the Lord and obeying the voice of the prophet. There is no dichotomy between the two. If one wants to hear the voice of God, one goes to the prophetic word. In Isaiah 30:2 God complains that his people's plans and decisions are made without consulting him. The phrase is more literally, "Without asking from my mouth." There is good reason to believe that the phrase "my mouth" refers to the prophetic voice.

Their obedience is attributed to their fear of God (1:12b). The fear of the Lord, in the Old Testament, is the key expression for a true and saving response to God and has to do with an affectionate reverence for God. God's word must sometimes make us uncomfortable. It has as one of its functions that of reproof (II Tim. 3:16). Haggai confronts God's people with the reality of their lives. They do not become angry with him. There are many times when people become hostile to the prophets, but here they do not because they see that what Haggai is saying is really what God is saying, and they respond in faith.

D.   God's Promise   1:13

Through the prophet, God gives his people a wonderful promise. The sequence of events in chapter one should be noticed. The prophet zeroes in on their sin. Then he gives them some motives for obedience, for changing their old pattern of life, and finally the narrative recounts the people's response in faith to his pleadings. We need to examine the relationship in Scripture between God's commands and God's promises. There are times when the commands need to be proclaimed loudly and clearly. At other times God's people need the comforting and reassuring words of promise.

When the commands need to be heard and when the promises of God need to be proclaimed is a tricky problem. The words "I am with you" contain the glorious news of the promise of the gospel. When the covenant is made with Abraham, God promises, "I will be your God" (Gen. 17:7). Later on in the covenant at Sinai the same terminology occurs: "I will be your God." But something is added — "You will be my people" (Ex. 6:7). God promises to dwell uniquely with his people (Ex. 29:45). These promises are powerful and unique stimulants to

Christian service and to Christian life. For God to promise *to be with us* is the greatest comfort that a human being can experience. How often do we think that way? Perhaps too often we act as if other things are far more important. And then only a crisis propels us passionately toward God. Our sense of need and perhaps some dose of enlightened self-interest drives us into the everlasting arms of the Lord (Deut. 33:27). So we need to cultivate the sense of his presence both "in the sunshine hour as well as when the storm clouds lower."

There is no greater comfort in life than to be a recipient of such a word from Almighty God. There is no greater source of strength to rely on than the promise of his presence. What does God tell Moses when he lacks the vision to lead the people of Israel out of Egypt? "I will be with you" (Ex. 3:12). What does our Lord say to us when he sends us forth with the command to go into all the world and preach the gospel? Jesus attaches a promise to the command, "And surely, I am with you, always" (Mt. 28:20b). What will carry us through the experience of trouble and tragedy and sorrow and heartache? Only the promise, "Never will I leave you, never will I forsake you" (Heb. 13:5). God guarantees to be with us in all our adversity. "When you pass through the waters, I will be with you" (Is. 43:2).

E.   The Gracious Intervention of God   1:14

> So the Lord stirred up the spirit of Zerubbabel son of Shealtiel, governor of Judah, and the spirit of Joshua son of Jehozadak, the high priest, and the spirit of the whole remnant of the people. They came and began to work on the house of the Lord Almighty, their God, on the twenty-fourth day of the sixth month in the second year of King Darius.

Would that all spiritual problems were as quickly resolved as this one! His word of reproof is delivered twenty-four days before their obedient response. What is the explanation for their quick reversal of spiritual priorities? It is seen in the quiet work of God within them. God is silently but graciously at work in the lives of his people. God *stirs up* his people. In Ezra 1:4 the verb is used with reference to God's hidden activity in the life of Cyrus, a Persian king, that leads him to make a proclamation allowing the Jews to return. God is at work behind the scenes. We may not always see it; we cannot always see it. We won't be able to look out at the events going on in the world and in each instance say, "Oh yes, I can see how God is at work." "As you do not know the path of the wind, or how the body is formed in a mother's womb, so you cannot understand the work of God, the Maker of all things" (Eccl. 11:5).

We can know the Lord is at work because his word says he is, but we never fully comprehend the details of how everything fits together. The God who works within heathen kings (Ezra 1:4; Is. 10:5) is also the God who works within the lives of his people. This we must reckon with, and it is something that should not make us lethargic and inactive.

The same word to "stir up" is used elsewhere, challenging us to *stir ourselves up* to take hold of God (Is. 64:7). We need to stir ourselves up to a holy resolve to love and serve God. We do so by listening to the exposition of his word and by encouraging one another in the warfare of faith (Heb. 3:12,13). We are to stimulate one another to good works, all the time reminding ourselves that if anything lasting is to be accomplished for God it will be the result of God's gracious work within us to will and to do of his good pleasure (Phil. 2:13).

III.   False Discontentment — Chapter Two

A.   Confronting the New Problem   2:1-3

In the second chapter a new problem soon surfaces; and it is the exact opposite of the previous problem. Contentment with second-rate lives and half-hearted obedience was the first temptation to which the people had succumbed. But now the opposite problem arises. They are discontented with their work for God because they don't consider service in little things to be important. The devil is very subtle and while at one time he moves us into certain attitudes that are wrong, later he manipuates us full circle in the other direction. "Who of you is left who saw this house in its former glory? How does it look to you now? Does it not seem to you like nothing?" (Hag. 2:3). This statement must be understood in the light of Ezra 3:12: "But many of the older priests and Levites and family heads, who had seen the former temple, wept aloud when they saw the foundation of this temple being laid." Now why do they weep? Probably because they are comparing the former

Solomonic temple in all of its external glory with the present temple and they can see even from the foundation that the present temple is no match for Solomon's temple. Thus they become discouraged.

Such a mood of discouragement often infects the Christian church. It results from evaluating one's ministry and one's service by false standards. If a false standard is used to evaluate service, it will be easy to become discouraged. The standard by which service is to be tested is not talent; it is not gifts; it is not results. Rather, it is our labor. "The man who plants and the man who waters have one purpose, and each will be rewarded according to his own labor" (I Cor. 3:8). Haggai meets their discouragement and disillusionment in the work by linking God's promises with his commands.

B.   The Promise: I Am With You   2:4b

Encouragement comes when our eyes are taken off the externals of circumstances and riveted to the promises of God. God is our God. We represent him. He promises to be with us. We are his fellow workers (I Cor. 3:9). We must then pray along with the Psalmist, "May your deeds be shown to your servants, your splendor (glory) to their children" (Ps. 90:16b). With such a vision, God's work becomes our work (Ps. 90:17). As a result, we may pray with confidence, "May the favor of the Lord our God rest upon us, establish the work of our hands for us, yes, establish the work of our hands" (Ps. 90:17).

Some of the oldtimers in Haggai's day have an idealized view of the past. Solomon's temple is a venerable part of the working of God within the covenant history, but it is only a small part of that history. The prophet reminds the remnant that God is present with them and so they don't have to worry about whether this temple is as externally impressive as the previous one was.

What they have to be concerned with is that God has commanded them to build, and thus what they are doing presently is in fulfillment of the past promise made when they came out of Egypt (Hag. 2:5). And what is that promise? Its essence is the relationship with God — the saving relationship with God contained in the statement, "I will be your God; you will be my people" (Ex. 6:7). The exile has apparently prompted some to believe that God's promise of salvation is derailed. Haggai tells them it proves nothing of the kind! In the rebuilding of his temple God is yet preparing for the messenger of the covenant, Jesus Christ, who will suddenly come to his temple (Mal. 3:1).

C.   The Promise: My Spirit is With You   2:5

The Spirit of God is the source of both purity of life (Ps. 51:10,11) and power for service. Micah spoke of the latter in his important statement, "But as for me, I am filled with power, with the Spirit of the Lord, and with justice and might to declare to Jacob his transgression, to Israel his sin" (3:8). Zechariah, a contemporary of Haggai, similarly encourages a discouraged people, " 'Not by might, nor by power, but by my Spirit,' says the Lord" (4:6). We need to know that it is not ultimately our own abilities that will make us successful. It is rather the promise of the presence of the Spirit in our work that will bring effectiveness to our endeavors. For Paul, it is the combination of human and divine energy that provides the key to effective service. "We proclaim him, admonishing and teaching everyone with all wisdom, so that we may present everyone perfect in Christ. To this end I labor, struggling with all his energy, which so powerfully works in me" (Col. 1:29).

D.   The Promise: Messiah is Coming   2:6–9, 20–23

Haggai knows that the people need something to overcome this false and nostalgic view of the past. They need to focus not on the past, but on the promise. This necessarily means that the future is the important thing, not the past, for God's promise of salvation is yet to come; the best is yet to be. Biblical prophecy is designed by the Lord to be a stimulus to faith and action *in the present* (I John 3:3). The certainty of what will be serves as a present catalyst to courage and a deterrent to indifference and lethargy in the Christian life.

The Old Testament's *history* of salvation begins with the promise of Gen. 3:15. Gen. 49:10 speaks of the kingly rule of the Messiah coming from the tribe of Judah (cf. also Rev. 5:5). A unique prophet is promised who will reveal God and speak his Word (Deut. 18:15,18). The Kingdom of God will come when one of David's descendants will be given an everlasting kingdom (II Sam. 7:11–16). The prophets elaborate on these earlier promises both in terms of the "sufferings of Christ and the glories that would follow" (I Peter 1:11b).

Many of the earlier prophets promise that salvation will come through the promised Messiah (Is. 9:6,7) and suffering servant (Is. 42:1–4; 50:4–9; 52:13–53). He will be the new David (Hos. 3:5; Ez. 34:23,24), the king from David's line of descendants (Jer. 23:5). His reign will be characterized by justice, righteousness and peace (Is. 32:1; 11:1–9; Ps. 80:4).

With the exile, however, comes a crisis of faith. The king is humiliated and deposed, the temple that symbolizes God's presence and promise is destroyed, and the people are dispersed from the land of promise. What had happened to the *sure* and *steadfast* mercies promised to David? (Is. 55:3). In this mood of despair and doubt Haggai is given a unique promise. "In a little while I will once more shake the heavens and the earth, the sea and the dry land. I will shake all nations, and the desired of all nations will come, and I will fill this house with glory, says the Lord Almighty" (Hag. 2:6,7). The "shaking" is clarified at the end of the chapter. "Tell Zerubbabel, governor of Judah, that I will shake the heavens and the earth. I will overturn royal thrones and shatter the power of the foreign kingdoms" (Hag. 2:21, 22). Here "shaking" clearly refers to the sphere of national kingdoms and of world politics (cf. Is. 13:13). God is the Lord of history and his purposes will yet be consummated.

Jehoiachin, the last legitimate Davidic ruler, is rejected by God (Jer. 22:24), but his grandson Zerubbabel has returned as the chosen one bearing the Lord's signet ring (Hag. 2:23) and as God's new servant. This enigmatic promise to Zerubbabel is evidently not made to him in his person, for he mysteriously vanishes from the scene, but rather in his office as a lineal descendant of the last Davidic ruler. It finds its fulfillment in Jesus Christ, the son of David, of whom Zerubbabel is also a lineal descendant (Mt. 1:13; Luke 3:27).

During and after the exile there are continual assurances given by the prophets of God's purpose to bring salvation through a coming king. During the exile both Ezekiel and Daniel speak of such a promise: "I will place over them one shepherd, my servant David, and he will tend them; he will tend them and be their shepherd. I, the Lord, will be their God, and my servant David will be prince among them" (Ez. 34:23, 24). Daniel assures God's people that though they may be buffeted for a while by foreign nations, in the end "the God of heaven will set up a kingdom that will never be destroyed, nor will it be left to another people. It will crush all those kingdoms and bring them to an end, but it will itself endure forever" (Dan. 2:44).

This kingdom centres in a figure referred to as the rock (2:45) and as a Son of Man. "He approached the Ancient of Days and was led into his presence. He was given authority, glory and sovereign power; all peoples, nations and men of every language worshiped him. His dominion is an everlasting dominion that will not pass away, and his kingdom is one that will never be destroyed" (Dan. 7:14). He will bring in everlasting righteousness, but only by means of being "cut off" himself (Dan. 9:24–27).

In addition to Haggai, the two other post-exilic prophets refer to the coming king. Zechariah speaks of "my servant the Branch" (3:8), an allusion to Jeremiah's statement of the Righteous Branch (23:5). The Branch is "he who will build the temple of the Lord, and he will be clothed with majesty and will sit and rule on his throne" (Zech. 6:13). "See, your King comes to you, righteous and having salvation" (Zech. 9:9). Malachi refers to the Coming One as "the messenger of the covenant" (3:1) and as "the sun of righteousness" (4:2).

Haggai speaks of the surpassing glory of the messianic age by contrasting the glory of the present temple being built with that of Solomon's temple. "The glory of this present house will be greater than the glory of the former house," (Hag. 2:9). To understand this promise one needs to understand the symbolism of the temple. "Then have them make a sanctuary for me, and *I will dwell among them*" (Ex. 25:8; 29:42–46; see also Ez. 10:18; 11:22, 23; 43:4, 5). This temple built under Joshua and Zerubbabel will be more glorious than that of Solomon because to this temple will come Jesus, the mediator of the new and more glorious covenant (II Cor. 3:11). The temple mediates the presence of God. Christ and his new covenant people are the fulfillment of the temple symbolism (John 2:19; Luke 2:32; Eph. 2:12). The glory of God is revealed in the face of Christ (II Cor. 4:6). "The Word became flesh and made his dwelling among us. We have seen his glory, the glory of the One and Only, who came from the Father, full of grace and truth" (John 1:14).

Along with the promise of a more glorious temple comes the promise of peace, "and in this place I will grant peace" (Hag.

2:9b). Messiah was called "Prince of Peace" (Is. 9:6). Peace was pronounced by the priests in conjunction with the offering of atoning sacrifices:

> The Lord bless you and keep you,
> The Lord make his face shine upon you and be gracious to you,
> The Lord turn his face toward you and give you peace.
> Numbers 6:24–26)

The prophets picture the Messianic Kingdom as one of peace and universal harmony within creation. "They will beat their swords into plowshares and their spears into pruning hooks. Nation will not take up sword against nation, nor will they train for war anymore" (Is. 2:4). "The wolf will live with the lamb, the leopard will lie down with the goat" (Is. 11:6). "Every man will sit under his own vine and under his own fig tree" (Micah 4:4).

The high-water mark of Old Testament revelation is reached when peace with God is seen as the result of the servant's death. "The punishment that brought us peace was upon him, and by his wounds we are healed" (Is. 53:5).

Christ gives the new covenant believer peace (John 14:27). He makes peace through the blood of his cross (Col. 1:20); and he is our peace (Eph. 2:14); all of which is received by faith, for "being justified by faith we have peace with God through our Lord Jesus Christ" (Rom. 5:1).

IV. Application

First, we must not give God what are the leftovers of our energies and efforts in commitment, service and worship. Sixty years after Haggai people were still offering to the Lord bargain basement religion. God does get tired of it all. Sometimes he reasons with his people as when he says, "Try offering them (your sacrifices) to your governor! Would he be pleased with you? Would he accept you?" (Mal. 1:8). How insulting to God this must be when we offer to him what costs us nothing (II Sam. 24:24):

> Give of your best to the Master, nought else is worthy His love.
> Howard Grose (1851–1939)

Rise up, oh men of God, Have done with lesser things, Give heart

and mind and soul and strength to serve the King of kings.
William P. Merrill (1867–1954)

The world keeps seeking to squeeze us into its mold and we
are often unconsciously affected by its voices. Our only re-
course is to be constantly insulating ourselves from its voices
by listening to the voice of the Lord. "Blessed is the man who
does not walk in the counsel of the wicked . . . But his delight
is in the law of the Lord, and on his law he meditates day and
night" (Ps. 1:1, 2).

Haggai speaks to us about our priorities, a battle in which
we are all engaged. Seek first the kingdom. Yes, but there are
so many other necessary things to do. Jesus addresses the issue in his word to Martha. Many things are important. One
thing is needed and vital (Luke 10:42). For the Psalmist, life's
highest calling was to know God, to dwell in the house of the
Lord, to gaze upon the beauty of the Lord, to seek Him in his
temple (Ps. 27:4), and that goal was worth pursuing with all the
intensity of his heart.

Second, the *reproving* nature of the word of God must be
equally emphasized along with the *comforts* of that word. Paul
talks about the comfort and encouragement of the Scriptures
(Rom. 15:4), but also about Scripture as being given for reproof
and correction (II Tim. 3:16). Haggai comes to God's people as
a reprover!

One of the most difficult things to do, humanly speaking, is
to *receive* correction. Scarcely less difficult is to *minister* reproof
in a biblical way. We are often unaware of the extent of the
biblical teaching on this subject. Some are temperamentally
and dispositionally predisposed to offer too much reproof, and
others, of a gentle and mild demeanor, to avoid it altogether.
Haggai is both an encourager and an exhorter! As a faithful
servant of God, he is willing to be unpopular and to confront
the problems he encounters in God's people. We must be willing to do the same under the cautions and conditions laid
down in the word of God.

In Scripture, children are spoken of as being in need of correction (Prov. 22:6; Eph. 6:4). Some very good people in the
Old Testament are criticized for failing to administer life-giving reproof to their children (I Kings 1:6; I Sam. 3:13). Kings
are also rebuked by prophets (I Kings 17:1; 18:18). How long
would David have taken to awaken to the horrors of his own

behavior had it not been for Nathan's penetrating words, "You are the man?" (II Sam. 12:70).

On occasion, sons have to reprove parents when they are clearly wrong. Jonathan's incisive remarks in defense of David are used at least temporarily to bring some moments of sanity into Saul's life (I Sam. 19:4–6). Even apostles need rebuke. Paul publicly reproves Peter when his practice of the truth (Gal. 2:14a) has falsified the gospel. His reproof does not lead to any long-term disruption of the relationship between them, since we find Peter acknowledging Paul as his beloved brother (II Peter 3:15). Jesus reproves the Scribes and Pharisees and his own disciples (Mt. 16, 23). What shall we then say to all this? The Scriptures, by teaching and example, stress the life-giving ministry of reproof. The Scriptures are profitable for reproof and correction as well as doctrine and instruction in righteousness (II Tim. 3:16). The Holy Spirit will reprove the world concerning sin (John 16:8). God himself, personified as wisdom, is a rebuker (Prov. 1:23–26). Proverbs contrasts the wise person with the fool, and one of the marks of a fool is his total unwillingness to receive correction. He is unteachable. On the contrary, the wise person is one whose "ear listens to the life-giving reproof" (Prov. 9:8, 15:31). To stand in need of correction is to admit one's limitations and sinfulness.

Now it needs to be observed that the Scriptures also provide us with the necessary cautions so that we do not become self-appointed guardians of everyone else's morality. We are not appointed to be spiritual busybodies! We must not be judgmental in spirit (Mt. 5:3–5; Gal. 6:1 — "considering thyself") or proud and harsh; rather, we should reprove with patience and instruction (II Tim. 4:2) and gentleness (II Tim. 2:25). Timing is critically important ("apt reply and a timely word" — Prov. 15:23).

Reproving words do not need to be many or loud! They must, however, come from a person who is "full of goodness complete in knowledge and competent to instruct one another" (Rom. 15:14). Prayer and reproof must be conjoined since that is at least implied in Paul's exhortation to those who are spiritual (Gal. 6:1).

Clear scriptural standards are the basis for reproof. We are not called to correct those with whom we disagree on secondary and peripheral issues of doctrine and practice. "Let the word of Christ dwell in you richly as you teach and *admonish* one another with all wisdom" (Col. 3:16). Reproof must not be personal, but rather, as much as possible, is to be directed against the deeds committed, not the person.

With these cautions in mind, however, all believers are called to be on the giving and receiving end of life-giving reproof. We minister reproof by means of our lives when we do not participate in the unfruitful deeds of darkness but instead reprove or expose them (Eph. 5:11; cf. also Luke 3:19). As receivers of reproof we put aside our wounded pride and seek to receive thankfully and graciously words of correction. Where there is no willingness to receive the life-giving reproof of the Word of God, the reason may well prove to be that given by Jesus himself:

> This is the verdict: Light has come into the world, but men loved darkness instead of light because their deeds were evil. Everyone who does evil hates the light, and will not come into the light for fear that his deeds will be exposed (reproved). (John 3:19, 20)

Third, God himself is the great motivator, and we need every motivation given by Scripture for serving God. One of the clarion calls of this little book is to "Give careful thought to your ways" (1:5,7; 2:15). There is need for the godly process of examining our lives in light of Scripture. Are we missing out in our Christian life by not walking each day closely with the Lord Jesus?

> Is there a thing beneath the sun that strives with Thee my heart to share? Oh, tear it thence and reign alone, the Lord of every motion there; Then shall my heart from earth be free when it has found repose in Thee.
>
> Gerhard Tersteegen (1697–1769)

Give careful thought to your ways. God motivates us by the appeal to enlightened self-interest. Yet the highest appeal to service is based on our desire to please God and to honor and glorify him. He is not asking for perfection in our service. Parents are pleased with their children when there is a *sincere* attempt to act in a way known to be pleasing to the parent. The doing "in my name" is what pleases the Father even when it is doing something as insignificant as offering a cup of water in his name (Mk. 9:41).

Fourth, it is comforting and reassuring to know that God is

at work within, "stirring us up" to good works. We may count on this and pray for this; however, not in such a way that allows us to remain passive and listless in his service. We are told this to *encourage* us when we are tired and discouraged and weary in well-doing, and to *humble* us when we have too much of a proud spirit (I Cor. 3:5; Josh. 8:2). Are we consciously reckoning with the promise, "My Spirit is with you"? Do we know that it's only as his Spirit is with us, empowering us for service and ministry, that our labor is not in vain? (I Cor. 15:58). The gospel we preach will fall on deaf ears unless it comes not "simply with words, but also with power, with the Holy Spirit and with deep conviction" (I Thess. 1:5). "Unless the Lord builds the house, its builders labor in vain" (Ps. 127:1).

Finally, as with the whole of the Old Testament, Haggai points us to Christ as the one who fulfills what the prophets have spoken (Luke 24:27, 44). He is the desired of all nations, the giver of peace (Hag. 2:7-9). He is the one who speaks of his body as the temple (John 2:21). We behold with unveiled face his glory and are being transformed into his likeness with ever-increasing glory (I Cor. 4:18).

God has spoken in Christ. We are not to refuse him who speaks (Heb. 12:25). He says, "I have set my King upon my Holy hill of Zion" (Ps. 2:6). It is ours to kiss the Son and take refuge in Him; to serve the Lord with fear and to rejoice with trembling (Ps. 2:11,12).

The good news for us, as the new covenant people of God, is that we are on the receiving end of his sovereign promise to shake the heavens and the earth (Hag. 2:21). That shaking happened first when Jesus "disarmed the powers and authorities and made a public spectacle of them, triumphing over them by the cross" (Col. 2:15). We participate in his triumph and acclaim him Victor and Lord. "Since we are receiving a kingdom that cannot be shaken, let us be thankful, and so worship God acceptably with reverence and awe" (Heb. 12:28).

Bibliography on Haggai — Commentaries

Baldwin, J. *Haggai, Zechariah, Malachi*. Tyndale Old Testament Commentaries. Downers Grove: IV Press, 1972.

Coggins, R. *Haggai, Zechariah, Malachi: Old Testament Guides*. Sheffield: JSOT Press, 1987.

Calvin, J. *Twelve Minor Prophets*, Vol. 4. Grand Rapids: William B. Eerdmans Publishing, 1950.

Craigie, P. *Twelve Prophets*, Vol. 2. Daily Study Bible Series. Philadelphia: Westminster Press, 1984.

Gaebelein, F. *Four Minor Prophets: Obadiah, Jonah, Habakkuk and Haggai*. Chicago: Moody Press, 1970.

Hengstenberg, E.W. *Christology of the Old Testament*. Edinburgh: T&T Clark, 1854.

Keil and Delitzsch. *The Twelve Minor Prophets*, Vol. 2. Grand Rapids: William B. Eerdmans Publishing, 1949.

Mauro, P. *The Last Call to the Godly Remnant*. Swengel: Reiner Publications, 1965.

Mason, R. *The Books of Haggai, Zechariah and Malachi*. Cambridge Bible Commentary. Cambridge: Cambridge University Press, 1977.

Meyers, C.L., and E.M.Meyers. *Haggai, Zechariah 1–8*, Anchor Bible. Garden City: Doubleday and Co., 1987.

Moore, T.V. *A Commentary on Haggai and Malachi*. Edinburgh: Banner of Truth, 1960.

Napier, J. *The Historical and Biblical Significance of the Messianic Passage in Haggai*. University Microfilms International, 1985.

Petersen, D. *Haggai and Zechariah 1–8*, Old Testament Library. Philadelphia: Westminster Press, 1984.

Tatford, F.A. *Prophet of the Restoration*. Eastbourne: Prophetic Witness Publishing, 1972.

Verhoef, P. *The Books of Haggai and Malachi*, New International Commentary. Grand Rapids: William B. Eerdmans Publishing, 1987.

Wolf, H. *Haggai and Malachi*, Everymans Bible Commentary. Chicago: Moody Press, 1976.

Wolff, H.W. *Haggai*, Minneapolis: Augsburg Publishing House, 1988.

Bibliography on Themes Within Haggai

1:8   *God's Honor or Glory*

Packer, J.I. *Hot Tub Religion*. Wheaton: Tyndale House, 1987: ch. 2.
Pentecost, J.D. *The Glory of God*. Portland: Multnomah Press, 1978.

1:12   *The Fear of the Lord*

von Rad, G. *Wisdom in Israel*, London: SCM Press, 1972: pp. 53–73.
Eichrodt, W. *Theology of the Old Testament*, Vol. 2. London: SCM Press, 1967: pp. 268–277.

1:12   *Remnant*

Hasel, G. *The Remnant: The History and Theology of the Remnant Idea from Genesis to Isaiah*. Berrian Springs: Andrews University Press, 1974.

Kittel, G. *Theological Dictionary of the New Testament*, Vol. 4. Grand Rapids: William B. Eerdmans Publishing, 1967: pp. 196–209.

1:14   *The Lord stirs up Zerubabbel, Joshua and the Whole Remnant*

Bridges, J. *Trusting God*, Colorado Springs: Navpress, 1988: ch. 4 and 5

2:3   *Successful or Unsuccessful Service*

Hughes, R.K., and B. *Liberating Ministry From the Success Syndrome*. Wheaton: Tyndale House, 1987.

2:5b   *The Holy Spirit*

Wood, L. *The Holy Spirit in the Old Testament*. Grand Rapids: Zondervan Publishing, 1976.

Warfield, B.B. "The Spirit of God in the Old Testament." In *Biblical and Theological Studies*. Philadelphia: Presbyterian and Reformed Publishing, n.d.: pp. 127–156.

Packer, J.I. *Keep in Step With the Spirit*. Old Tappan: F.H. Revell, 1984.

2:6–9   *Messianic Prophecy*

Briggs, C. *Messianic Prophecy*. Peabody: Hendrickson Publishers, 1988.

Hengstenberg, E.W. *Christology of the Old Testament*. Edinburgh: T&T Clark, 1854.

Kaiser, W. "Messianic Prophecies in the Old Testament." In *Dreams, Visions and Oracles*, C. Armerding and W. Gasque, editors. Grand Rapids: Baker Book House, 1977.

Kaiser, W. *Toward Rediscovering the Old Testament*, Grand Rapids: Zondervan Publishing, 1984: ch. 5.

2:17   *Yet You Did Not Turn to Me — Repentance*

Thompson, J.A. *The Book of Jeremiah*, The New International Commentary. Grand Rapids: William B. Eerdmans Publishing, 1980: pp. 76–81.

Sibbes, R. *The Returning Backslider: An Exposition of Hosea 14*. Evansville: Sovereign Grace Book Club, 1957.

Questions on Haggai

For the biblical background and lead up to the time of this prophet's ministry, read Ezra 1–4:6. Note the description of the remnant in Hag. 1:14; Ezra 3:1; 3:2–6 and 3:11. How do these verses describe the people called remnant and what would be the contemporary equivalent to them?

How does the fact of the opposition to the work of the rebuilding of the temple (cf. Ezra 4:1–5), help us to understand more completely all the reasons for the remnant's sidetracking from their task? What sidetracks us today, and hinders us from a whole-hearted commitment to the task of evangelism and the work of God's kingdom? (Cf. Mt. 6:33).

What "pastoral methodology" did the prophet use to solve the problem of the work stoppage on the temple?

Discuss the phrase "give careful thought to your ways" (1:5, 8; 2:15). Do you agree with the statement, "Disciplined self-examination before God, in order to learn one's weaknesses, blind spots, and deepest needs, is an ongoing necessity . . . Self-examination brings the self-knowledge that spiritual realism requires" (Packer, *Hot Tub Religion*, p. 180). Discuss.

Note the phrase "the Lord stirred up" in 1:14. See Ezra 1:4 and Isaiah 64:7. What New Testament verses might bear on that activity of God?

What are the fundamental lessons concerning service taught in this book?

Study the Messianic sections 2:6–9 and 20–23 and look at Hebrews 12:25–29. Note how the Haggai passages are used in the New Testament.

VII.   The Message of Malachi

The contemporary world is much concerned, and rightly so, about the problems of environmental pollution. Such concerns are highlighted in a *Reader's Digest* article, November, 1973 entitled "the Genesis of Pollution," by historian Arnold Toynbee. He lays the blame for environmental pollution squarely at the feet of the hierarchical view of man, which he perceives, erroneously, to be taught by Genesis. The religious view of man as the highest creation of God is the cause of our environmental problems. Genesis is responsible for the pollution crisis! While concern for the pollution of the environment is proper and should be shared by Christians, the Hebrew prophets were concerned with another kind of pollution; namely, the pollution of the heart which leads to polluted worship and a polluted lifestyle:

> Moral pollution works the same way as environmental pollution. The waste products of careless living work insidiously into the soil of thought and the streams of language, poisoning every part of society (E. Pederson, *Run with Horses*, p. 63).

Malachi, the last of the canonical prophets, argues with the covenant people of his day and accuses them of offering polluted worship, thus profaning the name of God (Mal. 1:7,12). This little book confronts us with a striking contrast between true and false religion and reminds us that not all worship of God is necessarily acceptable. This is made clear by the key passage in Chapter 3:16–18 where the righteous remnant, i.e., those who fear the Lord and honor his name and serve him, are distinguished from another group. Presumably the latter is made up of those whose attitudes and actions are being depicted in the main body of the book. It is the former group who are identified by the term "treasured possession" (Mal. 3:17b), which, until this time in the Old Testament, has been used of the whole of the covenant nation (Ex. 19:6). Malachi then sets forth the marks that distinguish a true believer from a false believer.

In order to understand his message, it is important to understand the background mood of the period in which he spoke and prophesied. From internal evidence the book can be dated at the time prior to the arrival of Ezra and Nehemiah in Jerusalem. The one historical reference in the book to the destruction of Edom in 1:3–5 most likely refers to that of the

Nabatean Arabs, who defeated the Edomites and set up a separate Idumean state in the place of Edom some time between 550 and 400 B.C. The closest we can come to dating the book, then, is to suggest that it fits the time period immediately preceding Ezra and Nehemiah.

The temple was completed in 516 B.C. and the established temple rituals had time to degenerate from an earlier period during which strict adherence to the letter of the law was followed. The conditions and problems with which Ezra and Nehemiah are confronted can also be found in the writings of Malachi. Both speak out against marriage to heathen wives (Mal. 2:11-15; Neh. 13:23-27). Both speak out against neglect of the tithe (Mal. 3:8–10; Neh. 13:10–14). Both speak out against the evils of a degenerate priesthood (Mal. 1:6–9 to 2:9; Neh. 13:7, 8) and both speak out against social sins (Mal. 3:5; Neh. 5:1–13).

Fortunately the absence of complete certainty in dating the book is not a hindrance to understanding its message. The book is distinguished by a "disputational" style consisting of an accusation made by the prophet against the people, a cynical querying of the accusation, in which the audience asks how what the prophet says is true, and a final rejoinder wherein the prophet elaborates and defines more specifically the nature of his (and God's) accusations.

In addition to the disputational style, which provides a key to understanding the message of the book, it is important to note the emphasis on covenant themes within the book. There are four explicit references to the covenant. There is the covenant of Levi (Mal. 2:5–9), the covenant of the fathers (2:10), the marriage covenant (2:14), and the messenger of the covenant (3:1). In addition to these direct references to covenant, the book begins by calling attention to Yahweh's love for his people (1:2–5), which should have evoked the covenantal response of loyalty, service and obedience. Instead, the prophet details the covenantal violations of the people and of the priests.

Yahweh is accused of unfaithfulness to the covenant (1:2–5) and in turn counters with the true picture of priestly incompetence and infidelity which erodes the faith of the common people. They are "profaning the covenant" (2:10) by breaking faith with one another in their marriages (2:11, 14:a) and in their social and economic relationships (3:5). Unless they repent (3:7), they will be under the curses of the covenant (3:9; Deut.

28:15–68; Lev. 26:14–46).

Another key to understanding the message of the book is the number of divine pronouncements in the form of first-person-singular statements. "I have loved you" (1:2). "If I am a Father, where is my honor; if I am a master, where is (my) respect?" (1:6). "I am a great king and my name is to be feared among the nations" (1:15). "I will send a curse upon you, and I will curse your blessings. Yes, I have already cursed them, because you have not set your heart to honor me" (2:2). "I hate divorce" (2:16). "I will send my messenger" (3:1). "I will come near to you for judgment" (3:5). "I the Lord do not change" (3:6). "I will spare them" (3:17). "I will send you the prophet Elijah before the great and dreadful day of the Lord comes" (4:5).

Malachi speaks to a disillusioned, discouraged and doubting people. The scenario glowingly portrayed in the second half of Isaiah does not unfold in the way the people expect. Nations have not yet come to Israel's light, nor kings to the brightness of their dawn (Is. 60:3). Furthermore, the wealth of the nations has not been brought to them by kings in triumphal procession (Is. 60:11), and rather than foreign nations becoming subservient to Israel, she is still taking orders from foreign powers. The nation waits for the fulfillment of Ezekiel's and Haggai's words about the glory of the new temple (Ez. 43 and Hag. 2:9). They have their own understanding of the coming of the Messianic Age with its unparalleled blessings, but their vision does not materialize. Instead, they experience poverty and drought, and are disillusioned with God and with their faith. In a sense, then, the book is a catechism for times of doubt and disappointment when religious people are tempted to disengage from God and give up their faith. The prophet's ministry is to rekindle the fires of faith in a discouraged people and set forth the continuing demands of the covenant upon those who truly know God.

Malachi's word confronts a people skeptical of the promises and therefore apathetic in their commitment to live in the light of those promises and to worship and serve the Lord with all their hearts. His pastoral concern is paramount as he unveils the precise nature of their heart attitudes and calls for them to return to God (Mal. 3:7b). Certainly the many first-person-singular statements on the character of God as loving, faithful (1:5), sovereign (1:14) and unchangeable (3:6), who acts in mercy to spare his treasured possessions, i.e., the righteous remnant (3:17), are part of the prophet's pastoral strategy to motivate them to their high and holy calling of being the people of God.

I. Disinterest In the Love of God   1:1-5

When properly understood from the Bible, the love of God is the most dynamic motivator to action. For this reason, the prophet begins with this amazing statement: "I have loved you" (2:5). He reminds those for whom religion has become a bore that they are the objects of electing love. To those nourished on the truth that only they among all nations of the earth are known by Yahweh (Amos 3:2), the words "I have loved you" are strangely ineffective. Such is their blindness to God's love that they respond with cynicism and even petulence. "How have you loved us?" (1:2b) they ask. Whenever we lose the sense of wonder and amazement at God's love and become complacent, then we may be sure that we have not really "understood" the love of God.

It is the great danger of orthodoxy that familiarity with the outward form of the truth breeds complacency and even occasionally contempt for the truth (Mal. 1:6b). God's love properly understood should never lead to moral complacency but to moral ambition. The nearness of God to Israel was to be the source of awe and amazement (Deut. 4:7, 8). Election should lead to doxology, to praise (Rom. 11:33; Eph. 1:12). "How great is the love the Father has lavished on us, that we should be called children of God" (I John 3:1). The wonder and uniqueness of God's love will be seen only when we pay particular attention to the objects of that love.

God loves sinners, those who by nature ought to be the objects of his displeasure and wrath (Eph. 2; 3; 4; Deut. 7:7, 8). He loves the world (John 3:16), and the world in the gospel of John is not a term of quantity. It refers to all that is intensely hostile to God. "God *so* loved the world." To say God *so* loves the world is not to suggest "that the world is so big that it takes a great deal of love to embrace it all, but that the world is so bad, that it takes a great kind of love to love it at all, and much more to love it as God has loved it when He gave His Son for it" (B.B. Warfield, *Biblical and Theological Studies*, 1952, p. 516). "Since God *so* loved us, we also ought to love one another" (I John 4:11). We sing the words of the famous hymn, "were the whole realm of nature mine, that were an offering far too small, love *so* amazing, *so* divine, demands *my soul*, my life, my all" (Isaac Watts, 1674–1748). When God's love is not appreciated there is a concurrent breakdown of human love within the community of faith which affects all relationships.

The lesson from this opening debate is clear:

> The complacency that may arise from the comfort of being loved must always be disturbed. One cannot relax in the atmosphere of divine love, being loved and yet not loving, hoping nevertheless that the pleasant atmosphere will continue forever. Love ever demands a response in kind, and if we truly love God, we cannot but seek to be channels through whom God's love is made known to the world (P. Craigie, *Twelve Prophets*, Vol. 2, 1985, p. 230).

The making known of God's love to the ends of the world is referred to at the conclusion of this section when Malachi says that the uniqueness of God's love will one day extend to the ungodly outside of the covenant nation (Mal. 1:5). God's love is not earned by those he loves, but it is the result of his character. It is not drawn out by human loveableness but it wells up like an artesian spring from the depths of the divine nature (I John 4:8,16). Love among people is awakened by something in the one loved, but God's love is free, spontaneous, unevoked and uncaused. "I will love them freely" (Hos. 14:9).

II.   Degeneration of the Priesthood   1:6–2:9

While the priests are addressed directly twice in this section (1:6; 2:1), at points the prophet's admonitions carry over and apply to the whole of the nation (1:13). One of the ways the priests "caused many to stumble" (2:8) was by their careless and half-hearted example. In an age of every-member involvement and ministry it still needs to be said that failure in leadership results in the spiritual decline of God's people. Hosea knew this when he wrote "like people, like priests" (Hos. 4:9). What attitudes are depicted by the prophet in his castigation of the leaders of his day? What specifically did the priests do for which they were reproved? What attitudes are revealed by these actions?

A. Attitudes

1. *Lack of Honor for the Name of God*   1:6a

Three times the Lord complains through his prophet at the failure of his priests to honor him (1:6; 2:2). Rather than honoring God in the conduct of their worship they have *acted contemptuously* against him (1:6b,7,12,13). The phrase "to act contemptuously" is often translated "to despise" in the book of Proverbs (cf. Prov. 1:7; 15:20; 23:22) or grouped with the term "to scorn" (Prov. 23:9). It is this strong term that the Lord uses to describe David's act of murder and adultery. David "despised" the word of the Lord and the Lord himself in his terrible sin with Bathsheba (II Sam. 12:9,10). The use of the same verb to describe both David's moral failure and the priests' ceremonial lapses might seem strange until we note that the latter sins also reflect a broken relationship with the Lord.

It is not fair to accuse the prophet of being a ceremonial purist, preoccupied with the minutiae of the law. Certainly he referred to "polluted offerings" but it is because such offerings reflect the pollution of the heart and mind. The emphasis upon the name of God (1:6b,11,14; 2:2, 5) suggests that the priests are being rebuked because at the heart of the lapses in their observance of the outward forms of religion is a flagrant disrespect and disregard for the honor of God himself.

The Old Testament prophets condemn ceremonial purity and ceremonial laxity. The former they castigate when it is divorced from a proper lifestyle. The latter, because it is clear evidence that what the Lord commands doesn't matter. Both sets of problems in worship reflect deeper problems in the life of the worshiper. For worship is expressed in the whole life lived in the presence of God. Ceremonial details in and of themselves are important only as they reflect an attitude of seeking to honor and glorify the Lord. For this reason the Old Testament prophets, when they speak of the future age, do so in two separate ways. They see the future as the past elevated to a new level of spirituality. For instance, Zechariah prophesies that "the survivors from all the nations that have attacked Jerusalem will go year after year to worship the King, the Lord Almighty, and to celebrate the Feast of Tabernacles" (Zech. 14:16). At other times the outward form of Old Testament worship is portrayed as being replaced by new ceremonies. "In

those days, men will no longer say 'the ark of the covenant of
the Lord.' It will never enter their minds or be remembered; it
will not be missed nor will another one be made" (Jer. 3:16).
That the Old Testament speaks concerning the outward forms
of religion both as if they are to be *reinstated* as well as *abolished* suggests that the Old Testament forms by themselves are
not important. Their importance lies in whether they serve as a
valid indicator or mediator of the spirit of the worshiper.

2. *Lack of Respect and Fear*   1:13a

As a father, the Lord has a right to honor. As a master, he
has a right to fear and respect (1:6). If in the future his holy
name is to be feared among the nations (1:14b) because he is a
great king, how much more in the present by those who profess to know him as covenant Lord and master. The distinguishing mark of Levi's priesthood is "that he revered me and
stood in awe of my name" (2:5).

Malachi notes the absence of such godly fear on the part of
priest and people in two areas. First, in the area of worship,
where priest and people apparently don't give a second
thought to offering the Lord that which cost them nothing (II
Sam 24:24). Imperfect animals are brought in sacrifice which
constitutes a clear violation of God's commands (Mal. 1:8,13b;
Ex. 12:5; Lev. 22:18–22; Deut. 15:21). Second, in the violations
of the moral laws of God (Mal. 3:6). It is impossible to claim to
know, love, and fear God and flagrantly disregard his commandments (Ps. 112:1; Gen. 22:12; Eccl. 12:13). Regardless of
whether those laws are viewed by us as governing crucial areas
of our lives or regulating the outward forms of worship, they
are important as indicators of our devotion and commitment
to the Lord and to express our fear of God. The fear of the
Lord is an affectionate reverence for him that influences our
conduct.

One who fears the Lord has a conviction that the favor of
the Lord is the greatest blessing in life and that the disapproval
of the Lord is the greatest tragedy in life. The one who fears the
Lord believes that his smile is to be sought at all costs and his
frown is to be avoided at all costs. The fear of the Lord, however, is not merely a belief. It is a conviction that leads one practically to seek God's favor as our highest good in life, and to
avoid his displeasure as our greatest evil. For this reason the

expression "the fear of the Lord" is often paralleled with the
phrase "to seek the Lord" (Ps. 34:9–10; II Chron. 20:3). The fear
of the Lord is seen then practically in our response to his word
(Ezra 9:4; Is. 66:2; II Kings 22:11). It will manifest itself in our
relationships and dealings with believers and nonbelievers
alike. It will be expressed in our speech (Ps. 34:11–14) and in
the exercise of charity (Neh. 5:9,15), in the treatment of the
poor (Lev. 25:43), the handicapped (Lev. 19:14), and the eco-
nomically disadvantaged (Lev. 25:26).

In summary, the fear of the Lord, while affecting our emo-
tional response to God, is best understood as that word in the
Old Testament that closely corresponds to faith in the New
Testament. As such it describes the comprehensive response to
God of intellect, emotion, and will. It incorporates love and
loyalty, obedience, service and worship (Ps. 2:11; Joshua 24:14;
I Sam 12:14; Ps. 5:7; 96:9; Heb. 12:28).

3. *Boredom* 1:13a

Enthusiasm in the performance of religious duties should
have been the mark of a true servant of God. One of the signs
of religious decline is boredom in carrying out religious rites
and responsibilities. The priests perform their holy services
but not as a labor of love. In the eighth century Micah complains that the worship and service of the Lord is perfunctory
and lackadaisical. So much so that the Lord condescends to
ask, "My people, what have I done to you? How have I bur-
dened you?" (Micah 6:3). The duties of the priests in Malachi's
time are seen as troublesome and bothersome and a burden to
be borne (1:13a) and are performed grudgingly and reluctantly.

When faith is cut loose from its moorings and the essence of
religion becomes the outward performance of a ritual, then it
is little wonder that joy gives way to drudgery and dullness in
worship. Such attitudes are an insult to God. They are worse
than having no religion at all, since at least in that case there is
no pretense of godliness. Thus the Lord calls for a stop to all
such religious pretense and hypocrisy. "Oh, that one of you
would shut the temple doors, so that you would not light use-
less fires on my altar!" (Mal. 1:10b). When such a spirit per-
vades the leadership, it is bound to infect the people.

The laity copy the priests and opt for cut-rate religion and
cheap grace. They choose the religion of appearance and out-

ward show. They vow to give perfect and unblemished animals as thanksgiving offerings (Lev. 22:19) but never deliver on their promise. Instead, inferior and less valuable animals are eventually substituted as offerings (1:14). Again the key question is, What attitudes are hidden behind such actions? When the outward forms of religion are substituted for the living relationship at the heart of the covenant ("I will be your God and you will be my people"), then such forms become a way of escape from God (cf. Amos 4:4) rather than acts offered to the Lord in humble obedience to his word. It is impossible to *sustain* commitment involving self-sacrifice without a proper understanding of grace and the meaning of faith.

"Give of your best to the Master, naught else is worthy *his love.*"
Howard Grose (1851–1939)

B. Priestly Instruction   2:7,8

In addition to the failure to honor and fear the Lord in the duties connected with worship, there is a second area in which the priests are recreant in the exercise of their responsibilities. It's an area not unrelated to the first in terms of cause and effect: namely, the *proper teaching* of the law of God. The lamentable failure of the people to worship the Lord heartily and in accordance with his revealed truth may be attributed to a considerable extent to their lack of instruction in the law and to the dismal failure of the priests to "make the teaching about God our Savior attractive" (Mal. 2:8, 9; Titus 2:10b).

It is a clear and oft repeated principle of biblical revelation that Scripture is an indispensable means of grace and that God has duly appointed and authorized his servants to teach and preach his word. The failure to do so is a tragedy of immense proportions.

The connection between the true knowledge of the Lord and instruction in his word by authorized servants is clearly taught in many places but perhaps most incisively in II Chron. 15:3: "For a long time Israel was without the true God, without a priest to teach, and without the law." Here we see the link between being without the true God and being without a priest to teach the word. In Malachi's day the priests are apparently doing God's work, but in reality there is no true instruction in their mouths. There is no walking with God in closed and intimate fellowship (2:6b; cf. also Gen. 5:22; 6:9, the only two other places where "to walk with God" is used). There is no harmonious unity between what they teach and say and how they live. The temper of their minds and the tenor of their lives are not of a piece with their doctrine or their profession. The priests may talk about God but they do not walk with God. Thus the word of God is not empowered by God to turn many from sin (cf. Mal. 2:6b; Ps. 119:9, 11).

The contrast between what God intends the priest to be and do and what the practice of the priesthood is in post-exilic times could hardly be more striking. "The lips of a priest ought to preserve knowledge" (Mal. 2:7). It is the prophet Hosea who says God's people will be destroyed from lack of knowledge (Hos. 4:6a). If they don't preserve knowledge, but reject it, the Lord will reject all such as his priests (Hos. 4:6).

Ezra, the priest, sets the ideal standard for the priesthood. He "devoted himself to the study and observance of the Law of the Lord, and to teaching its decrees and laws in Israel" (Ezra 7:10). Nehemiah tells us that priests "read from the book of the law of God, making it clear and giving the meaning so that the people could understand what was being read" (Neh. 8:8). The purpose of such godly instruction was to turn people from sin (Mal. 2:6b). The priest serves as the messenger of the Lord Almighty to guard and preserve the truth. "Every priest of God is a priest of truth, and it is very largely by the Christian ministry's neglect of their intellectual duties that so much irreligion prevails" (Smith, *The Book of The Twelve Prophets*, Vol. 2, p. 361).*

Sadly, the priests in Malachi's times are miles removed from what they are supposed to be. In their own personal lives, they have "turned from the way" (Mal. 2:8a, 9b). "The way" is used in Old and New Testament to refer to the walk of faith, the life of faith, the obedience of faith. It is a term signifying conduct (Ps. 1:6; Rom. 1:5; Acts 6:7). Sometimes it is used synonymously with the laws of God: "For I have kept the ways of the Lord; I have not done evil by turning from my God. All his laws are

---

* Smith's words are not outdated by the passage of time. He pinpoints two extremes in religion that the Christian priesthood must avoid. It must reject "the limitation of the ideal of priesthood to the communication of a magic grace, and its evaporation in a vague religiosity from which the intellect is excluded as if it were perilous, worldly and devilish." *The Book of the Twelve Prophets*, vol 2, p. 361.

before me. I have not turned away from his decrees. I have been blameless before him and have kept myself from sin" (Ps. 18:21–23; cf. also Gen. 18:19).

The priests in Malachi's day fail to guard their own lives from the ravages of moral failure and consequently their teaching, rather than turning people from sin, is actually a cause of stumbling for the many who listen to them and observe the disparity between their lives and their teaching (Mal. 2:8a). In the New Testament, Paul exhorts young Timothy to guard and watch over first his life and then his doctrine (I Tim. 4:16).

It is sobering to realize how our lives affect others either for good or for evil. In particular, leaders are called to serious accountability for their teaching (cf. James 3:1). Jesus levels stern warnings against any who lead others astray, in particular little children (Mt. 18:5, 6). The third commandment calls upon all believers to represent the Lord faithfully.

God's people are those who are "called by God's name" (Is. 43:7). Here is a phrase which means that his name, i.e., his person, is to be revered and honored in the faithful lives of his people (cf. Deut. 28:10). This representation of God takes place on two levels: In the arena of our lives we are called upon to represent the Lord; failure then to live consistently with our profession of faith causes the name of God to be blasphemed (Rom. 2:24). But we also represent God in what we say about him in our teaching. Malachi accuses the priests of misrepresenting the Lord first by their lives and then by their instruction. They have "shown partiality" in matters of the law (cf. Mal. 2:9b; Lev. 19:15). They have not applied the law indiscriminately to all, which may mean that they curried the favor of men. They may have been selective in the application of the whole truth to the rich and powerful strata of society. As messengers of the Lord Almighty (2:7) they are charged with teaching and applying the truth without fear or favor.

When prophets are commissioned to herald the word, they are often warned not to look at people's faces; that is, not to be afraid of those to whom they speak, knowing full well that great pressure will be brought to bear upon them to hold back some of what the Lord had given to them (Jer. 1:8,17; Is. 30:10,11). So also priests are to teach and apply the truth impartially and not for a price (Micah 3:11). We know that Paul more than once calls for a disinterested proclamation of the truth of the gospel. The gospel, he says, is entrusted to him and

therefore the servant of the Lord must not be motivated by
covetousness or by the desire to please men. Such motives are
to be scrupulously rejected, and the single goal of all ministry
is to please God (I Thess. 2:4–6).

C. Divine Declarations to the Priests   1:8

What is the Lord's response to a faithless and profane
priesthood? How does he react? What does he say through his
prophet to these leaders and to the people who pick up their
attitudes and follow in their footsteps? The first thing he does
is to label their actions for what they are. They are not harm-
less violations of the details of the ceremonial law. The rejection of the ceremonial statutes reveals an attitude of heart toward God, and it is not accidental that from their contempt for
the sacrificial laws they go on to break the moral law. When
men take it upon themselves to act contrary to clearly revealed
laws, they are setting themselves up as higher authorities than
the Lord. They are guilty of despising God's name (1:6); they
do not take worship seriously.

Jesus differentiates between the ceremonial and moral components of the law but without relegating the ceremonial to the
trivial or to the insignificant. In fact, he says to the teachers of
the law who tithe their spices, "you have neglected the more
important matters of the law — justice, mercy and faithfulness.
You ought to have practised the latter, *without neglecting the former*" (Mt. 23:23b).

By his rhetorical question, "Try offering them (impure sacrifices) to your governor. Would he be pleased with you? Would
he accept you?" (1:8). The priests are made aware that their
activities and attitudes are an *insult* to the living God. They apply standards of conduct toward human figures of authority
that are totally overlooked when it comes to the Lord himself.
They wouldn't offer second-rate gifts to the governor, but with
the Lord it is "anything goes." Such an attitude is completely
unacceptable, and has been so from the beginning of human
history when it was first exhibited by Cain (Gen. 4:6,7).

The prophet introduces a bit of irony and sarcasm into his
admonitions. He urges the priests, "implore God to be gracious to us" (1:9). With the kind of offerings you have been
bringing, will he accept you? Can you seriously expect to be
the kind of mediator I've appointed you to be and bring the

people before me and plead their case? In fact, all such worship is so damaging and harmful to those who bring it, to those who offer it, because it isn't worship at all, but deception. It is so damaging that it would be much preferable to do away with all such worship (Mal. 1:10). Such strong words of disgust and rejection of worship are almost unparalleled in the Old Testament. For Amos, the attempt to replace the moral law with the ceremonial law merits equally strong condemnation. He calls the religious worship at Bethel and Gilgal "sin." "Go to Bethel and sin; go to Gilgal and sin yet more. Bring your sacrifices every morning, and your tithes every three years" (Amos 4:4). The sacrifices are an act of sin, not an act of worship. The Lord hates and despises their feasts and can't stomach their solemn religious assemblies (Amos 5:21).

Secondly, Malachi depicts the seriousness of priestly sins against the backdrop of three statements in which the Lord speaks of himself. He says, God is a father to the covenant nation and deserving of honor (1:6). He is a master and deserving of respect (1:6). He is a great King and deserving of fear (1:14).

As father he loves them and calls them out of Egypt (Hos. 11:1). Lovingly he directs their young steps and patiently teaches his infant son how to walk (Hos. 11:3). As a loving parent, God tenderly nurtures his son, his only son, and yet the son rebels against him (Is. 1:2b). Honor and obedience should be the natural response to such love (Ex. 12:20), but they are not forthcoming. In the song of Moses one finds a similar reproof:

> They have acted corruptly toward him; to their shame they are no longer his children, but a warped and crooked generation. Is this the way you repay the Lord, O foolish and unwise people? Is he not your Father, your Creator, who made you and formed you? (Deut. 32:5, 6)

Isaiah links God as Father with God as Redeemer. "You, O Lord, are our Father, our Redeemer from of old is your name" (Is. 63:16). By using the word "father" Malachi returns the people to the covenant relationship and all that covenant mercy should have meant to them.

God is not only a father (Ex. 4:22) but is also a master. He is the covenant Lord to whom fear and respect are due (Is. 8:13). He is a great king. The idea of God as king enters early in Old

Testament religion (Num. 23:21; 24:7; Ex. 5:18; Deut. 33:5). There are numerous references in the Psalms to Yahweh as king (Ps. 5:2; 29:10; 48:2). The enthronement psalms (93–100) particularly describe God as governor of the world and therefore as the one who vindicates his willing subjects and punishes all who brazenly oppose his ways. In Isaiah 40–66 God is portrayed in his majesty as the real ruler of the world. He is not just the king of Jacob and Israel (Is. 41:21; 44:6) but he is the king of nations, and his kingship is linked with the coming eschatological act of salvation (Is. 52:7,10). His kingship is not so much a future hope but a present fact (cf. I Chron. 29:11; Ps. 103:19;145:13; Jer. 10:7,10 and Mal. 1:14). The prophet, having spoken of God as Father, as Master and as Lord and as coming King, thus seeks to correct the degenerate practices of the leaders of his day by an appeal to the *character of the God* they profess to believe in but have seemingly forgotten.

Finally, he appeals to the future glorious kingdom in which the promises of Messiah will come to fruition. "My name will be great among the nations" (Mal. 1:11). The RSV translates with the present tense: "My name is great." With this translation the prophet is castigating the worship practices going on *inside* Israel by pointing to the sincere and genuine worship of God presently taking place *outside* the covenant nation. Under this view he is trying to shame Israel out of their present lethargic worship patterns by comparing their perfunctory performance to the sincere worship of God going on in the surrounding nations. The present tense view of the RSV, however, is not at all likely. First, because the Old Testament universally dismisses the gods and worship of the surrounding nations as worthless. God is the incomparable one who tolerates no rivals. If the prophet is to be understood as saying that heathen worship when sincere is, in reality, true worship and acceptable to the Lord, then why does he later condemn intermarriage outside of the covenant in such strong terms? Several lines of thought in chapter one point to the necessity of interpreting 1:11 as a statement of what *will* transpire in the future, not what was *presently* happening.

The prophet has already pointed to the fact that in the future, the name of the Lord will be great beyond the borders of Israel (Mal. 1:5). The use of the phrase, "From the rising to the setting of the sun" in 1:11 (Ps. 50:1; Ps. 113:3; Is. 45:6; Is. 59:9) points to the future eschatological intervention of God toward the whole of the inhabited world.

The reference to the name being great in 1:11 rules out the idea that heathen worship presently offered to God is in view. "Name" stands for the divine character. Malachi in no way is saying that heathen worship is being offered to the thrice holy God. He is instead looking to a time, as many of the other prophets did, when the nations would come to know God. His message is that one day "in every place incense and pure offerings will be brought to my name" (1:11a). During the messianic age the heathen nations will indeed serve the Lord, but generally this is portrayed as taking place in Jerusalem (Is. 2:2–4; Zech. 14:16–21; Amos 9:12; Is. 66:19–21).

Two things are unique about Malachi's prophesy of the Messianic age. Those offering pure sacrifices are not the priests in Jerusalem but the followers of the Lord spread throughout all the nations. The place where this worship is ascending to the Lord is not in Jerusalem but "in every place" (Mal. 1:11b):

> Impure reluctant service will be exceeded by the pure, acceptable worship that shall come up to God from the peoples all over the earth (W. Kaiser, *Malachi: God's Unchanging Love*, 1984, p. 46).

In the future the pure offerings will exceed the old offerings in both worthiness and efficacy.

It remains to ask what significance the future glory of the messianic kingdom has for the present deplorable worship of the covenant people. The answer seems to be that we are spurred on to a greater level of commitment, service and worship by the certainty of the *ultimate* triumph of God's kingdom. An additional example of this type of thinking is the reference to the future triumph of God when the nations will come and identify with him and his laws (Is. 2:2–4). This future reference is followed by an appeal to the contemporary nation. "Come, O house of Jacob, and let us walk in the light of the Lord" (Is. 2:5). The future promise of what will be is a prod and spur to present endeavor. This principle is alluded to by the apostle Paul when he says, "Salvation has come to the Gentiles to make Israel envious" (cf. Deut. 32:21; Rom. 11:12). Certainly the New Testament also appeals to the future reality as a motivation for the present, for the improvement of present moral desires and performance. "We know that *when* he appears, we shall be like him. And everyone who has this hope in him purifies himself just as he is pure" (I John 3:3; cf. II Pet. 3:11,13).

III. Dissolution of the Marriage Covenant and Its Commitments   2:10-16

It is no accident that following the degeneration of the priesthood the prophet next has to confront the area of human faithfulness and unfaithfulness. Lack of faithfulness toward God inevitably leads to breakdowns in human relationships. Corrupt practices are the genuine fruit and product of corrupt principles. The section begins with general admonitions not to "profane the covenant of our fathers by breaking faith with one another" (Mal. 2:10). The specific illustration of such faithlessness is in the area of marriage and divorce. The connection between this new section and what precedes in the book illustrates two biblical principles. First, it shows the clear relationship which the Scriptures presuppose between doctrine and life, between our relationship to God and our relationship to our fellowman, between religion and ethics. Secondly, it shows practically how the unfaithfulness of *leaders* leads to dire results in the lives of God's *people*.

Malachi begins the section with a reference to God as father and creator. That these terms refer to the redemptive covenant is obvious from the statement that follows. (See also Is. 43:1; 63:16). God calls a people to himself and when he does so, he calls them not only into a relationship with himself but into a new community — the people of God. There is a *progression* of unfaithfulness, from unfaithfulness to the Lord (profaning the covenant), to breaking faith with one another (Mal. 2:10b), to breaking faith with the wife of your youth (Mal. 2:14).

A.   Foreign Marriages Strenuously Attacked   2:10–12

In 2:10–12 the prophet contends against marriages outside of the covenant. He labels their action of breaking faith by marrying the daughter of a foreign god a "detestable thing" (2:11). It is a particularly strong expression by which the prophet expresses his abhorrence of what they were doing. When used in Deuteronomy, "detestable thing" refers almost exclusively to idolatrous religious practices (7:25, 26; 12:21; 13:14; 18:12). This has led some to reject a more literal view of what is meant by "marrying the daughter of a strange god" and taking the phrase to refer to the acceptance of a foreign cult of worship within the covenant nation. The passage is quite difficult but is best understood as attacking not the faithlessness involved in taking over non-Israelite religious worship practices but the faithlessness in marrying outside the covenant (cf. Neh. 13:23–27; Ezra 10:18). This allows for a more natural transition between the problem resulting from marriages contracted outside the covenant community to the associated problem of divorce that follows in the text. It is also true that the term "detestable thing" as used in Leviticus and Deuteronomy sometimes refers to sexual offences (Lev. 18:22, 26, 29, 30; Deut. 24:4).

The Old Testament contains many warnings against marrying foreign women, not from any exclusivist racial bias but because of the link to pagan worship (Gen. 24:3,4; Ex. 34:12–16; Deut. 7:3,4; I Kings 8; 11:1–8; Josh. 23:12). This is the best explanation of "marrying the daughter of a foreign god." The woman is an idolatress, a daughter (follower) of a foreign god.

Three elements in the passage, then, point to the extreme seriousness of marrying outside the faith. The first is the twofold reference describing the action as a "profaning of the covenant of our fathers" and as "desecrating the sanctuary the Lord loves" (2:10b, 11b) The translation "sanctuary" is by no means certain. A study of the verb "to profane and to desecrate" shows that it is possible to profane the Lord's name (cf. Amos 2:17b). It is particularly important in Ezekiel's message to explain why God will intervene on behalf of his people. "I had concern for my holy name, which the house of Israel profaned among the nations where they had gone" (Ez. 36:31). The verb is also used for profaning the sanctuary (Ez. 7:22, 24; 24:20), the sabbath (Ez. 20:13), the covenant (Ps. 89:34), the land (Jer. 16:18), and profaning the law (Ps. 89:31). Thus the word refers to any action which contravenes God's established order.

Several options present themselves in understanding the phrase "profaning the sanctuary which the Lord loves." Judah profanes the sanctuary by taking over the idolatrous practices of the wives. Since God dwells in the temple the presence there of people and practices contrary to God profanes the temple. But the phrase that follows "profaning the sanctuary" (which the Lord loves) makes that view less likely. Some suggest the word does not refer in this context to the "sanctuary" but to the "holiness" of God. That view, however, still has the problem of the latter phrase, "the holiness of God which he loves." It is best to understand the sanctuary in terms of people. It is not the temple that is in view or the divine attribute of God's holiness, but God's people. They are a holy people (Ex. 19:5-6) and they are loved by God.

This usage is supported by reference to the practice of intermarriage, mentioned by Ezra in 9:2. "They have taken some of their daughters as wives for themselves and their sons, and have mingled the holy race with the peoples around them." So this seems to be rather strong support for interpreting Mal. 2:11b, "they have profaned the people of God by introducing the foreign wives into the people of God whom the Lord loves." Verhoef comments: The mixed marriages were a desecration of the "sanctuary of God," a violation of Israel's spiritual existence as covenant people. Through these marriages the frontiers between covenant people and heathen, between church and world were obliterated (P. Verhoef, *The Book of Malachi*, 1987, p. 270).

The second pointer to the seriousness of what they were doing is the verb "to break faith" used in 2:10b and 11a. It is used predominantly in Jeremiah and Malachi with reference to marital unfaithfulness. Jeremiah says, "Like a woman unfaithful to her husband, so you have been unfaithful to me, O house of Israel" (Jer. 3:20). Unfaithfulness in marriage is one kind of covenant unfaithfulness. "To break faith," then, is often used with other verbs like "to rebel" or "to transgress" or "to sin." It is a treacherous act against the Lord to profane his ordinances and not to listen to his testimonies. It is an act of treachery or breaking faith (Ps. 119:158). As used in Proverbs the verb "to break faith" alternates with the verb "to be wicked" and is contrasted with the upright who live in harmony with the divine order (Prov. 2:22). Rejection of God's ordinance for marriage, then, violates and profanes the divine order for mankind.

The third indicator of the seriousness of violating the command not to intermarry is found in the curse pronounced against those who do so. The curse is that all who do so, who commit such sin, will be excommunicated from the covenant community (2:12).

B.   Divorce of Jewish Wives   2:13–16

The prophet's second example of unfaithfulness comes to light in 2:13-16. Verse 15 is extremely difficult to interpret because of textual problems. But, the main thrust of the passage is clear. Some men within Judah are dealing faithlessly with their marriage partners. They are divorcing them possibly for social reasons. When the Jews return to Jerusalem many will have been on the lower end of the social and economic scale and thus tempted to marry to upgrade their social standing. The condition for these marriages, demanded by the fathers of the women, is the divorce of their Jewish wives (no longer young as implied in the phrase, "the wife of your youth," v. 14). In this way the newer wife would not be neglected in the interests of the Jewish wife (cf. Beth Glazier-McDonald, *Malachi The Divine Messenger*, 1987, p. 114). Such behavior is not acceptable and forms the basis for the rejection of their prayers and their worship.

Acceptable worship requires an acceptable lifestyle! The prophet tells them several things about the divine perspective on marriage and divorce. First, that God witnesses their actions and is aware of what they are doing. Second, that their actions toward their wives are clear violations of God's covenant (i.e., acts of unfaithfulness toward him). The divorce of a faithful wife is not only an act of cruelty toward her but an act of disloyalty to God. Third, that the wife in marriage is a *friend* and a *companion*. NIV translates using "partner." The masculine form of the word is translated "friend" in Proverbs. Fourth, that marriage is itself a covenant (2:14b; cf. Proverbs 2:17). Fifth, that the purpose of marriage is to be seen in the godly seed, the product of the marriage union; and sixth, that the Lord hates what they are doing and therefore they need to guard themselves against the attitudes of unfaithfulness that manifest themselves within marriage and in other areas of life as well.

In our narcissistic culture, it is good to remember the standards to which the followers of the Lord are called in the area of marriage. The Lord's people are not to mimic the world in its quest and preoccupation with self-fulfillment. We are not to be absorbed in pleasing ourselves, but in keeping covenant with God.

IV. Divine Displeasure Over Sin   2:17–3:5

The prophet chides a bored, disillusioned and cynical generation of religionists for the way in which their behavior is an affront to God. Isaiah tells us that our offences weary the Lord (Is. 43:23b). One such offense is this petulant spirit that constantly places God on trial. Two specific examples of such backtalk are given. God's moral government is rejected; indeed the cynics imply a total reversal of good and evil (2:17; cf. Is. 5:20). To say, as they were saying, that the Lord delights in or is pleased with evil-doers is the height of blasphemy. God delights in the knowledge of himself (Hos. 6:6) and in justice, loyalty and humility (Micah 6:8). He delights in truth in the inward person (Ps. 51:8) and in those who obey his laws (Is. 56:4). But some are saying that the God of justice is nowhere to be seen in the world. These despairers have become practical atheists. They are asking, Where is the God of justice? They mean by this, why aren't the promises of a glorious future for the nation being fulfilled according to our expectations and within our time frame? Almost 100 years have gone by since the return from exile in 539 BC. They want to know where the evidence is that God is with them, controlling the destinies of nations and leading the chosen nation into its glorious future. Their conclusion is either that God acts unjustly or that there is no God.

While God alone infallibly knows the heart, it is crucial to understand who is asking these questions and in what spirit they are being asked. Every parent and teacher knows that questions can be posed in quite different ways. They can be asked humbly, sincerely or defiantly. The questions by themselves do not indicate unbelief. Otherwise Abraham, Job, Moses, the Psalmist, Jeremiah, and Habbakuk would have to be relegated to the category of unbelievers. The key to resolving this problem resides in the correct understanding of Malachi 3:16-18. There the prophet contrasts two groups, the righteous and the wicked — those who serve God and those who do not; those who fear the Lord and those who do not. From this passage, we must say that the complaints are not coming from weak believers who are momentarily succumbing to the pressures of their lives. Rather, the words have the ring of the unbelief of mockers and scorners who brazenly put God on trial. Their concerns don't arise out of an aversion to wickedness. "They did not complain through zeal for what was right, but because they would have God bound to them to undertake their cause like earthly patrons" (Calvin, *Twelve Minor Prophets*, Vol. 5, p. 565).   Blindly these cynical, religious unbelievers are trying to dictate to the Lord the course of his providence.

A. The Messenger of the Covenant Brings Judgment

To their mocking questions (2:17) the prophet replies that the Lord is indeed coming to his temple and that this event will be preceded by his sending a messenger (3:1). The Jews are looking for the Lord to judge the nations, thereby bringing the covenant nation into its destined position of power and glory. Malachi tells them that when the Lord comes in judgment, as he most certainly will, he will exercise judgment not against the heathen nations but against the godless within the covenant nation (Mal. 3:2-5). The Lord, whom they are seeking, would come suddenly to his temple as God and King to dwell among his people (Ez. 43:7; 37:26-27). That was the essence of the covenant promise from its inception (Ex. 25:8; Lev. 26:11-12). But that glorious presence brought with it the blessing of his true people, the righteous, and the punishment of the ungodly. Simeon's prophecy over the Christ child revealed the same truth: "This child is destined to cause the falling and rising of many in Israel" (Luke 2:35).

When the Lord comes in judgment, there will be some unpleasant surprises because judgment always *begins* with the house of God (I Peter 4:17). A study of the biblical usage of the adverb "suddenly" indicates that the word is almost universally associated with an unhappy and calamitous circumstance. Such an experience will come upon the unrighteous who will not be able to abide the day of the Lord's coming. "The Lord of glory comes as a thief in the night to those who sleep in their sins" (Keil and Delitzsch, *The Twelve Minor Prophets,* Vol. 2, p. 458).

It is the ungodly who will find the coming of the Lord intolerable. The tragedy is that, as in the case of the people in Amos's day who were waiting expectantly for the day of the Lord to come (Amos 5:18), so here is a false confidence. Though they clamor for his coming, they are not prepared for it. The only thing to prepare them for the coming of Christ the

Messiah is repentance. The messenger promised by Malachi will be involved in preparing the way. The phrase "to prepare the way" is used *prominently* in Isaiah (40:3; 57:14; 62:10) and points to the removal of that which would prevent and retard the coming of the Lord to his people. "The announcement of this messenger therefore implied that the nation in its existing moral condition was not yet prepared for the reception of the Lord, and therefore had no ground for murmuring at the delay of the manifestation of the divine glory but ought to murmur at its own sin and estrangement from God" (Keil and Delitzsch, *The Twelve Minor Prophets*, Vol. 2, pp. 457-458).

B. The Messenger of the Covenant Brings Purification

The passage speaks not only of *judgment* but of *purification*. In the refining process the pure metal is separated from the dross. The purpose of the Lord is to refine his people and in particular the sons of Levi. The picture of the Lord as a refiner is a common one with the Old Testament prophets (Is. 1:25; 48:10; Jer. 6:29-30; Ez. 22:17-22; Zech. 13:9). It is the pretended members of the covenant who will be purged and it is the remnant who will be purified. Since the priests are attacked in 1:6 and are the cause of much of the spiritual malaise of the day, the renovation and purification will begin with them and extend outwardly to the rest of the people. The sons of Levi represent all those devoted to praising God and employed in his service.

As a result of the work of the Messenger of the Covenant (Mal. 3:2), proper worship will again be offered since the hearts and lives of the offerers will be purified and righteous worship presented to the Lord. Malachi speaks of offerings in righteousness (Mal. 3:3-4), just as he spoke in 1:11 of "pure offerings in every place" to emphasize genuine and true worship of God. In doing so he employs terms for worship known in his own day. The basic principle in sacrifice by which God operates in both the Old and New Testaments is the one announced from the earliest point of Old Testament revelation in Genesis 4:4. "The Lord looked with favor on *Abel* and on his *offering*." No *performances* in religion are acceptable unless our *persons* are acceptable. Therefore the Lord purifies his people so that they may offer to him worship in righteousness (Ps. 4:5). "Then will I purify the lips of the peoples, that all of them may call on the name of the Lord" (Zeph. 3:9).

The Lord Jesus Christ is the messenger of the covenant who makes us acceptable (Mal 3:4) through his atoning sacrifice by which he brings us near to God (Eph. 1:6; I Pet. 3:18). We are accounted righteous in our persons on account of his sacrifice on our behalf (Rom. 3:25-26). As chosen by God and precious to him, God's people are being built into a spiritual house to be a holy priesthood offering spiritual sacrifices acceptable to God through Jesus Christ (I Peter 2:5). Paul remarks that he is given grace "to be a minister of Christ Jesus to the Gentiles, with the priestly duty of proclaiming the gospel of God, so that the Gentiles might become an offering acceptable to God, sanctified by the Holy Spirit" (Rom. 15:16).

This section (2:17-3:5) begins with the religious cynics accusing the Lord of injustice. It ends with the Lord bringing a lawsuit against covenant lawbreakers in which he lists a series of their injustices. They ask, Where is the God of justice? But they will live to regret their pretentious and reckless words. When they ask for justice, they will get it. For he will "come near" for judgment (3:5a). And if they believe the wheels of justice grind too slowly, then he will be quick to testify against them (3:5b). The image of the refining process leads to the idea of judgment, for the dross is removed so that the pure metal may emerge:

> They justify themselves, and, their sins having been artfully concealed, hope to escape punishment for want of proof; but God, who sees and knows all things, will himself be witness against them, and his omniscience is instead of a thousand witnesses, for to it the sinner's own conscience should be made to subscribe, and *so every mouth shall be stopped* (*Matthew Henry's Commentary: Isaiah to Malachi*, p. 1494).

The omniscience of God ought to operate as a deterrent against sin to all who seriously consider this truth. "For they have done outrageous things in Israel; they have committed adultery with their neighbors' wives and in my name have spoken lies, which I did not tell them to do. I know it and am a witness to it, declares the Lord" (Jer. 29:23). God is the refiner who comes to purify the faithful and to remove the unfaithful who will not be able to stand before him (Ps. 1:5), but will become part of the dross to be purged and cast away.

The specific sins mentioned in 3:5 are those clearly marked out by the law of God. The serious nature of these sins is seen in the fact that many were punishable by death. Many of the transgressions listed are sins against the social order. Like the rest of the prophets, Malachi sees no gulf between responsibilities to God and responsibilities to our fellowmen. The first three sins may refer to their relationships with their wives. Sorcery possibly could be a reference to some of the worship practices associated with their pagan wives. Adultery, as well, may be tied in with the taking of other wives and discarding their Jewish wives. Swearing falsely would be a failure to keep the covenant promises.

In addition to these sins the powerful are accused of exploiting the weak and helpless classes of society. Presumably these sins are reasonably common in Jewish society at this time. This in itself testifies to the blinding effects of sin. These religious scoffers brazenly reproach God for not acting and call into question the very justice of God: all the while they are oblivious to their own sins. "Let then everyone, who implores God's judgment, be his own judge, and anticipate the correction which he has reason to fear" (Calvin, *Twelve Minor Prophets*, Vol. 5, p. 578).

The root cause of their sins is the absence of the fear of God (Mal. 3:5b). It is the source from which all other sins flow. If the fear of God were present in their lives it would cause them to hate evil and to follow after and delight in God's commandments (Gen. 22:12; Ps. 112:1; Prov. 8:13).

When the world ignores and violates the moral laws of God, it is to be expected. When a people pretending to know God do so, it is truly tragic because such willful defiance of divinely revealed truths will bring with it fearful consequences (II Peter 3:20-22). Malachi is called upon to speak out boldly against such evils because

> even when such rampant evil cannot be contained, it must be denounced . . . But the very act of the prophet's proclamation changed the shape of society: when few knew any longer the distinction between good and evil, one man affirmed the good and declared the final end of evil (Craigie, *Twelve Prophets*, Vol. 2, p. 240).

The prophet sees the mission of Christ, the messenger of the covenant, as a whole. The first and second comings of Christ are not differentiated:

It is also self-evident that this ultimate fulfilment is neither to be looked for in his state of humiliation, nor his state of exaltation alone, but that the two are rather to be regarded as constituting together an inseparable whole. The advent of Christ in humiliation contains the germ of all the blessings which he bestows, and all the punishment which he inflicts, in his subsequent exaltation (Hengstenberg, *Christology of the Old Testament*, Vol. 2, p 1209).

V.   The Divine Desire to Bless   3:6–12

Having denounced the sin rampant in his day, Malachi proclaims the message of an unchanging God (Mal. 3:6). The Hebrew particle "ki," translated "for" (3:6a), connects the statement with what has gone before. The threat of judgment in verse 5 is explained in verse 6. Neither God nor Israel change. Israel continues to sin, which reflects her pattern from the very beginning of the covenant. The Lord continues to deal with her patiently and to call her to repentance (Mal. 3:7). Because Jehovah is unchangeable in his purposes Israel, as the people of God, will not perish. The wicked within the covenant nation will be judged and the remnant will be refined and shaped to perform its true calling. The connection with what has gone before is that Yahweh is the unchanging one, the compassionate and gracious God, slow to anger, and abounding in love and faithfulness and forgiving of wickedness, rebellion and sin (Ex. 34:6,7). Because of this, the sons of Jacob (a term that accentuates the weakness and changeability of human nature) do not cease to exist, i.e., they are not destroyed (cf. Jer. 30:11).

A. God's Unchanging Character   3:6

The connecting thought with what follows in the next section (3:7-12) is that in the light of the Lord's unchanging patience and compassion and righteous purposes, the people will be called to repentance. God's attitude toward sin is the same now as it was when he drove Adam and Eve from the garden. His attitude is the same as when he held out his hands all day long to an obstinate people who walked in ways not good, pursuing their own imaginations (cf. Is. 65:2).

God cannot change for the better, for he is perfect, and being perfect he cannot change for the worse. He is the one who reveals himself to Moses as "I Am who I Am" (Ex. 3:14).

All that God is he has always been, and all that he has been
and is he ever will be (cf. Ps. 102:27 and James 1:17). We
change according to our moods and according to new information that comes our way. God isn't subject to changes in
mood. Our own understanding of truth changes. Sometimes
we don't even know our own thinking. What comfort would it
be to pray to a God who changed like an earthly potentate who
granted one thing one day and denied it the next? However
unstable I may be and however fickle my friends may be, God
does not change. If he varied as we do, if he willed one thing
today and another tomorrow, if he were capricious, would we
confide in him? God does not compromise or alter his truth.

The permanence of his character guarantees the fulfillment
of his promises. His truth does not change. "All men are like
grass, and all their glory is like the flowers of the field . . . The
grass withers and the flowers fall, but the word of our God
stands forever." (Is. 40:6b, 8). His word is forever settled in
heaven (Ps. 119:89). He stands behind his promises but also
behind his demands and his warnings. His purposes do not
change (Is. 46:10). "The plans of the Lord stand firm forever,
the purposes of his heart through all generations" (Ps. 33:11).
"Because God wanted to make the unchanging nature of his
purpose very clear to the heirs of what was promised, he confirmed it with an oath. God did this so that, by two
unchanging things, in which it was impossible for God to lie,
we who have fled to take hold of the hope offered to us may be
greatly encouraged" (Heb. 6:17, 18). Those purposes are
accomplished in his Son who does not change, but is the same
yesterday, today, and forever (Heb. 13:8). This unchanging
God, through the gospel, produces radical changes in our lives
through the new birth. We have become new creatures in
Christ. We have turned from darkness to light.

B. Money Matters   3:8–12

The prophet proceeds to talk about tithes and offerings (3:8-
12), in other words, about giving and about money. According
to George Bernard Shaw, money is indeed the most important
thing in the world. "When money speaks, truth is silent."
Sadly, this is often the case. But isn't this one area in which the
people of God are to be significantly different? Isn't it true that
when a person is converted, so also is his pocketbook? Yes, it is

true because giving is an evidence of love and we love him
because he first loves us (I John 4:19). God so loved that he
gave. Giving makes us like God. The Scriptures teach that giving is a form of honoring the Lord. When we give we honor the
Lord (Prov. 3:9-10). Giving of the first fruits is also an evidence
of faith, since we are giving the first fruits without any guarantee that more of the material blessing will necessarily follow.
Giving is also an activity whereby we share in the work of
God.

God is the source of all we have. "Remember the Lord your
God, for it is he who gives you the ability to produce wealth"
(Deut. 8:18. See also I Chron. 29:12-14; Ps. 15:11-12; Hag.
2:8).When we deny this truth in our daily lives, we engage in a
practical form of idolatry. Sometimes within the covenant
nation, this idolatry took the form of looking to Canaanite fer-
tility deities as the source of material well-being (Hos. 2:8). At
other points it was a more humanistic type of idolatry. "My
power and the strength of my hands have produced this
wealth for me" (Deut. 8:17). In either case, it was a slap in the
face of the living God.

The Scriptures never underestimate the peculiar tempta-
tions connected with wealth. Wealth often competes with God
for our attention and energy (Jer. 9:23). It makes promises of
security and happiness that can only be fulfilled by the Lord.
It has a deceptive power that seduces (Mark 4:19). It competes
with God for the love (I Tim. 6:10), honor (Jer. 9:23), and trust
(I Tim. 6:17) of his people. Money tempts toward pride and
independence (Prov. 28:11; 18:11, 30:9a). When confronted
with the clear choice between God and wealth, many choose
wealth (Mk. 10:23; Luke 12:21; Mt. 6:24).

There is a lighter and brighter side to wealth, however.
Material blessings are to be a ladder by which our thoughts
are raised to God in gratitude for the furnished table that he
has provided (Ps. 23:5).* They are part of "everything" the

---

* Calvin's remarks on Ps. 23 are very wise and balanced: For this reason,
  we ought the more carefully to mark the example which is here set before
  us by David, who, elevated to the dignity of sovereign power, surrounded
  with the splendour of riches and honours, possessed of the greatest abundance of temporal good things, and in the midst of princely pleasures, not
  only testifies that he is mindful of God, but calling to remembrance the
  benefits which God had conferred upon him, makes them ladders by
  which he may ascend nearer to Him. (J. Calvin, *Commentary upon the
  Book of Psalms*, vol. 1, 1949, p. 391.)

Lord has given us for our enjoyment (I Tim. 6:17). Material things are also a responsibility, however, because the law specifies ways in which generosity toward and care of the poor are to be shown. Thus God's people participate in his work through their gifts. (Deut. 24:29ff; Lev. 19:ff; Lev. 19:9ff; Deut. 15:9ff).

It is instructive that Malachi's teaching about money (i.e., tithes and offerings) is given as an illustration of the need to repent. So often repentance is viewed as an emotional thing, feeling a certain degree of sorrow for sin. Here it is clearly volitional. It is a change of *attitude* manifesting itself in a change of *action*. Faith always influences both our affections and our actions. One such action is to acknowledge by the practical means of the tithe and offering that everything belongs to the Lord. Setting aside the part symbolizes that *all* is given by God. David saw this clearly as he praised the Lord in the presence of the whole assembly. "But who am I, and who are my people, that we should be able to give as generously as this? Everything comes from you, and we have given you only what comes from your hand" (I Chron 29:14).

C. Sin — The Great Robbery   3:8,9

To sin is to engage in the great robbery (Mal. 3:8). Failure to bring the tithe and offering is not just robbing God of the money that rightfully belongs to him. The cattle upon a thousand hills belong to him, and he is not in need of our gifts (Ps. 50:10). Sin and disobedience rob the Lord of the honor and the glory to which he as sovereign is due (Ps. 96:8; Prov. 3:9). Giving honors the Lord as an act of obedience, recognition, and acknowledgement of him as the source of all that we have. It is the heart that God cares about, not the money. Failure to give the tithes, part of which went to the Levites to support them in the work which they did in serving at the tent of meeting, shows how little heart the people had for the worship of God.

Since the tithes were at least partly used for the poor (Deut. 14:28-29; 26:12), it can be said as well that the poor are robbed, and since God so closely identifies with the poor, he is thereby defrauded. Tithing is God's way in the Old Testament of involving his people in his own redemptive activity, in his own concern for the poor. Just as he shares his blessing with his

people, so those who received those blessings must share them
with those who are less fortunate.

D. Encouragement to Repent   3:7b

The prophet connects his command to repent with a gracious promise. "Return to me and I will return to you" (Mal
3:7; cf. Zech. 1:3). The latter verbal idea stresses the intention
behind the action. Even though a persistent pattern of turning
from the Lord and his ordinances has characterized them in
the past, it is not too late if they will turn to him in repentance.
"God is said to *return* to us, when he ceases to demand the
punishment of our sins, and when he lays aside the character
of a judge, and makes himself known to us as a Father" (Calvin, *Twelve Minor Prophets*, Vol. 5, p. 582). It is an encouragement for the wayward wanderer to return home. "Come near
to God and he will come near to you" (Js. 4:8). It is only sin
that separates from God and causes him to hide his face (Is.
59:2). No one, however, can and will repent apart from an
awareness of sin.

The bad news (sin) always precedes the good news (the gospel). Thus the tragic blindness of their reply, "What have we
done that we need to repent?" This implies that they feel no
need to turn to God. They are pure in their own eyes (Prov.
30:12). The Jews of a later period have the same attitude when
they are urged to repentance by John. They are warned not to
think that repentance is not for them because they had Abraham as their father (Mt. 3:9).

How ready are many to acknowledge themselves in a vague
and general way to be sinners, but they never get down to
repent of *specific* sins. To enable the rich young ruler to see his
true need of a Savior, Jesus warned him against the sin of covetousness (Luke 18:18–27). So here the prophet lays specific
charges against the people in the area of tithes and offerings.

In preaching repentance, he addresses the entire nation
(3:9a) who were apparently guilty of giving God their second
best. He tells them to bring the *whole* tithe into the storehouse
(3:10a). The word "whole" is being emphasized. *Part* of the
requirements of the law of tithes were being followed:

> We then see that it is no new or unusual thing for men to pretend
> to do the duties they owe to God, and at the same time to take

away from him what is his own, and to transfer it to themselves, and that manifestly, so that their impiety is evident, though it be covered by the veil of dissimulation (Calvin, *Twelve Minor Prophets*, Vol. 5, p. 589).

If we wish to experience the blessing of God, we will need to be concerned with detail in the performance of our duties.

By failing to honor the Lord in bringing their tithes and offerings, the Levites, who served the Lord, were without their proper portions and withdrew from the service of the temple (Neh. 13:10). Undoubtedly this is what is meant by the phrase, "that there may be food in my house" (Mal. 3:10). Thus the principle that "those who preach the gospel should receive their living from the gospel" is being violated (I Cor. 9:14). Though the priests had shown themselves to be untrustworthy in God's service, the Lord will not allow his people to disobey the law requiring their support. Their full tithes and gifts must be brought to the storehouse; i.e., a room within the temple for the storage of such gifts (II Chron. 31:11; Neh. 10:38-39; Neh. 12:44; 13:12).

God invites the people of that day to test him! This is a reversal of common biblical usage. God normally tests man in the Old Testament (Ps. 11:5; 26:2; 66:10; Prov. 17:3). There are only a few instances of men being invited to test God; i.e., to prove his claims and justify his commands (Is. 7:11-12; Judg. 6:36-40). Of course it is true that the proof of the pudding is in the eating. The Psalmist who recounts his own experience of the goodness of the Lord invites his hearers to taste and see that the Lord is good (Ps. 34:8). There are warnings, however, against a wrong kind of testing of God (cf. Ps. 95:8-11).

A note of caution and reserve is needed here. Certainly the text contains no ironclad formula for material success. It is not an open-ended promise to bless materially:

It cannot be reduced, as sometimes happens, to a formula for success in business: if you give such and such, you can be sure that your profits will rise phenomenally year after year! The principle is rooted more in the health of the relationship a person has with God (Craigie, *Twelve Prophets*, Vol 2, p. 244).

While the text from Malachi about tithing must be rejected as a formula for material prosperity, there are important principles arising from it. True faith and giving are intertwined.

Little faith and little giving logically go together (Mt. 6:30).
"Small giving and small faith lay the foundation for small
receiving" (Craigie, *Twelve Prophets* Vol. 2, p. 243). So also Paul
writes "whoever sows sparingly will also reap sparingly, and
whoever sows generously will also reap generously" (II Cor.
9:6).

VI. The Destiny of the Righteous and the Wicked   3:13–4:6)

The closing section of Malachi provides the key for understanding the book and in some sense the whole of the Old Testament. From an early period the Old Testament has been
moving in the direction of identifying the remnant within
Israel as the true people of God. With the last book of the Old
Testament one meets with an explicit identification. Malachi
employs the term *"segullah"* (treasured possession), not of the
nation as a whole, as it is used in Exodus 19:5-6 at the inaugu-
ration of the covenant. Rather, he applies it to the "God-
fearers" within the nation. "They will be mine in the day when
I make up my treasured possession" (Mal. 3:17). The contrast
between the godly and the ungodly within the covenant nation
comes very strongly to the fore in this final section of the book.
It can be divided into five parts:

A. The Harsh Words and Attitudes of the Doubters   3:13-15
   1. Disillusioned in Service   3:14a
   2. Doubtful Concerning Divine Retribution   3:15b

B. The Godly Conduct of the True Israelites   3:16
   1. Their Relationship to God
   2. Their Relationship to Fellow Believers

C. Distinguishing the Righteous from the Wicked   3:17-18

D. The Rewards of Good and Evil in the Coming Day   4:1-3
   1. The Triumph of Good Over Evil   4:1a
   2. Judgment Upon Evil-doers   4:1b
   3. The Blessed Future of the Righteous   4:2

E. Two Old Testament Foundations for the Righteous — Law
   and Prophecy   4:4-6

A. The Harsh Words and Attitudes of the Doubters   3:13-15

Unbelief has reached a climax here with strong statements from the lips of these impudent cynics. "It is vain to serve God," they say. There is no benefit in keeping the divine commandments. Those who challenge God (put him to the test) escape. Such expressions have not been heard previously in the Old Testament by those people of faith who wrestled with their doubts. They go beyond those well-known experiences of doubt and frustration found scattered throughout the Old Testament (Job; Ps. 73; Habakkuk). The word "vain" in the statement, "it is vain to serve God," is the term used in the third commandment and means emptiness. It is empty and without reward. It is without value and importance to serve God. Such a mercantile spirit is condemned in the Bible; rather disinterested service to the covenant God is a distinguishing mark of true faith (Mal. 3:18).

It doesn't pay to observe the commandments, they say. What "profit" (NIV uses the word "gain") is there in keeping the covenant laws? (Mal. 3:14). The noun "profit" or "gain" is often employed negatively of the greedy person or of the one striving for unjust gain. It is used as one of the disqualifying characteristics of a leader (Ex. 18:21) and is condemned by the prophets in the strongest terms (Ez. 22:27; Jer. 8:10; Is. 56:11). The desire for personal gain in service is the very opposite of desiring God's truth. Thus the Psalmist prays that his heart would be turned toward the divine statutes and not toward selfish gain (Ps. 119:36; cf. Is. 33:14-16). In fact, the desire for selfish gain will dull all true hearing of God's word (Ez. 33:11). The inevitable end of all who make such personal gain their ambition is destruction (Prov. 1:19). The essence of worldliness is to measure the good life by the standards of time and not by those of eternity, by the things seen and not by the eternal weight of glory (II Cor. 4:17).

God himself lays no heavy burdens of service upon his people. False notions of God lead to erroneous ideas of service. When we really know who the Lord is, then there is joy in serving Christ. His yoke is easy. His service brings perfect freedom (Mt. 11:28). Service arises out of a love relationship. "Jacob served seven years to get Rachel, but they seemed like only a few days to him because of his love for her" (Gen. 29:20).

One wonders how such distortions of true faith can arise

within the religious community of Israel. They are diametrically opposed to the perspective of true belief and practice. Peoples' values or perspectives are based upon three inverted beatitudes: Blessed are the proud; blessed are the evil-doers because they will succeed in life; and blessed are those who thumb their noses at God, for God is too weak to do anything about it.

B.   The Godly Conduct of the True Israelites   3:16

Throughout the whole of redemptive history, even at those points where the cause of God and truth is at its lowest ebb, God has a remnant who never bow the knee to Baal (I Kings 19:18). The godliness of the remnant in Malachi's day is displayed in two areas; first in their relationship with God, and second, in their relationship with each other.

1.   *Their Relationship to God*

Three things are singled out. They *feared* God (3:16a; 16b; cf. 1:6b and 1:14). This is not a fear of dread but of affection and is the characteristic term for faith in the Old Testament. That verse 16 begins with "then" should not go unnoticed. The conversation and conduct of those who fear God are occasioned by the preceding words of murmuring and are placed in *contrast* to them. The godly accept that the Lord whom they follow is the Holy One, the just judge who will by no means leave the guilty unpunished or the righteous unrewarded (Ex. 34:6). Their fear of God should be understood, therefore, in this context.

They *honor* his name. They esteem his name, unlike the priests who despise his name (1:5). The word "esteem" suggests the engagement of the mind. But it is not a mere thinking about the name but proper esteem and regard for the person. This is in sharp contrast to the wicked who have no room for God in their thoughts (Ps. 10:4) and have no fear of God before their eyes (Ps. 36:1). The godly place a high value on the *name*, which is none other than the revealed character of God. When they "remember the name of God" it serves as a deterrent to sin (Ps. 119:55). The opposite is also true. Forgetting God for days without number (Jer. 2:32) allows one to sin with impunity.

They *served* God with the disposition of children (Mal. 3:17-18). "If we serve God with the disposition of children he will spare us with the tenderness and compassion of a father" (*Matthew Henry's Commentary, Isaiah to Malachi*, p. 1500). Service is performed out of the principle of love (Gen. 29:20). It is a delight, not merely a duty. It becomes an integral part of our character as God's children to bind ourselves to the Lord to serve him and to love the name of the Lord (Is. 56:6). With such a loving father-child relationship as a basis for service, we will not offer to the Lord that which costs us nothing.

2. *Their Relationship to Fellow Believers*

The ungodly are speaking among themselves (3:13b) *against* the Lord. The godly determine to take their stand for the Lord, and such a stand begins with fellowship among themselves as a means of encouraging one another in faith. The proud words of the ungodly summon the piety of the god-fearing. When evil is rampant, standing for the truth becomes much more difficult (cf. Amos 5:13). Under such circumstances the fellowship of God's people takes on even more significance and importance.

A fire, where the coals are in danger of being extinguished, is best revived by placing the dimly burning embers close to each other. So also at times when the fire of faith burns dimly, the Spirit uses the encouragement and stimulation from fellow pilgrims and followers of the Lord to revive the people of God.

In the face of the upsurge of secular and militant humanism, with its accompanying rejection of any biblical absolutes, it will be all the more necessary to learn to stand together for the truth without exhibitionism and to speak simply, naturally, and forthrightly about the essentials of our faith.

In being valiant for the truth (Jer. 9:3) against a pluralistic and secular society in which an absolute claim to truth is regarded suspiciously and skeptically, the church must avoid internal warfare and learn to distinguish between the central and secondary aspects of truth. In times of religious declension and apostasy, the Lord takes special notice of "those who grieve and lament over all the detestable things" done in his name (Ez. 9:4). He sees and is vitally concerned about the difference between true faith and false faith. He observes his people's fellowship with one another and their God-honoring thoughts. Their names and actions will not be forgotten (cf. Ex. 32:32; Ps. 69:28; Ps. 56:8; Is. 4:3; Dan. 12:1). The background to the Lord's "Book of Remembrance" (Mal. 3:17) may be the practice of Persian kings recording the faithful activities of their loyal subjects for an appropriate future reward (cf. Esther 2:23; 6:1-3). The reference to the Lord's "Book of Remembrance" should give encouragement to those persevering in faith and going against the tide of unbelief since the knowledge that God remembers is a stimulant to faith (cf. Ex. 2:24; Ps. 103:13,14; Ps. 139).

In Malachi, then, we see two sources of encouragement to godliness in the face of the forces of cynicism and despair. One is the encouragement that comes from fellowship with those of like precious faith. The second is the encouragement that comes from knowing that God sees and that "he is not unjust; he will not forget your work and the love which you have shown him" (Heb. 6:10):

> However absent God might appear to be from a society's life, he was in reality present, observing how people lived and noting those who did good and those who practised evil (Craigie, *Twelve Prophets*, Vol. 2, p. 246).

C. Distinguishing the Righteous from the Wicked   3:17-18

The scandal of the Bible to modern thought is that it makes clear and precise distinctions between truth and error, light and darkness, good and evil, heaven and hell, distinctions based on the unchanging character of God. Radical and dramatic social changes do not change or obliterate the character of God. Elections may be determined by the vote of the electorate, but goodness and truth aren't determined by the ballot.

From the earliest human history, God makes a distinction between Cain's and Abel's offerings. The first was not acceptable; the second was. The Lord makes a distinction between the Egyptians and the Israelites at the time of the Exodus (Ex. 8:23; 9:4; 11:7).

Later in the Old Testament there is a clear line of demarcation between the worship of Baal and the faith of Israel. They are two entirely different and separate religions with no possible way of integrating the two perspectives (I Kings 18:20). Malachi tells us that there is a clear distinction between the righteous and the ungodly. To the Bible student this is not startling or surprising, because throughout the whole of biblical revelation these two groupings are clearly and emphatically present. In terms of the Old Testament the contrast is expressed by the terms "righteous" and "wicked" (Ps. 1; 37; Prov. 10:6; Hab. 2:4). In the New Testament the two terms are the church or the people of God and the world.

It is much more startling, however, to have to make these distinctions among people who outwardly profess to know God. But such is what comes clearly into focus in Malachi 3:17-18. God's true people, his treasured possession (Ex. 19:5; Deut. 7:6; 14:2; 26:18) are the God-fearers, the remnant, those who value his person, honor his name, those who truly serve him. "These will be mine" (Mal. 3:17). This is one of the hard sayings of Scripture (John 6:60). "Not everyone who says to me, 'Lord, Lord' will enter the kingdom of heaven, but only he who does the will of my Father who is in heaven" (Mt. 7:21). Such a distinction is the missing ingredient in much recent teaching within evangelicalism.

There is a tendency, arising probably out of charity or fuzzy thinking, to equate faith with a profession of faith. This is a serious error. Jesus never does so (Mt. 7:21-22). Paul doesn't (II Cor. 13:5; II Tim. 1:5). Peter doesn't (II Pet. 1:5-11). John doesn't, otherwise why does he give tests whereby regeneration could be known (I John 2:29-5:13), and why would he call people who say that they know God, but don't, "liars"? (I John 4:20).

Belief always influences behavior. Faith influences our affections and our actions. "Faith without works is dead" is not merely a New Testament truth. It is clearly proclaimed in Malachi that those who *know* God are those who *serve* him. The true sons are those who serve. Of course, doing service doesn't earn the forgiveness or the sonship. The basis for forgiveness is found in the verb "to have compassion upon" or "to spare."

It is also not the perfection of the service that makes it acceptable (cf. Luke 17:10). We must be sons before we can be servants. "I will spare them as in compassion a man spares his son who serves him" (Mal. 3:17b). When we are sons, we will serve out of a principle of love and delight to do our Father's will. And as a Father, "God will not be extreme to mark what we do amiss, but will make the best of us and our poor performances" (*Matthew Henry's Commentary, Isaiah to Malachi*, p. 1500).

This truth is taught clearly in the historic Westminster Confession of Faith in the following statement:

> Yet notwithstanding, the persons of believers being accepted through Christ, their good works also are accepted in him, not as though they were in this life wholly unblameable and unreprovable in God's sight, but that He, looking upon them in His Son, is pleased to accept and reward that which is sincere, although accompanied with many weaknesses and imperfections.

As children of Adam, we are servants of sin (Rom. 6:16-20). Through Christ and his death, we become servants of righteousness (Rom. 6:18-19). In Adam, we naturally worship and serve created things rather than the Creator (Rom. 1:25). We are enslaved to various kinds of passions and pleasures (Titus 3:3). But when we come to know Christ we turn to God from idols to serve the living and the true God (I Thess. 1:9).

In the context of the whole book of Malachi then, there are six distinguishing characteristics of the remnant:

(1) They honor and fear God's name (1:6; 1:14; 2:2, 5; 3:16; 4:2).
(2) They keep the covenant (2:8; 3:14).
(3) They follow him in observing marriage commitments (2:11-15).
(4) They are able to discern and discriminate between good and evil (3:5).
(5) They honor God through the giving of money (3:9-12).
(6) They serve him (3:18).

D. The Rewards of Good and Evil in the Coming Day   4:1-3

1. *The Triumph of Good Over Evil*   4:1a

A day is coming! These words ring out across the centuries. They ring out a familiar cry beginning with Amos 5:18-27 in the eighth century B.C. and culminating with Malachi in the fifth century. Their familiarity should not obscure their radical message to our modern way of looking at life. Of course, it is all too easy to caricature the Bible's teaching on a future judgment. It is even possible for Bible-believing people to distort the eschatology of the Bible and regard it merely as a blueprint giving inside information on what is going to happen in the future. But these words are primarily addressed to the community of faith under siege from the forces of pessimism, cynicism, narcissism and doubt.

The real people of God appear to be forsaken by a God who is hidden. His involvement within history is nowhere evident. This prophet, like the others before him, counters the problem by an appeal to the coming day in which there will be a great and drastic reversal. God will no longer be hidden, but his presence will be unmistakably evident. There will be a day in which he acts to vindicate his treasured possession (3:17b), a day in which proud evil-doers will be dealt with resolutely.

2. *Judgment Upon Evil-doers* 4:1b

No doctrine of biblical revelation requires more careful study or a more resolute determination to think God's thoughts after him. Many of the teachings of Scripture oppose human reason and human wishes. There are some difficult things found within Scripture (II Peter 3:16); there are some hard sayings (John 6:60). Yet we believe in the doctrine of the Trinity not because it is an easy doctrine to understand or because it makes sense, but because it is taught in Scripture.

The incarnation is incontrovertibly mysterious (I Tim. 3:16) but is clearly taught in the New Testament, and therefore faith affirms what is revealed. But the doctrine of the anger and wrath of God eventuating in divine judgment is hard for the natural man and hard for the Bible-believing Christian. It is at this point that the child of God needs to ask some questions. How do I know anything about God? Only by divine revelation. Do I wish to make my mind the final arbiter of what can or cannot be true about God? If not, then I will seek to gird up the loins of my mind and allow Scripture to dictate to me and not I to dictate to it. The passage under consideration provides, therefore, a test case in this matter of submitting our minds to the truth of God's revealed word. Before looking at the passage, it will be helpful to listen to the practical words of a wise and respected Christian thinker:

No doubt it is true that the subject of divine wrath has in the past

been handled speculatively, irreverently, even malevolently . . .
Yet if we would know God, it is vital that we face the truth concerning His wrath, however unfashionable it may be, and however
strong our initial prejudices against it. Otherwise, we shall not
understand the gospel of salvation from wrath, nor the propitia-
tory achievement of the cross nor the wonder of the redeeming
love of God. Nor shall we understand the hand of God in history,
and God's present dealings with His own people; nor shall we be
able to make head or tail of the book of Revelation; nor will our
evangelism have the urgency enjoined by Jude; "save some by
snatching them out of the fire" (Jude 23). Neither our knowledge of
God, nor our service of Him will be in accord with His word.
(Packer, *Knowing God*, p. 174).

Malachi uses two images of fire to describe God. One is of a
refining fire (3:2). The other in our passage is a destroying fire
(4:1). This latter imagery is common in the prophets (Joel
2:3,10; Is. 10:16; 30:27; Amos 7:6-9; Jer. 21:14; Zeph. 1:18; 3:8).
The New Testament uses similar imagery (Heb. 12:29; II
Thess. 1:7). Psalm 21:9b makes the connection between the
imagery of fire and the wrath of God: "In his wrath the Lord
will swallow them up, and his fire will consume them."

Those upon whom wrath will come are called the arrogant
(the proud) and evil-doers (4:1). The eyes of unbelief saw these
groups in a different light (3:15) and called such people
blessed!

Malachi informs us that there will be no escape from this
judgment. "Not a root or a branch will be left to them" (4:1).
The reference to the root and branches presupposes a tree
(Amos 2:9) that will be consumed down to the roots, i.e., totally
destroyed.

The reality of a divine judgment must impinge on the way
we live our lives. Very simply put, if we believe in such a judgment then the conclusion of the matter will be to "fear God
and keep his commandments, for this is the whole duty of
man. For God will bring every deed into judgment, including
every hidden thing, whether it is good or evil" (Eccl. 12:14).
Because God is our judge, he has authority. He made the
world and we must adjust to the way he made it, not assuming
that we know what is best. This will mean that because in love
he wants the best for us, in love to him we will want to follow
his laws. As judge, he will do what is right and good. "Will not
the judge of all the earth do right?" (Gen. 18:25b).

God has our good in mind in giving us his laws. "And now,

O Israel, what does the Lord your God ask of you but to fear the Lord your God, to walk in all his ways, to love him, to serve the Lord your God with all your heart and with all your soul, and to observe the Lord's commands and decrees that I am giving you today for your own good?" (Deut. 10:12-13). God does not make mistakes, because he is wise and infinite of understanding. And therefore he knows the secrets and hidden motives of men. He, the Lord, is not some impotent potentate helpless to effect his purposes. He is the Almighty God with infinite power to carry out his sentence. Despite appearances he is in charge and sovereign and therefore all proud defiance of him will one day be eradicated from the world. So the future for all human presumption and pride is bleak indeed (Is. 2:6-22).

In a world without God, anything is permissible. In a world created by God, man is accountable to him in a final judgment:

> The doctrine of final judgment enshrines many important truths. It stresses man's accountability and the certainty that justice will finally triumph over all the wrongs which are part and parcel of life here and now. The former gives a dignity to the humblest action, the latter brings calmness and assurance to those in the thick of the battle. This doctrine gives meaning to life. The Greek idea of history as a cyclic process shut men up to a treadmill in which they might strive mightily, but neither gods nor men could advance. The Christian view of judgment means that history moves to a goal. . . . Judgment protects the idea of the triumph of God and of good. It is unthinkable that the present conflict between good and evil should last throughout eternity. Judgment means that evil will be disposed of authoritatively, decisively, finally. Judgment means that in the end God's will will be perfectly done (L. Morris, *The Biblical Doctrine of Judgment*, 1960, p. 72).

Using Malachi's image the righteous will win out in the end. "You will trample down the wicked; they will be ashes under the soles of your feet on the day when I do these things" (Mal. 4:3). The wicked will become Christ's footstool (Ps. 2:1). The saints will rule with him and the Lord will bruise Satan under their feet (Rom. 16:20). Christ promises "to him who overcomes and does my will to the end, I will give authority over the nations — He will rule them with an iron scepter; he will dash them to pieces like pottery — just as I have received authority from my Father" (Rev. 2:26-27).

3. *The Blessed Future of the Righteous*   4:2

The righteous are the beneficiaries of the purifying and invigorating rays that emanate from the "sun of righteousness." The image of the sun is applied in several instances to the Lord (Ps. 85:11; Num. 6:26; Is. 60:19). The Davidic king would reign in righteousness (Is. 32:1) and would be referred to as the "Righteous Branch" (Jer. 23:5) who would be called the Lord, our Righteousness (Jer. 23:6). He is also referred to as the "Righteous Servant" (Is. 53:11b) and a "Righteous God and a Savior" (Is. 45:21). "The Sun of Righteousness" points forward to Christ. He is the light of the world and it is his peculiar office as our prophet to enlighten darkened minds (John 1:9; 8:12; Eph. 5:14). "Christ is peculiarly called light with regard to all the faithful, whom He delivers from the blindness in which all are involved by nature, and whom he undertakes to guide by his Spirit" (Calvin, *Twelve Minor Prophets*, Vol. 5, p. 618).

The spiritual light that comes from this "sun of righteousness" cannot be divorced from righteousness. He is the source of all our righteousness. Christ has become for us righteousness (I Cor. 1:30) and by his regenerating spirit he causes us to hunger after righteousness (Mt. 5:6) and to become servants of righteousness (Rom. 6:18).

God alone can bring healing (Ex. 15:26; Deut. 32:39). Healing is sometimes synonymous with forgiveness (II Chron. 7:14; Ps. 103:3) and even with deliverance from the grave (Ps. 107:20). Jeremiah cries out to the Lord, "Heal me, O Lord, and I shall be healed. Save me and I shall be saved (Jer. 17:14). The parallelism between healing and saving demonstrates that healing may be used here in a comprehensive way for salvation. Such is the meaning of the healing procured by the wounds and stripes of the suffering servant (Is. 53:5).

The wings of the sun (Mal. 3:2b) refer to its rays:

As the rays of the sun spread light and warmth over the earth for the growth and maturity of the plants and living creatures, so will the sun of righteousness bring the healing of all hurts and wounds which the power of darkness has inflicted upon the righteous (Keil and Delitzsch, *The Twelve Minor Prophets*, Vol. 2, pg. 469). (cf. Ps. 36:7; 91:4; Mt. 23:37.)

Christ rescues us from the dominion of darkness and translates us in his kingdom of righteousness (Col. 1:13). "He gave himself for our sins to rescue us from the present evil age" (Gal. 1:3).

"Then you will trample down the wicked" (Mal. 4:3a). The saints participate with Christ in the fruits of his victory (II Tim. 2:10; Rom 16:20). When the Lord redeems and delivers his people, it involves the destruction of their enemies. Redemption always culminates in the destruction of God's enemies (Gen. 3:15; Ex. 15; Rev. 20). The text is clear, however, to say that this destruction will be accomplished by the Lord himself. Victory will come "on the day when *I* do these things" (Mal. 4:3b). To overcome all despondency based on the short-term outward success of the wicked, the Lord strengthens the patience of his saints by telling them that the success of the ungodly is only temporary and short-lived. The day of the Lord will bring vindication to all those who fear his name:

> Christ, whose glory fills the skies,
> Christ, the true, the only Light,
> Sun of righteousness, arise,
> Triumph o'er the shades of night;
> Day-spring from on high, be near;
> Day-star, in my heart appear.

Charles Wesley (1707–88)

E. Two Old Testament Foundations for the Righteous — Law and Prophecy (4:4–6)

The past and the future come together in this passage, which furnishes a fitting conclusion to both the book of Malachi and the whole of the Old Testament.

"Remember the law of Moses." The Old Testament speaks often of remembering. It is a favorite term used in Deuteronomy (9:7, 27; 24:9; 25:17; 32:17). Jeremiah raises the complaint from the Lord: "My people have forgotten me days without number" (2:32). To remember means to be directed and influenced in the inner core of one's being and in one's actions. Malachi points to obedience to the law as the only sure path to blessing (2:8–9; 3:7, 9,10–12; 3:22). It is the norm and unchanging authority for the entire community.

It is critical to understand the relationship of law and grace in the Old and New Testaments. The Ten Commandments are revealed in the context of the covenant, the gracious gift of salvation that God gives his people. The law isn't an alternative route to salvation. It isn't to serve as a ladder whereby one might climb into the divine presence. The Ten Words are given to a people who had already been redeemed out of the land of Egypt (Ex. 20:1, 2) as a means of expressing their gratitude to God for his mercy and grace to them.

The way we understand the law-grace question will profoundly influence both the way we preach the gospel and what we say concerning the requirements of God's law. It will have a significant bearing on the place of obedience in the life of a professing believer.

Three positions are present within the church today. One regards obedience as an *optional extra* to belief with no necessary connection between belief and behavior. Believing is kept rigidly separate from obeying. To be sure God will be pleased and we will receive much more blessing if we go the additional mile and sign up for the obedience course. Our salvation, however, is not in question and remains intact because it is by grace and is received by faith, and faith is defined as belief and nothing more. Bonhoeffer called this erroneous theology "cheap grace." It is grace without disciplineship, forgiveness without repentance, privilege without responsibility, comfort without the cross.*

The second position sees obedience in a somewhat stronger way. It is a *desirable sequel* to faith. Desirable to whom, it needs to be asked? Of course God desires it and that's why he revealed himself and calls for obedience. Since his laws are a revelation of his character, it goes without saying that from God's point of view obedience is a desirable sequel to faith. It is also true that obedience is desirable from the point of view of the person believing. Since God's laws are for our good (Deut. 10:3; Rom. 7:12) we will receive much more blessing and good if we obey them. Still, to call obedience merely the desired sequel to faith falls short of a biblical understanding of faith.

The third position sees obedience as an *indispensable and necessary component of true faith*. Grace is interpreted not only in terms of the objective events of redemptive history such as

---

* D. Bonhoeffer, *The Cost of Discipleship*, 1964, p. 35 begins his study by remarking, "Cheap grace is the deadly enemy of our Church. We are fighting today for costly grace."

Christ — his incarnation, his perfect obedience and sinless life, his vicarious and substitutionary death, his resurrection and ascension to the right hand of God, his coming again. Under this view grace is also seen in the subjective response to the gospel:

> 'Twas grace that taught my heart to fear and grace my fears relieved; how precious did that grace appear the hour I first believed. Grace taught my wandering feet to tread the heavenly road and new supplies each hour I meet, while pressing on to God.
>
> J. Newton (1725–1807).

While faith is seen to involve believing certain truths, it is also to be understood as a personal trust or commitment that leads to obedience. Faith gives evidence of itself in the commitment to follow and obey. The works of faith are the lived-out reality of faith. Election secures the obedience. The obedience of faith is not an optional extra, nor even a desirable sequel to faith, but the necessary outworking of true faith. Faith without works is dead! "If anyone is in Christ, he is a new creation; the old has gone the new has come!" (II Cor. 5:17). Where true faith is present it energizes (Gal. 5:6). The God who *reckons* us righteous through faith, based on the atoning work of Christ, *purifies* our hearts by faith (Acts 15:9).

To some, the fact that the Old Testament ends on a note of calling for obedience to divine laws is an embarrassment. To others, it simply proves that we need to move on from the Old Testament to the higher ground of the New Testament. In reality the way the Scriptures handle the law-grace question is essentially the same in both testaments. God takes the initiative in grace. Gratitude for the gift of salvation inspires God's people to act in a way pleasing to God. When we fail to do so, we are all the more enabled to see that salvation can come only as a gift. The marvel of God's freely offered forgiveness is the most powerful propellant to a godly life.

One current writer on evangelism and discipleship calls our attention to the dreadful attrition rate in modern decisionistic Christianity and calls for a *long* obedience in the same direction:

> It is not difficult in such a world to get a person interested in the message of the gospel; it is terribly difficult to sustain the interest. Millions of people in our culture make decisions for Christ, but there is a dreadful attrition rate. Many claim to have been born

again, but the evidence for mature Christian discipleship is slim. In our kind of culture anything, even news about God, can be sold if it is packaged freshly; but when it loses its novelty, it goes on the garbage heap. There is a great market for religious experience in our world; there is little enthusiasm for the patient acquisition of virtue, little inclination to sign up for a long apprenticeship in what earlier generations of Christians called holiness.

Religion in our time has been captured by the tourist mindset. Religion is understood as a visit to an attractive site to be made when we have adequate leisure. For some it is a weekly jaunt to church. For others, occasional visits to special services. Some, with a bent for religious entertainment and sacred diversion, plan their lives around special events like retreats, rallies and conferences. We go to see a new personality, to hear a new truth, to get a new experience and so, somehow, expand our otherwise humdrum lives. The religious life is defined as the latest and the newest: Zen, faith-healing, human potential, para-psychology, successful living, choreography in the chancel, Armageddon. We'll try anything — until something else comes along (E. Peterson, *A Long Obedience in the Same Direction*, 1980, p. 12).

Perhaps we need to rediscover the gospel and offer Christ to people in the biblical way of Prophet, Priest, and King rather than merely inviting them to come to Christ as their personal Savior. If we did so it would become clearer what people are signing on for. Perhaps we need to preach repentance and faith (Acts 20:21). Perhaps we need to preach justification and the sanctification. Perhaps we need to tell sinners that Christ saves them from both the penalty and the power of sin (Mt. 1:21). Perhaps in addition to telling sinners to believe, we might also try telling them that faith is the gift of God (Acts 18:27; Eph. 2:8,9). Only the authentic gospel is a big enough message to incline the hearts of men and women to sign up for a long apprenticeship with God.*

The second focus of this concluding section is to reiterate the impending day of the Lord previously mentioned in chapter 3:1. The language of 4:5 corresponds to that of 3:1, at several points. It is therefore likely that the messenger of 3:1, who

---

* For an interesting and informative discussion of these issues and the nature of saving faith, see John MacArthur, Jr., *The Gospel According to Jesus*, 1988, and the reply by Charles Ryrie, *So Great Salvation*, 1989, and Zane Hodges, *Absolutely Free*, 1989.

prepares the way for the Lord, is to be identified with Elijah in 4:5. Both passages begin with "behold," both contain the same verbal form, "I am sending," and in both cases the purpose of the mission of the forerunner is to preach repentance and turning from evil. "To prepare the way" or "to clear the way" (Mal. 3:1; cf. also Is. 40:3) pictures the arrival of a reigning monarch and urges the removal of all spiritual and moral impediments in anticipation and expectation of his arrival. The verb used in 4:6, "turn," is the commonly used verb for repentance in the Old Testament.

The synoptic gospels identify John the Baptist as Elijah (Mt. 11:14; 17:10–13; Mk. 9:11–13). "He will go on before the Lord, in the spirit and power of Elijah, to turn the hearts of the fathers to their children . . ." (Luke 1:17). Of course this one fulfillment at the first coming of Christ does not, of necessity, preclude the possibility of a later fulfillment (cf. Rev. 11:33–12).

It is interesting to notice that these same two (Moses and Elijah) figures appeared to Jesus on the Mount of Transfiguration (Mk. 9:2–8). They represent the two-fold foundation of the Old Testament law and prophecy. The law reminds us of our responsibilities and commitments to God. The prophets prod and cajole and exhort us to obedience. They call us from the false ways to which we turn and urge us to return to God.

This prophet began with preaching the electing love of God (1:1–5) and ended with the threat of the curse (*herem*, 4:6b). Some find this distressing. Several things need to be noted. While this is no idle threat, it is nevertheless not a "curse pronounced but a curse threatened . . . It is the last appeal of love aimed at averting calamity by announcing it as the natural sequence of disloyalty and sin" (G.C. Morgan, *Malachi's Message for Today*, 1972, p. 113). It is an act of condescension and great mercy for the Lord to issue warnings, no matter how terrible they are. The Day of the Lord is a great and awesome day, and it is better to face the reality that God will bring every act unto judgment (Eccl. 12:14) than to put our heads into the sand and go on blindly in our sin. "Often the sternest and most terrifying warnings of God are the tokens of his deepest love. He warns us because he loves us and desires to save us" (J. Benton, *Losing Touch with the Living God*,1985, p. 127). God's warning bell of judgment may serve to become the wedding bell of our betrothal and marriage to Christ (II Cor. 11:3).

The doctrine of the "day of the Lord" that Malachi preaches

points to the extreme importance and significance of our choices. How we act is important! How we live in time determines how we will live in eternity. Secularists may refer to this teaching sneeringly as "pie in the sky when we die," but the one who follows Scripture will be conscious that his or her life is being lived in the presence of a holy God.

Rather than being exclusively an Old Testament teaching, the message of the day of the Lord reminds us of the Pauline statement, "Consider therefore the kindness and sternness of God" (Rom. 11:22). The most solemn warnings and threats of future punishment are not sounded in the Old Testament but come from the lips of Jesus himself (Mt. 23:15).

Malachi ends this section by giving a concrete example of what it means to listen to the warnings of the Word of God. Repentance and turning to God will be seen in the restoration of family relationships, in the transformation of hearts wherein love is in evidence. The fathers' *hearts* will be turned "to their children, and the hearts of the children to their fathers" (4:6a). True faith produces love (Gal. 5:6; I John 4:16). "Heaven is indeed a world of love, and only as we learn to love are we being prepared to enter that place. We are only prepared for the day of the Lord as we have faith in Jesus which is shown by practical love" (Benton, *Losing Touch With the Living God*, p.132).

Bibliography on Malachi — Commentaries

Achtemeier, E. *Nahum — Malachi Interpretation:* A Bible Commentary for Teaching and Preaching. Atlanta: John Knox Press, 1986.

Baldwin, J. *Haggai, Zechariah, Malachi.* Tyndale Bible Commentaries. Downers Grove: Inter Varsity Press, 1972.

Benton, J. *Losing Touch with the Living God — The Message of Malachi.* Welwyn Commentary Series. Welwyn: Evangelical Press, 1985.

Calvin, J. *Twelve Minor Prophets*, Vol. 5. Grand Rapids: William B. Eerdmans Publishing, 1950.

Craigie, P. *Twelve Prophets*, Vol. 2. Daily Study Bible. Philadelphia: Westminster Press, 1985.

Deutsch, R. *Malachi — A Call to Obedience.* Grand Rapids: William B. Eerdmans Publishing, 1987.

Kaiser, W. *Malachi — God's Unchanging Love.* Grand Rapids: Baker Book House, 1984.

Laetsch, T. *The Minor Prophets.* St. Louis: Concordia Publishing Co., 1956.

Mason, R.A. *Books of Haggai, Zechariah, Malachi.* Cambridge Bible Commentary. Cambridge: Cambridge University Press, 1977.

Glazier-McDonald, Beth. *Malachi — The Divine Messenger,* SBL Dissertation Series 98. Atlanta: Scholars Press, 1987.

Morgan, G.C. *Malachi's Message for Today.* Grand Rapids: Baker Book House, 1972.

Moore, T.V. *A Commentary on Haggai and Malachi.* Edinburgh: Banner of Truth, 1960.

Pusey, E. *The Minor Prophets*, Vol. 2. Grand Rapids: William B. Eerdmans Publishing, 1950.

Smith, R.L. *Micah — Malachi*, Vol. 32: Word Biblical Commentary. Waco: Word Books, 1984.

Verhoef, P. *Haggai, Malachi.* New International Commentary. Grand Rapids: William B. Eerdmans Publishing, 1987.

A very useful resource for teaching and preaching from Malachi is Vol. 84, No. 3 (1987), of the *Review and Expositor*, published by Southern Baptist Theological Seminary in Louisville, Kentucky.

Bibliography on Themes Within Malachi

God's Love   Mal. 1:5

Morris, L. *Testaments of Love*. Grand Rapids: William B. Eerdmans Publishing, 1981.
Packer, J.I. *Knowing God*. London: Hodder and Stoughton, 1973: ch. 12.
Warfield, B.B. *Biblical & Theological Studies*. Philadelphia: Presbyterian & Reformed Publishing Co., 1952: ch. 2, "God's Immeasurable Love."

Worship   Mal. 1:6–2:9

Foster, R. *Celebration of Discipline*. New York: Harper & Row, 1978: ch. 11.
MacArthur, J. *The Ultimate Priority: On Worship*. Chicago: Moody Press, 1983.
Webber, R. *Worship is a Verb*. Waco: Word Books, 1985.
———. *Worship Old & New*. Grand Rapids: Zondervan Publishing, 1982.

Marriage and Divorce   Mal. 2:10–16

Atkinson, D. *To Have and To Hold*. Grand Rapids: William B. Eerdmans Publishing, 1979.
Foster, R. *Money, Sex & Power*. San Francisco: Harper & Row, 1985.
Smedes, L. *Sex for Christians*. Grand Rapids: William B. Eerdmans Publishing, 1976.
Stevens, R.P. *Marriage is for Good*. Downers Grove: Inter Varsity Press, 1986.

Giving   Mal. 3:8–12

Brown, B. *The Health and Wealth Gospel*. Downers Grove: Inter Varsity Press, 1987.
Catherwood, F. *Time, Talent, Money*. Downers Grove: Inter Varsity Press, 1987.
Ellul, J. *Money & Power*. Downers Grove: Inter Varsity Press, 1984.

Fee, G. *The Disease of the Health and Wealth Gospel*, Spiritual Counterfeits Project Newsletter, Spring, 1985.

Foster, R. *Money Sex & Power*. San Francisco: Harper & Row, 1985.

Mitchell, C. *Stewardship of Money*. Downers Grove: Inter Varsity Press, 1951.

Packer, J.I. *Hot Tub Religion*, Wheaton: Tyndale House, 1987: ch. 4.

Verhoef, P. "Tithing — A Hermeneutical Consideration." In *the Law and the Prophets*, J.H. Skilton, editor. Philadelphia: Presbyterian & Reformed Publishing, 1974.

Meditation   Mal. 3:16b

Foster, R. *Celebration of Discipline*. New York: Harper & Row, 1978: ch. 2.

Toon, P. *From Mind to Heart — Christian Meditation Today*. Grand Rapids: Baker Book House, 1987.

Serving God   Mal. 3:17

Boice, J.H. *God the Redeemer*. Downers Grove: Inter Varsity Press, 1978: ch. 7.

Foster, R. *Celebration of Discipline*. London: Hodder & Stoughton, 1980: ch. 9.

Swindoll, C. *Improving Your Serve*. London: Hodder & Stoughton, 1981.

Wrath of God   Mal. 4:1–3

Morris, L. *Biblical Doctrine of Judgment*. Grand Rapids: William B. Eerdmans Publishing, 1960.

Packer, J.I. *Knowing God*. London: Hodder & Stoughton, 1973: ch. 14 and 15.

Toon, P. *Heaven and Hell*. Nashville: Thomas Nelson, 1986.

Righteousness   Mal. 4:1–3

Hengstenberg, E.W. *Christology of the Old Testament*. Edinburgh: T&T Clark, 1854.

Snaith, N. *The Distinctive Ideas of the Old Testament*. New York: Schocken Books, 1964: ch. 3.

God's Law   Mal. 4:4

Boice, J.M. *God the Redeemer*. Downers Grove: Inter Varsity Press, 1978: pp. 55–107.
Packer, J.I. *I Want to be a Christian*. Wheaton: Tyndale House, 1977: pp. 245–316.

Questions on Malachi 1–2:9

1. Using a concordance, study some of the passages in Deuteronomy that speak of the divine love which originated the covenant relationship. Study Deuteronomy 7:6–9 in more detail. How is it possible to react so indifferently to God's electing love?

2. Note the descriptions of the Divine character in verses 3 (love and hate), 4 (wrath of the Lord), 6 (father-son and servant-master), and 14 (I am a great King). What are the different responses that these aspects of the Divine character are intended to evoke? Discuss.

3. What specific attitudes are displayed by the religious leaders (priests, see v. 6) that contribute to the ungodly response of the people? What were the proper duties of the priests? Cf. Mal. 2:6,7.

4. Study Malachi 1:11. What is the significance of the threefold emphasis on God's name becoming great?

5. How serious a matter is it when religious leaders fail in the performance of their duties? In answering this note the verses that speak of the Divine response to the priests (2:1-3,9). Are there N.T. statements which severely rebuke religious leaders for their failures in life and doctrine?

Questions on Malachi 2:10–16

1. Israel was the nation with whom God had established his covenant. Malachi accuses the nation of profaning the covenant and breaking faith with one another. What evidence of this is mentioned in this passage?

2. a) What is the significance of "marrying the daughter of a foreign god"? (see Deut. 7:1–6).
   b) Can you think of anything which for a Christian would be equivalent to this particular sin? (see II Cor. 6:14–18).

c) How could such sin be prevented? (see II Cor. 7:1).

3.   Mal. 2:13,14 shows that they have compounded their sin.
   a) Compare the people's complaint in v. 13 with God's
      promises in Deut. 7:12–15. Why the lack of blessing?
   b) What do you consider to be blessing from God in your
      life?
   c) Have you ever noticed a pattern of lack of blessing result-
      ing from lack of obedience? How do you react in such a
      situation?

4.   All divorce is failure to reach God's ideal for marriage.
   a) What in particular does God hate about the divorce men-
      tioned in this passage?
   b) Is this passage adequate grounds for an unqualified con-
      demnation of all divorce? (compare with Ezra 10:1–4,18).

5.   Mal. 2:15b, 16b speaks of "guarding yourself in your spir-
      it" (NIV) as a preventative to marriage breakdown.
   a) What might that mean for a man or woman in our cul-
      ture?
   b) How can we as the church be helpful to one another in
      this area?

6.   In your opinion how relevant is this passage to the late
      20th-century church?

Questions on Malachi 2:17–3:5

1.   Things were not going well for the returned exiles. They
      had returned with memories of the messianic prophecies
      of earlier years and the expectations of a powerful cham-
      pion who would throw off all oppressors. This had not
      happened.
   a) What was their response? (2:17)
   b) What attitude is demonstrated?
   c) Why does their response "weary the Lord"?
   d) What are some ways Christians "weary the Lord"?

2. a) What is 3:1 talking about?

b) Who is the first mentioned "messenger"? See ch. 4:5 and Mt. 11:7–15

c) Who is the "messenger of the covenant"? (see immediate context)

3. a) In light of their expectations how do you think Malachi's hearers would have responded to verses 2–5?

b) What had they failed to understand about the Messiah?

c) What do these verses tell us about God's intention for his people?

d) Are modern Christians ever guilty of false expectations concerning Christ's return? Support your answer.

Questions on Malachi 3:6–15

Three areas of God's protest against his people in this book are:

Polluted Priesthood
Mixed Marriages
Rebellious People

1. Why did God not destroy rebellious Israel? (v. 6) Consider and discuss why this attitude of God is so important for each one of us to remember when God does not judge us instantly for sinful acts.

2. What promise does God make in verse 7? Though this sounds simple, why is it so difficult today? (as it would be then).

3. In your own words, what two accusations did God make against them? (vs. 8,13)

4. Do they acknowledge they are wrong? (vs. 8,13) What does this tell us today about our awareness of sinful acts? cf. Romans 2:1–8; Rev. 2:4, 5; 14–17; 3:14–19.

5. What is God's amazing promise to these people (and us) if we stop doing unrighteousness and obey him? Apply and give insights and testimony to this truth.

82317

Questions on Malachi 3:16–4:6

In spite of all the rebellion and challenges to God from his people — what do we find taking place in verse 16?

1.   Will God really judge people who ignore him? (vs. 1–3) What does the New Testament say? Mt. 25:40–46, Rev. 21:7, 8.

2.   How should the teaching of God's judgment affect:
     a) our lives?
     b) our attitude toward helping others see the good news of the gospel when they ignore or disbelieve in God?

3.   What special promise does God make in verse 5? When was this promise fulfilled? (cf. Mt. 11:14) What two events will follow this person's death? (v. 5b, 6) Where does this put our age and these prophecies then? Discuss.

Those must expect to be smitten with a sword, with a curse, who do not turn to Him that smites them with a rod.

                                        (Matthew Henry on 4:6b)